Building XNA 2.0 Games

A Practical Guide for Independent Game Development

James Silva and John Sedlak

Apress®

Building XNA 2.0 Games: A Practical Guide for Independent Game Development

Copyright © 2008 by James Silva and John Sedlak

ISBN-13 (pbk): 978-1-4302-0979-9

ISBN-13 (electronic): 978-1-4302-0980-5

Printed and bound in the United States of America 9 8 7 6 5 4 3 2 1

Lead Editor: Ewan Buckingham
Technical Reviewer: Fabio Claudio Ferracchiati
Editorial Board: Clay Andres, Steve Anglin, Ewan Buckingham, Tony Campbell, Gary Cornell, Jonathan Gennick, Kevin Goff, Matthew Moodie, Joseph Ottinger, Jeffrey Pepper, Frank Pohlmann, Ben Renow-Clarke, Dominic Shakeshaft, Matt Wade, Tom Welsh
Project Manager: Beth Christmas
Copy Editor: Marilyn Smith
Associate Production Director: Kari Brooks-Copony
Production Editor: Ellie Fountain
Compositors: Susan Glinert and Octal Publishing, Inc.
Proofreader: Nancy Sixsmith
Indexer: Carol Burbo
Artist: Kinetic Publishing Services, LLC
Cover Designer: Kurt Krames
Manufacturing Director: Tom Debolski

Distributed to the book trade worldwide by Springer-Verlag New York, Inc., 233 Spring Street, 6th Floor, New York, NY 10013. Phone 1-800-SPRINGER, fax 201-348-4505, e-mail orders-ny@springer-sbm.com, or visit http://www.springeronline.com.

For information on translations, please contact Apress directly at 2855 Telegraph Avenue, Suite 600, Berkeley, CA 94705. Phone 510-549-5930, fax 510-549-5939, e-mail info@apress.com, or visit http://www.apress.com.

Apress and friends of ED books may be purchased in bulk for academic, corporate, or promotional use. eBook versions and licenses are also available for most titles. For more information, reference our Special Bulk Sales–eBook Licensing web page at http://www.apress.com/info/bulksales.

The source code for this book is available to readers at http://www.apress.com

This book is dedicated to my mom and dad,
who were always supportive of my game development obsession.
—James Silva

Contents at a Glance

Contents

About the Authors

 **JAMES SILVA** has been creating games as a hobbyist developer for nearly a decade, but he never took himself quite seriously enough until his latest work, *The Dishwasher: Dead Samurai*, got some attention. The Dishwasher won the Microsoft Dream-Build-Play 2007 contest and earned James an Xbox Live Arcade contract. He was approached with the concept of creating a book focused on techniques used to create The Dishwasher.

James holds a Master's Degree in Computer Science from State University of New York Institute of Technology. He lives in Utica, New York, with two cats who he swears are trying to kill him. James is still hard at work on The Dishwasher, which will soon be making its debut on Xbox Live Arcade.

 **JOHN SEDLAK**, a Microsoft MVP for XNA/DirectX, got his start in game development when he was just 11 years' old, with the help of Microsoft's Visual Basic. After completing a few games with BitBlting techniques, it was time to move on and learn the .NET Framework and all DirectX had to offer. Since then, John has placed a great deal of effort into understanding the design of frameworks and engines. From the first release of the XNA Framework, he has worked to grow the community through tutorials, code snippets, and complete open source games, such as GW3 and Domination.

In his spare time, John enjoys cycling on the open road and driving long distances, and has even been known to take a few photos along the way.

About the Technical Reviewer

FABIO CLAUDIO FERRACCHIATI is a senior consultant and a senior analyst/developer. He works for Brain Force (http://www.brainforce.com) in its Italian branch (http://www.brainforce.it). He is a Microsoft Certified Solution Developer for .NET, a Microsoft Certified Application Developer for .NET, and a Microsoft Certified Professional.

Fabio is a prolific author and technical reviewer. Over the past ten years, he has written articles for Italian and international magazines and coauthored more than ten books on a variety of computer topics. You can read his LINQ blog at http://www.ferracchiati.com.

Acknowledgments

I would like to acknowledge John Sedlak, who saved this book from certain doom, as well as all of the great guys in the XNA community and Microsoft XNA team, who helped me with all of my stupid programming questions. (That is actually the term used—"stupid programming question"—and it is a question that one should not have to ask if one has been approached to write a book about the subject.)

James Silva

There is an incredibly long list of people who should be thanked—a list that would probably be longer than this book.

First and foremost, I would like to thank James for developing The Dishwasher, an amazing game that truly deserves all the honors it has received. I look forward to losing many nights' sleep playing the game on my Xbox. I would also like to give thanks to the people behind the scenes at Apress. They truly are an amazing team of people, who have been incredibly patient while we strived for excellence.

Special thanks to all the hard-working developers and readers out there. Without you, this book could not exist. I hope you all learn something from this book, and I hope many more take what we cover and produce some original and amazing games with XNA.

John Sedlak

Introduction

We're in an amazing era of video games; high-definition, complex shader-powered, highly immersive 3D content is the norm. The games industry is bombarded by titles of incredible quality month after month. While the end product is great for gamers, it can be a bit disheartening to aspiring game developers with great ambitions and little experience.

Being in this crazy era, it's easy to make a number of mistakes while trying to jump into game development. Most are due to not really fully grasping the scope of a game development undertaking. For instance, it's easy to look at a lot of big-name games and start thinking in terms of cut scenes; or, a bit worse, to start thinking of massive multiplayer anything. Creating something simple, like a bouncing sprite, and then getting overwhelmed while trying to introduce bigger game-play concepts is a fairly common pitfall. James will readily admit to making all of the main mistakes at one point or another (though to be fair, it was in an era before MMORPGs).

When we set out to make this book, we intended to describe the process of creating a game very much like James's game, The Dishwasher: Dead Samurai—a platforming, combat-heavy 2D game with good controls, clean animation, and polished presentation. We could have introduced you to a smattering of math-intensive 3D concepts like BSP trees and volumetric lighting, but we wanted to give you something you can easily be productive with, because that's the fun part of game development. And that's the essence of what we're doing here: having fun. That's why we got into this business in the first place.

In this book, we take all of the main aspects of development from The Dishwasher and put them into a new game we'll be making called Zombie Smashers XNA. We'll take little, chapter-sized modules of functionality—things like map and character editors, basic platforming, particle effects, exploding zombie heads, and so on—and really give you a feel for what we're doing and, more important, what you can do. When it's all said and done, you'll have an excellent foundation for going anywhere with any sort of game of this scope: puzzle platformer, coin-op style beat-'em-up, story-driven role-playing game, and so on. Just don't expect to learn how to make a first-person shooter (FPS) here. Of course, that's not to say that the fundamentals we'll cover in this book won't help you should you decide to confront something as ambitious as an FPS (still, there's a reason most well-funded FPS developers don't use in-house engines!).

We'll be using Microsoft XNA Game Studio 2.0 to build a side-scrolling beat-em-'up game. XNA 2.0 is a great framework for game programming. It is extremely powerful, yet well suited for amateur, independent, and hobbyist developers. This book, of course, is written by amateur/indie/hobbyist developers for amateur/indie/hobbyist developers. Throughout the next several hundred pages, you'll get to see XNA really shine in this respect. We'll be focusing on techniques for good presentation and fast development, such as through fluid animation and eye-catching particle systems, where you'll see the most payoff for time invested.

We'll start off by covering some programming basics, and then jump right in to XNA with our version of a Hello World program: XNAPong! After the brief, two-chapter crash course on all things basic, we'll kick off the start of our Zombie Smashers XNA game with a map editor and character editor, and then start working directly with our game. We'll implement a solid platforming engine, particle systems, audio, and menus, before moving on to some advanced stuff like postprocessing effects and networking.

The really nice bit is that you can download the final projects now. In fact, you had better do it right away. The link is `http://apress.com/book/view/1430209798`.

This way, you'll be able to see exactly where we're headed before we get there. We find it kind of annoying and troublesome to keep writing code without getting much visual payoff. We like to see what we're doing! So snag the code online, fire up Zombie Smashers XNA in Visual Studio, run it on Windows, and see where we're headed. With all of the fully completed projects in hand, you shouldn't have to feel in the dark when we throw hundreds of lines of convoluted tools, particles, and who knows what else at you in the chapters to come.

Of course, we will skip around a lot—more in some chapters than in others. That's just the nature of the beast. We may want to add a bit of functionality to one area, but in doing so, we find we need to update a tool, introduce some global states, and so on. So bear this in mind while following the final projects: there may be code that the text doesn't cover yet. It's safe to ignore; we'll get to it all eventually.

All that said, it's probably safe to dive in!

CHAPTER 1

■ ■ ■

A .NET Snapshot
Coding 101

Prior to writing a game, or any application for that matter, it is extremely important to know how to program! This chapter provides a brief overview of some core programming concepts as they pertain to .NET and the C# language. If you are not familiar with C#, .NET, or object-oriented design, we suggest that you first spend some time reading and exploring other books dedicated to those subjects. If you have some experience developing on the .NET platform, you may wish to skip this chapter entirely. You won't miss much if you just want to develop a sweet game!

The .NET Platform

All of .NET (pronounced "dot net") is called a *platform*, because it is much more than some code, a software development kit (SDK), or a set of languages. The platform consists of a set of goals developed by Microsoft to tackle cross-platform development and create a way to enable rapid application development. In marketing terms, .NET makes developers' jobs easier by letting them focus on implementing functionality rather than developing the core mechanics of an application.

The goal of .NET is to provide a large umbrella for which *managed* languages can be written, compiled, and run with greater ease than ever before. One of the major strengths of the .NET platform is that it is inherently cross-platform.

The platform encompasses a wide range of three-letter acronyms (TLAs), a few of which you should know and understand while programming.

When you or some other developer writes an application or library in a .NET language, it is compiled into an *assembly*. This assembly, no matter what type, can be used by other .NET assemblies. This allows developers to easily reference and use code written in multiple managed languages, such as C#, Visual Basic .NET (VB .NET), or Managed C++. This is due to the fact that the code written in these languages compiles down into the *Common Intermediate Language* (CIL), a low-level language that resembles assembly. CIL is not an assembly language, however; it represents the code itself, rather than CPU-specific instructions. The fact that CIL represents the actual code, instead of optimized and cryptic assembly code, allows it to be decompiled easily into a high-level language. The CIL is a very important middle step in the platform because it unifies all the languages under the umbrella, providing interoperability, so that the multiple pieces of software can communicate.

How is the CIL used and why is it so inherently cross-platform? Because the CIL provides the middle ground between a high-level language and machine code, which is platform-specific, the .NET platform needs to some layer that can interpret the code and run it. Assemblies written for the platform run under the *Common Language Runtime* (CLR), which compiles and uses CIL code *just-in-time* (JIT) for execution, as illustrated in Figure 1-1. One of the strengths of executing code in this way is that it makes for incredibly easy debugging. It allows a developer to stop execution at any time and run code line by line.

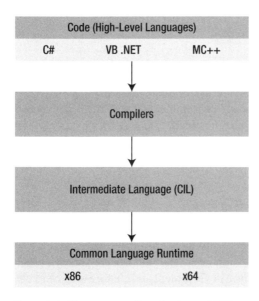

Figure 1-1. *The process of producing a .NET assembly from source code*

What about the languages, then? You now know that languages fit under some umbrella called the CIL and that the intermediate language can be run on a special runtime, but how does this all play out? It turns out that the glue that holds the languages together is yet another TLA. The *Common Type System* (CTS) provides a base layer of types and functionality that is global to all .NET languages. Figure 1-2 provides a high-level view of how the type system and languages are laid out.

The CTS is provided by another assembly, mscorlib.dll, which can be referenced in any .NET project. Using Lutz Roeder's .NET Reflector (which can be downloaded from http:// www.aisto.com/roeder/dotnet/), it is possible to look at what mscorlib.dll actually contains. If you do look at it, you will notice all the common types for each language, such as Boolean, Int32, and Byte. Figure 1-3 shows an example of the Boolean type within the CTS library.

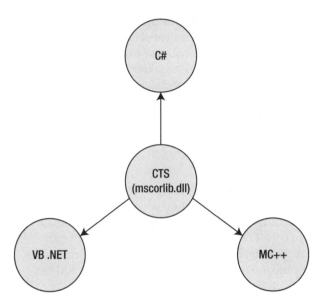

Figure 1-2. *How the CTS relates to your source code*

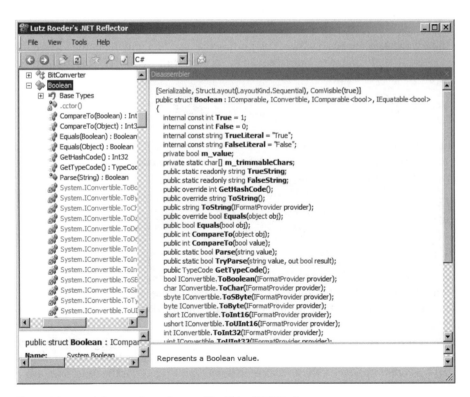

Figure 1-3. *A quick snapshot of mscorlib.dll in .NET Reflector*

Now that you understand what the `mscorlib.dll` library provides, you know one part of what is called the .NET Framework. In general, a framework is a set of libraries composed of types, methods, algorithms, and resources that developers can use to create applications. Inverting the diagram shown in Figure 1-1, you can see that assemblies reference and use each other to actually create a program. These libraries and all this technology are useless without some knowledge of how to use them. This is where object-oriented programming and design come in and guide us to the greener side of application development.

Variables

As developers, we use *variables*, *fields*, *members*, or whatever else you decide to call them to hold stuff for us. When we wish to count from one to ten, or know when a user has clicked something, we use variables to hold the data. Each variable has what we call a *type*, which determines exactly what the variable can hold. For example, a variable of type `int`, or an integer, can hold whole numbers. A variable of type `double` or `float` can hold decimal values. C# is very specific about how we declare and use these variables. For instance, we add two numbers in a certain way:

```
int myValue = 4;
int myValue2 = 3;
int myResult = myValue + myValue2;
```

Notice how we always declare a variable by putting the type first and the name second. It is important to note that the name of a variable can never start with anything but a letter. Thus, the following are illegal declarations:

```
int 3myValue;
int #myValue;
```

After the first character, you can use numbers and underscores. The capitalization does not matter and is done in a certain way for readability. The general convention is to start each word with a capital letter. Here are some valid declarations:

```
int my_VALUE;
int m_value;
int myvalue;
int MyValue;
```

After declaring a variable, we can assign it a value by using the equal sign. The variable we are setting is always to the left of the equal sign, and the value we are generating is to the right. So, in the first example in this section, we are setting the variable `myResult` equal to the sum of `myValue` and `myValue2`.

We can separate the declaration of a variable from when we set it. These types of variables are known as *value types* due to how they are stored in memory. Basically, there are two places a variable can be stored: the stack and the managed heap. Value types, for the most part, are stored on the stack because it is quick and dirty. Bigger types, known as *object* or *reference types*, are stored on the heap and require the use of the `new` operator, as you will see in examples later in this chapter. Table 1-1 shows a short list of common types and their uses.

Table 1-1. *Some Common .NET Types*

Type	Example	Use
bool	bool myBoolean = true;	True or false; represents a bit (0 or 1)
byte	byte myByte = 3;	Eight bits in length;. whole number between 0 and 255
short	short myShort = 3;	Small integers (–32,768 to 32,767); 16 bits in length
int	int myValue = 3;	Whole numbers; 32 bits in length
double	double myDbl = 3.0;	Precise real numbers
float	float myFloat = 3.0f;	Real numbers
char	char myCharacter = '3';	Single ASCII characters
string	string myString = "333";	Many characters

What if we want to convert from one variable type to another? A problem exists with going from types like an int to a byte. Clearly, all the data inside an int cannot fit inside a byte. Similarly, a string cannot just fit inside a char, because a string is many characters put together. Fortunately, we have type casting to help us fit in as much as possible. To type cast, we put the type we want to cast to in parentheses in front of the variable we wish to cast, as in the following example:

```
int myInteger = 254;
byte myByte = 1;
myByte = myInteger; // This is invalid!
myByte = (byte)myInteger; // This will work!
```

Be warned that when you move from a more precise type like int or double to a less precise type like byte or float, you can lose some of your data. Furthermore, when doing mathematical operations, it is possible to overflow or underflow a variable. Let's rework the previous example to demonstrate how this works:

```
int myInteger = 254;
byte myByte = 10;
myByte += (byte)myInteger;
```

In this case, the byte, myByte, will actually roll past 255 and be set back to zero because 254 + 10 is more than the total amount (255) a byte can hold. Similarly, a char can hold only one character from a string.

You may also have noticed a new way to do addition. It is possible to combine math operations and set operations into a single operator. The previous example uses the += operator because we want to add myInteger onto what myByte already is.

Playing around with these variables can be interesting, but in order to have some real fun, you need to be able to create and use objects.

Object-Oriented Programming

For now, we are concerned only with C# 2.0, which is available in Visual Studio 2005 and later. This is due to the fact that the XNA Framework does not support C# 3.0 or the .NET 3.5 Framework natively, especially on the Xbox 360, where a custom version of the Compact Framework is used. C# (pronounced "cee sharp") is known as an object-oriented programming (OOP) language because it relies on the ability to format code within sections called *objects*.

You can think of objects as anything you can perform an action on or anything that has an attribute associated with it. Relating to the real world, we can consider physical items as objects. Consider the idea of representing a box as an object. The core idea behind OOP is the notion of relationships. In the case of a cardboard box, we can say that a cardboard box *is a* box. The *is a* relationship tells us that something can be classified as something more generic. This relationship is called *inheritance* and is essential for OOP languages. When one object inherits another, it takes on some of its properties and methods as its own. Here is how our box object looks in C# code:

```
class Box
{
    /// <summary>
    /// Describes the height of the box.
    /// </summary>
    public int Height;

    /// <summary>
    /// Describes the width of the box.
    /// </summary>
    public int Width;

    /// <summary>
    /// Describes the length of the box.
    /// </summary>
    public int Length;
}
class CardboardBox : Box
{
    /// <summary>
    /// Describes the thickness of the cardboard.
    /// </summary>
    public int Thickness;
}
```

This code also contains a second essential part of OOP: the *has a* relationship. In the case of a box, we can say that Box *has a* Height, Width, and Length. In the case of a CardboardBox, we can say it *has a* Thickness, Height, Width, and Length. The *has a* relationship can give us a lot of information about an object or allow us to perform an action on an object.

Boxes are boring unless they have something inside them! Let's say that we ordered something from our favorite online store and it just arrived. How would we open it in code? We can do this by giving the Box object a *method*, which is a block of code that can be called from inside or outside the object. Defining a method is incredibly simple. We name it and then define what it does.

Before you read the next block of code, we should cover something that is important to understand from here on out. We can say that any object can be considered as a *type*. A type describes the name of the object, as well as what it contains, what it is, and what it can do. In our example, we say that the Box is a class type and has a Width, Height, and Length. When we declare a method, we need to give it what is referred to as a *return type*. When the method is called by code somewhere, it should do some work and then return some value. In the following example, we use a special type called void, which describes nothing; that is, the method does not need to return a value.

```
class Box
{
    // ...

    /// <summary>
    /// Opens the box.
    /// </summary>
    public void Open()
    {
    }
}
```

You may have noticed the use of the public keyword in the code examples. Another big idea in OOP is the notion of *scope*. In essence, scope defines who can do what from where. In the previous code examples, we have made everything public so that code outside the Box and CardboardBox classes can use the defined items. The following are a few other scopes:

- *Public*: Anyone can call the method or use the member.

- *Private*: Only the class itself can see, call, or use the item.

- *Protected*: The class itself as well as child classes (CardboardBox is a child class) can see, call, or use the item.

- *Internal*: Similar to public, but only code within the assembly can see, call, or use the item.

These scopes are very useful when writing code. The following is an example where the Box class uses *properties* instead of public fields to hold and maintain data. Properties are a quick way of writing access methods for a private field and can contain any standard code.

```
class Box
{
    // ...
    private int height;
```

```
/// <summary>
/// Gets or sets the height of the box.
/// </summary>
public int Height
{
    get { return height; }
    set { height = value; }
}
}
```

This block of code shows the `Height` property. The `Width` and `Length` properties are written in a similar manner.

Our `Box` class is awesome in that it has the ability to be opened, but it doesn't do anything. Let's add a new property to the class that lets us know whether the box has been opened. We then will change this property in the `Open` method, essentially opening the box!

```
class Box
{
    // ...
    /// <summary>
    /// Describes whether or not the box has been opened.
    /// </summary>
    private bool isOpened = false;

    /// <summary>
    /// Opens the box.
    /// </summary>
    public void Open()
    {
        if (IsOpened)
            return;

        IsOpened = true;
    }

    /// <summary>
    /// Gets whether or not the box has been opened.
    /// </summary>
    public bool IsOpened
    {
        get { return isOpened; }
        private set { isOpened = value; }
    }
}
```

Here, you see a few other OOP concepts. The first is that we can set the scope of both the getter and setter individually. *Getters* and *setters* are used, unsurprisingly, to get and set fields. They come in handy by letting us control how data is accessed. In the preceding example, we can check the IsOpened value from outside the class, but if we want to set it, it must be done from within the class.

We check the value of the IsOpened property in the Open() method, to see if the box has already been opened before trying to open it. The if statement uses what is known as *Boolean logic* to decide what to do.

Controlling Flow with Boolean Logic (If Statements)

A Boolean value can be either true or false, on or off. Thus, if the IsOpened Boolean is true, the method returns. If the IsOpened Boolean is set to false, it opens the box by setting the IsOpened Boolean to true. This means that we are able to open the box a maximum of one time.

We can combine several Boolean statements to create larger and more complex statements. This is done with Boolean operators. The two main operators are And, which requires both statements to be true, and Or, which requires at least one of the statements to be true. When considering two statements, A and B, Table 1-2 describes how you can combine them.

Table 1-2. *How Boolean Logic Works*

A	B	A && B (And)	A || B (Or)
True	True	True	True
True	False	False	True
False	True	False	True
False	False	False	False

Suppose that we allow a Box to take on a new attribute describing whether or not it has a top. Clearly, we cannot open a box that does not have a top, so a check to see if the Box is opened *or* has no top is necessary when trying to open it. The following code is based on a Box class with a new Boolean property named HasTop.

```
class Box
{
    // ...
    public void Open()
    {
        if (IsOpened || !HasTop)
            return;

        IsOpened = true;
    }
}
```

Notice that in this case, we want to check the opposite of what the HasTop property provides. We do this using the negation operator (!), which makes a true value false and a false value true. We read the if statement here as "if the box is opened or does not have a top, we cannot open it."

What if we also want to remove the top when a Box is opened? We would need to handle the case where the box isn't opened and does have a top. We can add on to the if statement using the keyword else, which allows us to extend the statement with alternative checks. Each if and else if statement is checked in order until an option evaluates to true or no options are valid.

```
class Box
{
    // ...
    public void Open()
    {
        // If it is opened or does not have a top, we can't do anything
        if (IsOpened || !HasTop)
            return;
        // Otherwise, if it is not opened and has a top, "remove" the top.
        else if (!IsOpened && HasTop)
            HasTop = false;

        IsOpened = true;
    }
}
```

Using the Box Object

Now that we have our awesome Box and CardboardBox objects, we should actually use them. Open a new instance of your favorite C# integrated development environment (IDE) and create a new console project. In Visual Studio 2005, this is done by choosing New Project on the startup screen or by selecting File ➤ New ➤ Project. Figure 1-4 shows the Visual Studio New Project dialog box with the Console Application template selected.

When the project is created, you should see a window to the right titled Solution Explorer. This window shows all the files included in your project and solution. A *solution* is simply a super project that can contain several projects. A *project* is a container for code and is compiled into a single executable or library. If you do not see this window, select View ➤ Solution Explorer.

Open Program.cs by double-clicking the file in Solution Explorer. This is the file that will actually run your application. Currently, it contains a single method called Main in a class named Program.

Now we need to add two files for our objects to the project. This can be done a few ways:

- By right-clicking the project and selecting Add ➤ New Item

- By clicking the Add New Item icon in the toolbar

- By selecting Project ➤ Add New Item

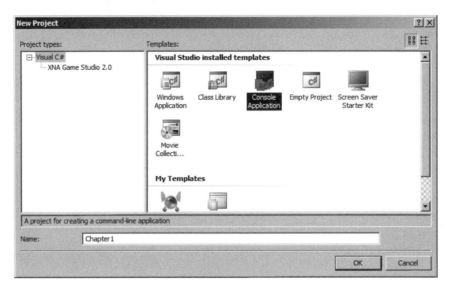

Figure 1-4. *Creating a console application*

You should see a dialog box similar to the one shown in Figure 1-5. Select Class, enter a name (we used Box.cs), and select Add. Repeat this process for the CardboardBox object.

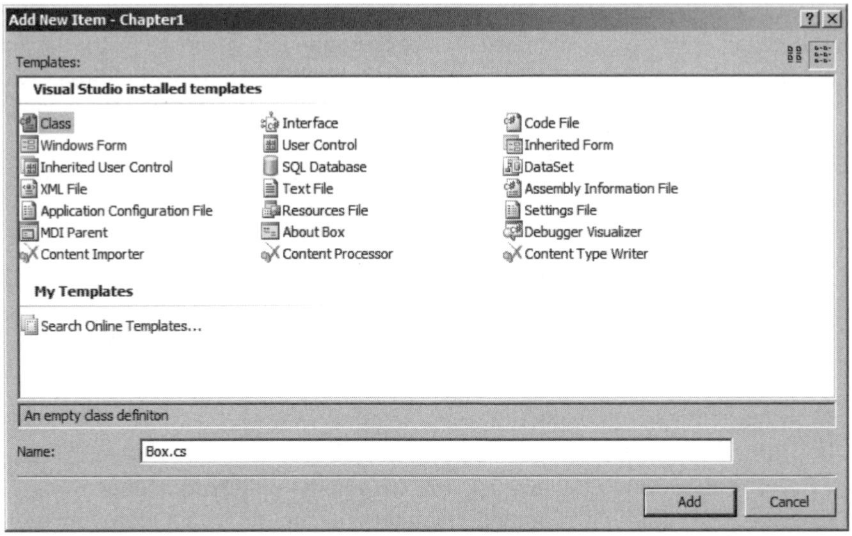

Figure 1-5. *Adding a class file*

Fill in the class files using the code provided previously in this chapter. If you run into trouble, remember that the full source code for all the examples in this book is available from the Source Code/Download section of the Apress web site (http://www.apress.com).

Now that we have two files with two objects, we need to write some code to actually do something. Open Program.cs again and in the Main method, add the following code:

```
class Program
{
    static void Main(string[] args)
    {
        Box box = new Box();
        box.Width = 10;
        box.Height = 10;
        box.Length = 10;

        CardboardBox cbBox = new CardboardBox();
        cbBox.Width = 10;
        cbBox.Height = 10;
        cbBox.Length = 10;
        cbBox.Thickness = 2;

        Console.WriteLine("Box Volume: {0}", box.Width * box.Height * box.Length);
        Console.WriteLine("Cardboard Box Volume: {0}",
            cbBox.Width * cbBox.Height * cbBox.Length - cbBox.Thickness * 6);
    }
}
```

Notice the use of a new keyword, new, which creates an instance of each object for us. We can use the object only after we have instantiated it. After creating each object, we set the Width, Height, and Length properties. Because a Box is not a CardboardBox, we cannot set the Thickness property (it doesn't exist). However, because a CardboardBox is a Box, we can set the Width, Height, and Length properties.

At the end of method, you see Console.WriteLine(...);, which is a call to a static method inside an object. A *static* method or property does not require the object to be instantiated in order to use it. Consider it to be an item that is unique and consistent across all instances of the object. In this case, we are using a method to write text to a console window, as shown in Figure 1-6.

After you are finished writing code, select Debug ➤ Start Without Debugging from the menu bar, or press Ctrl+F5.

Debugging

When you start an application without debugging, you are telling Visual Studio to run the application and ignore errors as much as possible. If an error occurs, it will not jump into the code and help you figure out what is going on. It will also ignore any breakpoints in the code.

A *breakpoint* is as simple as it sounds: a point in the code where Visual Studio will stop execution and jump into the code, allowing you to manually step through it line by line. Test this by inserting a breakpoint on the line where the first Box is created. You can do this by clicking in the gray area to the left of the text editor; a red circle should appear. Now simply run the program with debugging by selecting Debug ➤ Start Debugging or pressing F5.

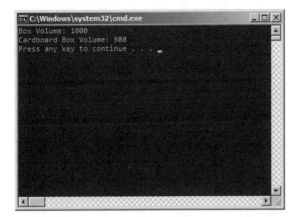

Figure 1-6. *Running our program*

When the application is run, it will immediately jump back into the code and highlight the current line it is on. You are now debugging your code! Move your mouse over various code elements, and you will see a box pop up, telling you more about each item. If you hover over box in Box box = new Box();, you will see that the pop-up reads null. This tells you that the box item has not been created yet.

In the Debug menu, look up the shortcut key for Step Over and select it. You will see the code start to execute line by line. As you continue to press the Step Over key, you can hover your mouse over objects and properties and see how they change.

Controlling Flow with Arrays and Looping

Now suppose that we have a lot of boxes to open. If you wanted to buy many copies of this book, each one coming in its own box, you would need a way to open them all easily. For this, we use an array.

An *array*, in its most basic form, is simply a collection of items maintained in one location. We can loop through the array, which allows us to visit each item in order. This can be done via the standard for loop:

```
Box[] boxes = new Box[10];
for (int i = 0; i < 10; i++)
    boxes[i] = new Box();

Box[] boxes = new Box[10];
for (int i = 9; i >= 0; i--)
    boxes[i] = new Box();
```

This code creates an array of ten boxes, loops through each item in the array, and instantiates it.

Each spot in the array is said to be at a certain *index*, or position in that collection. In C#, arrays are *zero-based*, meaning that the first element is always index 0 and the last element has an index of *length* – 1.

The for loop can be dissected into three distinct elements:

- *Initialization*: Sets up the counter field.

- *Continuing condition*: Provides a Boolean statement that decides whether or not the loop can continue.

- *Incrementing statement*: Moves the counter field toward a value that makes the continuing condition evaluate to false.

Loops are useful anytime many instances of the same object need to be stored. These objects are stored in arrays, lists, or collections.

There are a couple of ways to declare and use arrays. The preceding code blocks show one way. There are also classes that can help maintain collections. Two notable classes are Queue and Stack, located in the System.Collections.Generic namespace. A *queue* is known as a first-in, first-out (FIFO) structure, because the first item to be put in the queue will be the first item taken out. This can be likened to how a line at a coffee shop works: the first customer in line is the first customer served. A *stack* is the opposite of a queue, in that it is a first-in, last-out (FILO). The stack structure can be likened to how a stack of lunch trays works in a cafeteria, where the first tray put on the stack is the last tray to be picked up, and the last tray to be put on the stack is the first to be used.

Instead of the for loop, we could also use a while or a do-while loop. This approach involves setting up a counter to help us index through the array. For an array of ten items, the indices of the items will range from 0 to 9, or one less than the total amount. The difference between a while and a do-while loop is when the check to exit the loop happens, as demonstrated in the following code:

```
int index = 0;
do{
     boxes[index].Open(); index++;
}while(index < boxes.Length);

int index = 0;
while(index < boxes.Length){
     boxes[index].Open(); index++;
}
```

But while loops are used much less often than standard for loops. One feature of the C# language that makes the handling of objects in a collection easier is called the foreach structure. This looping method allows us to pick out certain types within a collection and use them without needing to worry about counters. Here is a simple example:

```
foreach(Box box in boxes)
     box.Open();
```

It really is that simple! However, there are some caveats to using the foreach loop in place of a normal for loop. The biggest problem is that you can't modify or remove objects from the collection. In order to do this, you should use a for loop as in the prior examples, but loop through the array backward. Having said this, the foreach is great for updating objects or drawing them, because it gives us quick and easy access to the objects we need.

There is one major flaw with how we have been creating our arrays so far: they aren't easy to modify. There is no simple way to add new elements or remove old ones. The next section describes how to use generics to create modifiable lists of a certain type.

Using Generics and Events

Generics, or *template classes*, are a way of defining a type such as a class based on another type. This relationship is known as the *of a* relationship, because you can say that you are declaring a variable as a "List of Box objects," where List is the generic class and Box is the class you are using.

Let's define our own little box collection using generics. First we need to create a class to handle items in a collection. Start up a new console application in Visual Studio and add a class called ListBase. Now we need to add the necessary namespaces and declare the class type. We use the letter T to signify the generic type, but you can use any other letter. In fact, it is possible to declare multiple generic types for a class.

```
using System;
using System.Collections.Generic;

namespace Generics
{
    class ListBase<T> : List<T>
    {
    }
}
```

Note that we do not do much with the generic parameter; we simply pass it on up to the base class. Now we need to create some functionality in this class.

One problem with the built-in generic collection types (List, Dictionary, Queue, Stack, and so on) is that they do not have events for when an item is added or removed. An *event* is a way of notifying code outside the class that something has happened. For example, in a Windows application, the window fires a MouseDown event whenever the user clicks the mouse on the window. This allows us to know about and handle events as they happen. To create an event, we use what is known as a *delegate*, which is nothing more than a function turned into a type. Here is the delegate we will be using (defined in System.dll):

```
public delegate void EventHandler(object sender, EventArgs e);
```

You should notice right away that much of this looks like a normal function. It has scope (public), a return type (void), a name (EventHandler), and two parameters (sender, e). The main difference is the addition of an extra keyword: delegate. This tells the compiler that this function is to be used as a type.

Let's use this delegate in our ListBase class to declare some events. We do this using another new keyword: event.

```
class ListBase<T> : List<T>
{
    public event EventHandler ItemAdded;
    public event EventHandler ItemRemoved;
```

```
    public ListBase()
    {
        ItemAdded += OnItemAdded;
        ItemRemoved += OnItemRemoved;
    }

    ~ListBase()
    {
        ItemAdded -= OnItemAdded;
        ItemRemoved -= OnItemRemoved;
    }

    protected virtual void OnItemAdded(object sender, EventArgs e)
    {
    }

    protected virtual void OnItemRemoved(object sender, EventArgs e)
    {
    }
}
```

A lot of things are going on here. First, we have declared our events with the new keyword. Next, in our constructor, we add our methods (event listeners) to the events using the += operator. After this, we declare the deconstructor for the class, which is called when the memory is being freed. It is good practice to always remove listeners from events when you are finished with them to make sure there are no lingering references. Last, but certainly not least, we declare the bodies of our event listeners. Do you notice anything familiar? The parameters and return type match that of the delegate definition. Also note that we have set the scope to protected and that it is possible to change the name of the parameters.

Now that we have events, we need to use them. Despite the ListBox class having many more methods for adding and removing items, we are going to rewrite only two of them. You can rewrite functionality provided by a base class by using the new operator.

```
public new void Add(T item)
{
    base.Add(item);

    if (ItemAdded != null)
        ItemAdded.Invoke(item, EventArgs.Empty);
}

public new bool Remove(T item)
{
    bool returnValue = base.Remove(item);
```

```
    if (ItemRemoved != null)
        ItemRemoved.Invoke(item, EventArgs.Empty);

    return returnValue;
}
```

Here, we have a method, `Add`, that uses the generic type as a parameter. Notice how it is used as a type (like `int`, `bool`, and so on). This is the meat and bones of using generics. After calling the base class's methods, we invoke the event and pass in the item as the first parameter and empty arguments as the second.

Now let's see how to use this class! In `Program.cs`, we will add some code to declare and use a list:

```
static void Main(string[] args)
{
    ListBase<int> myIntegers = new ListBase<int>();
    myIntegers.ItemAdded += OnItemAdded;

    myIntegers.Add(3);
}

static void OnItemAdded(object sender, EventArgs args)
{
    Console.WriteLine("Item added: {0}", sender);
}
```

We declare a variable of a generic type in much the same way as we declare any other variable, except for the addition of the extra type inside the carets. After coding this, the output should be pretty clear. It should say `Item added: 3`.

As an exercise, we suggest playing around with events and the `ListBase` class to add functionality for the other `Add` and `Remove` methods. You can test these by adding event handlers and trying to add and remove items in different ways.

Conclusion

This chapter was intended to give you a little taste of what .NET and C# can do. In the coming chapters, we will be applying the ideas we have discussed here to game development. As you progress through this book, the core concepts you have read about here will become increasingly important. Thankfully, we will not need to introduce many more core concepts and can get right down and dirty with creating a game with the XNA Framework. Now let's make some games!

CHAPTER 2

■■■

A Crash Course in XNA Pong: The Hello World of Game Development

Programming primers often start with some derivative of "Hello World"—a terrifically simple program whose sole purpose in this world is to greet it. For example, a Hello World program in BASIC would read something like this:

```
10   PRINT "HELLO WORLD."
20   END
```

The point of Hello World is to illustrate some language or medium as simply as possible. Because the medium we're using here is a game development tool set, we might as well use the first popular video game to be created as a simple introduction. We're speaking, of course, of Pong. Before we start developing though, you need to get XNA Game Studio 2.0 up and running, so we'll begin by installing it.

Installing XNA Game Studio 2.0

XNA Game Studio 2.0 is essentially a bunch of tools that we'll be using with Microsoft Visual C# 2005 Express Edition. As of the second version of XNA Game Studio, you can choose to develop games in any version of Visual Studio 2005, including Express, Standard, and Professional. We have chosen to write the source code in Visual Studio Express because it is free, but the steps are similar, if not the same, for any other version.

To get up and running, first install Visual C# 2005 Express Edition. The installer can be downloaded from http://www.microsoft.com/express/2005/download/default.aspx. Once the installer is downloaded, run it to install Visual C# 2005 Express.

Next, install XNA Game Studio 2.0. You can download the installer from http://www.microsoft.com/downloads/details.aspx?FamilyId=DF80D533-BA87-40B4-ABE2- ➥ 1EF12EA506B7&displaylang=en.

Now that you have everything installed, you can get started by running Visual C# 2005 Express Edition.

Building XNAPong

Creating XNAPong should be fairly simple and straightforward. The procedure will go something like this:

1. Create the project.

2. Create some graphics.

3. Load the graphics in the project.

4. Set up the program structure.

5. Handle joystick input, update the ball's movement, check for collisions, and detect scoring.

6. Set up rendering.

7. Add force feedback (rumble).

8. Implement audio.

Although it will end up being a bit longer than the BASIC incarnation of Hello World, it will also be slightly more impressive (*slightly* is a relative term). When all is said and done, you should be familiar enough with XNA and the XNA Game Studio 2.0 environment to create your own projects.

Creating a New Game Project

With a new instance of Visual Studio opened, select File ➤ New Project. In the New Project dialog, select Windows Game. Enter a name—we'll use XNAPong for this example, as shown in Figure 2-1. For your own games, you will also probably want to specify a location close to root (we prefer d:\dev\). Click OK, wait a few seconds, and you're ready to go!

■**Note** If you do not see the project templates for XNA Game Studio 2.0 in the New Project dialog, make sure you have installed both XNA Game Studio 2.0 and Service Pack 1 for Visual Studio 2005.

Congratulations, you've just completed what could have constituted a few hours of ugly work before the advent of XNA Game Studio. XNA Game Studio has set you up with a standard game framework, including a render loop, content loaders, input handling, and a lot more. You will be dropped into the Visual Studio integrated development environment (IDE) with the XNAPong solution opened to class Game1.cs. Your brand-new solution should look like Figure 2-2.

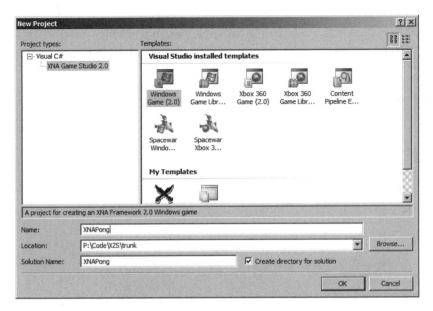

Figure 2-1. *Unleashing a new imagining of Pong on the world*

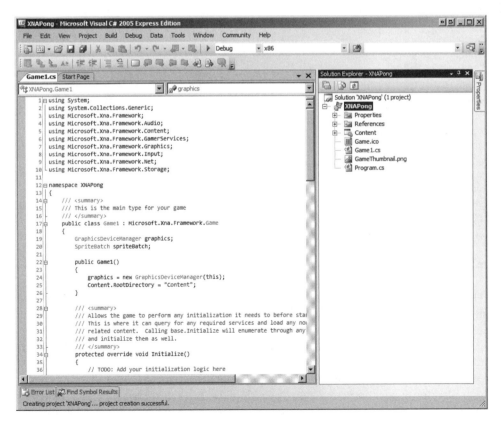

Figure 2-2. *A nice, fresh solution in the Visual Studio IDE*

We'll cover some of the functionality that has been created for your game project, but bear in mind that you don't really need to understand a substantial amount of what's going on. This is where XNA really shines—the framework exposes functionality that we really like, so we can focus on game building, not tedium.

One of the biggest concerns beginning developers have is how to create the actual game window. Countless articles have been written about this issue—many of them longer than this book. Fortunately, creating a window with XNA Game Studio is as simple as creating a project. As you will soon find out, the framework does all the work necessary for creating and maintaining a window for your game. Furthermore, the same method for creating a game for Windows can be applied for the Xbox 360. Again, the framework knows how to set everything up for you. For the uninitiated, learning how to do this and writing the pages of code necessary to open a window correctly could take hours.

Instead of diving into exactly how all of this is handled, we'll just run our bare-bones project. Click Start Debugging to run it. Behold, our amazing cornflower blue game, as shown in Figure 2-3.

Figure 2-3. *Cornflower blue: the game*

Here's our game in action. It doesn't look like much, but there is a lot going on here. The graphics device and content manager are initialized, and a frame loop is working, furiously rendering a cornflower-blue background 60 times per second. If you have an Xbox 360 controller plugged in, XNAPong will also be polling to make sure you haven't pressed Back, which will exit the application.

A game works quite differently from a desktop application such as Notepad or Internet Explorer. Desktop applications are generally developed to be event-based; they will sit forever, doing nothing except waiting for the user to press a key or click the mouse. In a game application, this tends not to work, since characters are always moving and new stuff is always happening.

Because of this, games employ a loop structure to continuously handle input while drawing items on the screen.

Loading Textures

Loading textures, and content in general, used to be a time-consuming task made even harder by nonstandard texture formats, which often required third-party libraries to load and use. XNA helps to fix this issue by introducing the Content Pipeline, a set of libraries devoted to loading, saving, and consuming content. As of XNA Game Studio 2.0, all of a game's content, including textures, is maintained by what is called the Content project. This project, a child of a game or library project, is responsible for holding related content and compiling it. This greatly reduces the work needed to add and use textures such as paddles for a Pong clone.

Since we're creatures of habit, we tend to put graphics on sprite sheets. A *sprite sheet* is a large graphic consisting of smaller images that are typically, but not always, contained in a grid. Using a sprite sheet, rather than separate textures, should provide some improvement in loading and rendering, but under typical levels of complexity, the performance improvement will probably be negligible. Also, sprite sheets have their own problems, such as the wasted space and the temptation to fit everything on *one sprite sheet*. That said, since we're making a very simple game here, let's put everything on a single sprite sheet.

In order to draw only the parts of a sprite sheet we want, we need to create an *alpha channel*. An alpha channel determines the opacity of the RGB (Red Green Blue) color to draw: a value of 0 is clear; a value of 255 is opaque. Our source images are shown in Figure 2-4.

Note All of the source images for the examples in this book, as well as the source code, are available from the Source Code/Download section of the Apress web site (`http://www.apress.com`).

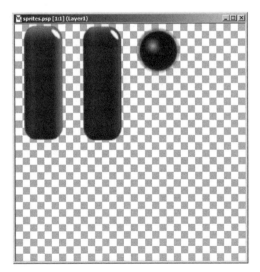 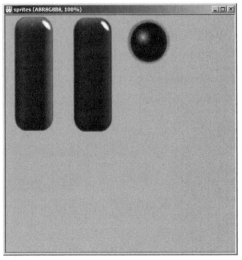

Figure 2-4. *Original image with alpha channel (left) and RGBA (right) in DirectX texture editor*

Figure 2-4 shows our original image as created in Paint Shop Pro and our composited final product in DirectX Texture Tool (DxTex). In the original image, all translucency is depicted as a gray-and-white checkerboard. The image on the right side of the figure shows what happens when we import the alpha-enabled PNG into DxTex. Because XNA is built on DirectX, this is *exactly* how it will look in the game. While we tend to be Paint Shop Pro fans, if you want to create graphics on the cheap, you just can't go wrong with the 100% free, plug-in enabled Paint.Net. You can download Paint.Net from `http://www.getpaint.net`.

■**Note** To get a fine, if somewhat meticulous degree of control on your alpha channels, you can save alpha and RGB images *separately*, and then composite them in DxTex. Using one image editor for creating bitmaps and alpha channels and then compositing them in DxTex is a somewhat cumbersome solution, but if you use it, here's a tip: save alpha bitmaps as `file_a.bmp` and save RGB bitmaps as `file.bmp` (replace `file` with your file name), then drag `file.bmp` into DxTex. DxTex will automatically composite the images into one RGBA image.

Back in XNAPong, you'll need to create a folder for graphics. Right-click the Content project in Solution Explorer and select Add ➤ New Folder. Name the folder `gfx`.

From our image editor, save the image as `sprites.png` in the folder you just created from within Visual Studio. If you are working with DxTex, save the image as `sprites.dds`. We used a DDS file, but you can use DDS and PNG interchangeably.

In Visual Studio, add the image you just saved to the project. With the Content project selected in Solution Explorer, ensure that Show All Files is enabled (through the Solution Explorer toolbar or Project menu) and open the `gfx` folder. Right-click `sprites.dds` and select Include In Project. In the Properties window, Build Action is now set to Compile, as shown in Figure 2-5. This means that when the project is built, `sprites.dds` will be sent to the Content Pipeline for preprocessing.

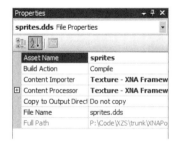

Figure 2-5. *The sprites.dds file ready for the Content Pipeline*

Now we're ready for some coding!

Loading and Rendering

Before we get to anything Pong-like, let's get the rendering set up. We'll need a `Texture2D` object to store our image file. Game Studio 2.0 already sets us up with a `SpriteBatch` to handle sprite drawing. We'll also need to load our image in `LoadContent()` and draw it in `Draw()`.

At the class-level declarations in the Game1.cs file, add the following:

```
SpriteBatch sprite;
Texture2D spritesTexture;
```

For 2D development, SpriteBatch is one of the most useful classes in the XNA Framework. When you draw anything on modern graphics hardware, it is done in 3D. Essentially, SpriteBatch takes some 2D drawing calls you give it, converts them into optimized, complicated calls that the 3D-geared hardware likes, and sends them along. For all things 2D, this is a huge time-saver.

SpriteBatch is not without its problems, however, and knowing how to efficiently use the SpriteBatch object can save you from spending a lot of time later on performance issues. The guiding rule behind using a SpriteBatch is to bunch as many Draw() calls together as possible. Consider it similar to building a five-lane highway but sending only one car down it at a time. This is highly inefficient, since four lanes are going unused; sending many cars at once will ensure that the highway is running efficiently.

Note that in the Game1 class constructor, two objects are instantiated:

```
public Game1()
{
    graphics = new GraphicsDeviceManager(this);
    Content.RootDirectory = "Content";
}
```

graphics is a bit of an all-inclusive graphics device management object. All things that have anything to do with graphics will have something to do with graphics or the actual device it manages, GraphicsDevice. When we discuss the GraphicsDevice object, we are talking about an object that provides an interface between our code and the graphics card on a user's PC.

Moving along through our new project, we have the following:

```
protected override void Initialize()
{
    // TODO: Add your initialization logic here

    base.Initialize();
}
```

Initialize() is where we'll be adding any game-initialization logic. We can leave it empty for now. Later, we'll be using it to initialize audio stuff.

Next up is LoadContent(), where we'll be loading content. Let's add a line to load our sprites texture:

```
protected override void LoadContent()
{
    // Create a new SpriteBatch, which can be used to draw textures.
    spriteBatch = new SpriteBatch(GraphicsDevice);

    spritesTexture = content.Load<Texture2D>(@"gfx/sprites");
}
```

When content is loaded through a content manager, you signify which type of object you want returned using what is called a *generic method*. In this example, we are passing in the

Texture2D type, since that is what we want to load. We then pass in the path to the content file, using the @ symbol to tell the compiler to ignore any escape sequences in the string.

Now that the texture file has been loaded into an object, we can use it to render the paddles. For now, we'll just render the entire image to show that it works. In Draw(), add the following:

```
protected override void Draw(GameTime gameTime)
{
    graphics.GraphicsDevice.Clear(Color.CornflowerBlue);

    spriteBatch.Begin(SpriteBlendMode.AlphaBlend);
    spriteBatch.Draw(spritesTexture, new Rectangle(0, 0, 256, 256),
        Color.White);
    spriteBatch.End();

    base.Draw(gameTime);
}
```

All the Game1.Draw() method did before we added these few lines was to clear the graphics device to a nice shade of cornflower blue, and then render the image to screen. We've added some lines to draw spritesTexture, entirely as is, onto the screen. Our initial success with graphics is shown in Figure 2-6.

Figure 2-6. *Loading and rendering success!*

This is exactly what we wanted: the images from our sprites The texture are rendering properly. If we had failed to set up the alpha channel correctly, a big, black box would have appeared behind our image.

SpriteBatch.Draw() is a fairly robust method for drawing 2D sprites in whatever way you desire. We're using the minimal overload here: indicating which Texture2D to use; which Rectangle, or size, to draw on the screen (x, y, width, height); and what Color to apply to the texture. The Color parameter will become increasingly important because it allows you to shade a texture a certain color as well as increase or decrease the transparency. Surrounding the SpriteBatch.Draw() method are two calls: spriteBatch.Begin() and spriteBatch.End(). This is the essence of the SpriteBatch: we use Begin() to set up the SpriteBatch for a certain type of rendering (more on this in Chapter 7), throw it as many Draw() operations as desired, and then use End() to finalize the deal and send it off to be drawn. Not only is this a great system for efficient sprite rendering on 3D hardware, but it's absolutely necessary—calling Draw() outside a Begin() ... End() block will result in a nasty crash.

Caution Be careful to finish what you start. Every spriteBatch.Begin() must lead to a spriteBatch.End() before base.Draw() is called. Calling spriteBatch.Begin() and then spriteBatch.Begin() again without ending the first batch will kill your game; calling spriteBatch.End() when no spriteBatch.Begin() has been called will do the same.

The Begin()/Draw()/End() requirement is due to how drawing any sort of graphic on the screen works with DirectX. When a developer calls SpriteBatch.Begin(), the object sets up the GraphicsDevice in a specific way and gets your graphics card ready to be used. Without doing this, both the GraphicsDevice and the SpriteBatch will not know how to draw sprites on the screen. When the call to SpriteBatch.End() is made, the object finishes any drawing that still needs to be done and either resets the GraphicsDevice to how it was before Begin() was called or just cleans up a bit. How, when, and exactly what is done at this point is highly dependent on the parameters used in the call to Begin(), but for now, you do not need to be concerned with that.

So far, we've created a project, created an image, loaded that image, and rendered it in a render loop. Granted, we've glossed over a bit, but we'll get to more details when we start doing some substantial game development in upcoming chapters. For example, you'll see more versatile SpriteBatch rendering in Chapter 4, and learn how to organize game entities using objects in Chapter 6.

Adding the Game Logic

Now we can start on the actual game logic. Game logic includes any code that actually makes the game play happen. It can be composed of physics, artificial intelligence, or gathering user input.

Because this is an extremely small project, we think it's safe to put everything in Game1. As a general rule, putting too much functionality in Game1 is a terrible idea, but for really small projects, it's forgivable. If we were making a larger game, or a game we might extend, we would want to put this logic in separate classes: one class for the ball and one class for the paddle.

The task list for the game logic goes something like this:

1. Create class-level variables to keep track of paddle locations, ball location and trajectory, and game state.

2. Handle gamepad input, update paddle locations, and handle game state.

3. Update ball location, check for paddle collisions, and check whether a point has been scored.

4. Draw!

We'll start with the class-level variables. At the class level (Game1.cs), add the following:

```
float[] paddleLoc = new float[] { 300.0f, 300.0f };
Vector2 ballLoc = new Vector2(400.0f, 300.0f);
Vector2 ballTraj = new Vector2();
bool playing = false;
```

Because we have two paddles, we might as well use a two-dimensional array for paddle location, paddleLoc[]. Both paddles will start at location 300.0f, which is vertically centered on our 800 × 600 screen. BallLoc, the ball location, is initialized as 400.0f, 300.0f, or dead center, and ballTraj, the ball's trajectory, is set to zeros. playing determines whether or not the ball is in play, and is set to false.

Paddles and Gamepad Logic

We'll just get the paddles moving around for now, and set up the collision and score-detection logic in the next iteration. We tend to work iteratively (that is, code, then run, then code, then run), because it's nice to have some visual confirmation that we're on the right track.

In Update(), add the following:

```
for (int i = 0; i < paddleLoc.Length; i++)
{
    GamePadState state = GamePad.GetState((PlayerIndex)i);
    paddleLoc[i] -= state.ThumbSticks.Left.Y *
        (float)gameTime.ElapsedGameTime.Milliseconds * 0.5f;
    if (paddleLoc[i] < 100.0f) paddleLoc[i] = 100.0f;
    if (paddleLoc[i] > 500.0f) paddleLoc[i] = 500.0f;

    if (!playing)
    {
        if (state.Buttons.A == ButtonState.Pressed)
        {
            playing = true;
            ballLoc.X = 400.0f;
            ballLoc.Y = 300.0f;
            ballTraj.X = ((float)i - 0.5f) * -0.5f;
            ballTraj.Y = ((float)i - 0.5f) * 0.5f;
        }
    }
}

base.Update(gameTime);
```

Here, we are iterating through paddleLoc[], updating each paddle location based on the associated gamepad. First, we'll grab the state of the gamepad with GamePad.GetState. Notice how we can cast index i to a PlayerIndex. GamePadState holds everything we need to know about the gamepad: analog stick positions, buttons pressed, the directional pad (D-pad), and so on.

The next few lines of code move our paddles around. The Update() method is set up with one parameter: gameTime. We use gameTime to determine how much time has elapsed since the last update. If we base all movements on gameTime, objects in the game will move at speeds independent from the frame rate. If we did not use gameTime while updating objects, we would end up with slowdowns reminiscent of old Nintendo days.

Because we're using time-based movement, we update the paddle location by decrementing its value by half the number of elapsed milliseconds multiplied by the left thumbstick's Y value. With GamePadState, up on the left thumbstick is 1, down is -1, and resting is 0. This is the opposite of how screen coordinates work (0 is top; 600 is bottom), so we use the inverse in updating paddle position. The left thumbstick's Y value is multiplied by half of gameTime's elapsed milliseconds to give us a good speed for time-based paddle movement.

The next two lines prevent the paddle from flying off the top or bottom of the screen.

The if clause that follows is the bit of code we'll use to control the game state. Basically, if the game state is playing = false, it checks if the current player has pressed the A button. If A has been pressed, the ball location is reset to dead center, and the ball trajectory is set to be diagonally away from the player who pressed A. The game state is switched to true.

This takes care of our first iteration in the logic department. Now let's do some rendering. In Draw(), add the following:

```
graphics.GraphicsDevice.Clear(Color.CornflowerBlue);

spriteBatch.Begin(SpriteBlendMode.AlphaBlend);
for (int i = 0; i < paddleLoc.Length; i++)
{
    Rectangle destRect = new Rectangle(
        (i * 736),
        (int)paddleLoc[i] - 64,
        64, 128);

    spriteBatch.Draw(spritesTexture, destRect,
        new Rectangle(i * 64, 0, 64, 128), Color.White);
}

spriteBatch.Draw(spritesTexture,
new Rectangle((int)ballLoc.X - 16, (int)ballLoc.Y - 16, 32, 32),
new Rectangle(128, 0, 64, 64),
Color.White);

spriteBatch.End();

base.Draw(gameTime);
```

We're not doing anything much different here from our first iteration. The only real difference is that the spriteBatch.Draw() method is using a different overload to allow us to specify a source rectangle. Remember how when we drew it the first way we ended up with the whole image? Specifying a source rectangle allows us to render just one area of the source image at a time.

We're defining the destination rectangle, destRect, to be relative to the location of each paddle. The (i * 736) will cause paddle 2 to appear on the right side of the screen, because for player 2, i will be 1, whereas for player 1, i will be 0. Pretty clever, right? We didn't think so either. The top Y value of destRect is (int)paddleLoc[i] - 64, which means that since the paddle will be 128 pixels tall, it will end up drawn perfectly centered at paddleLoc[i]. The overload we're using for spriteBatch.Draw() here is as follows:

```
spriteBatch.Draw(Texture2D texture,
    Rectangle destination,
    Rectangle source,
    Color color)
```

After the paddles are drawn, we draw the ball. The Draw() call does a similar thing here—offsetting the top-left location of the destination rectangle by half of the rectangle's width and height.

Run it and see our moving paddles in action. Figure 2-7 shows an example.

Figure 2-7. *Your paddles should now move.*

This is good progress, and all in a couple dozen lines of code. Now we can add the ball update logic.

The Ball Logic

To update the ball, we need to do a few things:

- Update ball location by trajectory.

- Let the ball go out of bounds; set the game state to not playing if it does. (We're not going to record scoring.)

- Let the ball bounce off walls.

- Let the ball bounce off paddles.

First and foremost, we'll check if playing == true. Here's the rest:

```
if (playing)
{
    float pX = ballLoc.X;

    ballLoc += ballTraj *
        (float)gameTime.ElapsedGameTime.Milliseconds;
    if (ballLoc.X > 800.0f) playing = false;
    if (ballLoc.X < 0.0f) playing = false;
    if (ballLoc.Y < 50.0f)
    {
        ballLoc.Y = 50.0f;
        ballTraj.Y = -ballTraj.Y;
    }
    if (ballLoc.Y > 550.0f)
    {
        ballLoc.Y = 550.0f;
        ballTraj.Y = -ballTraj.Y;
    }

    if (ballLoc.X < 64.0f) TestBallCollision(0,
                (pX >= 64.0f));
    if (ballLoc.X > 736.0f) TestBallCollision(1,
                (pX <= 736.0f));
}

base.Update(gameTime);
```

We'll use the variable pX to store the previous x coordinate of the ball's location. This will come in handy for telling whether the ball has hit a paddle dead-on or on the side. If it hits on the side, we won't want to return it.

After updating the ball's location by ballTraj, we check to see if the ball has gone out of the left bounds (ballLoc.X < 0.0f) or the right bounds (ballLoc.X > 800.0f), and set playing to false if this has happened. If the ball hits the upper (ballLoc.Y < 50.0f) or lower (ballLoc.Y > 550.0f) boundaries, we move the ball to the location of that boundary and reverse vertical speed.

The next section contains a function, testBallCollision(), which we define as follows:

```
private void TestBallCollision(int i, bool reverse)
{
    if (ballLoc.Y < paddleLoc[i] + 64.0f &&
        ballLoc.Y > paddleLoc[i] - 64.0f)
    {
        if (reverse)
            ballTraj.X = -ballTraj.X;
        ballTraj.Y = (ballLoc.Y - paddleLoc[i]) * 0.01f;
    }
}
```

This is a nifty little function. The parameter i refers to the index of the paddle being tested (0 = left; 1 = right), and reverse indicates whether a collision will result in the ball's horizontal trajectory being reversed. Basically, if reverse is false, the ball's most recent update did not cross over the paddle's leading edge, meaning that the ball has glanced off the side of the paddle. If the ball's most recent update *did* cross over the paddle's leading edge, this means we just had a direct hit, and the paddle should return the ball.

To test whether the ball crossed over, we call testBallCollision() with the following:

```
if (ballLoc.X < 64.0f) TestBallCollision(0,
                (pX >= 64.0f));
```

Here, we're testing if the ball's X location is less than the left paddle's leading edge, and testing for collision while considering whether or not the ball has just crossed over this leading edge. If ballLoc.X < 64.0f is true, TestBallCollision() is called with the reverse parameter true if the ball's previous location is >= 64.0f. The next line of code basically does the same thing for the right paddle.

We have our fully functional, slightly Spartan XNAPong now, as shown in Figure 2-8.

And that's it! Run it, and be enthralled by what we have called XNAPong.

We're missing a few things, so we might as well continue our crash course, briefly touching a few other XNA features. XNAPong 2.0, here we come!

Figure 2-8. *XNAPong 1.0 in all its glory*

Adding a Background Image

XNAPong looks like it's begging for a background image that is something other than corn-flower blue, so let's give it what it wants. We're not going to introduce anything novel and new here. We just want to illustrate one of the fun cases where a game can be made to look several times better in no time.

Create an 800 × 600 image to fit snugly as our background. For our image, we added white lines on the top and bottom as the "walls," as shown in Figure 2-9.

Figure 2-9. *Source image for the background*

You won't need an alpha channel for this image—we can draw the whole rectangle—so it's safe to save it as a bitmap in your gfx folder. Within Visual Studio, make sure you include the background image by right-clicking in Solution Explorer and choosing Include In Project. We've saved it as background.bmp.

Ready to add a background image in three lines of code? At the class level (again, everything is going in Game1.cs), add the following:

```
Texture2D spritesTexture;
Texture2D backgroundTexture;
SpriteBatch spriteBatch;
```

In LoadGraphicsContent(), add this:

```
spritesTexture = content.Load<Texture2D>(@"gfx/sprites");
backgroundTexture = content.Load<Texture2D>(@"gfx/background");
```

Finally, in Draw(), add this:

```
spriteBatch.Begin(SpriteBlendMode.AlphaBlend);
spriteBatch.Draw(backgroundTexture, new Rectangle(0, 0, 800, 600),
    Color.White);
```

```
for (int i = 0; i < paddleLoc.Length; i++)
```

That's it! We've done a real commendable job of making XNAPong less ugly and are well on our way to making XNAPong 2.0. XNAPong in all its glory is shown in Figure 2-10.

Figure 2-10. *Less-ugly XNAPong*

Adding Rumble

As we continue tearing through the simpler features of the XNA Framework, force feedback (rumble) is one we shouldn't pass up. We can take care of it in a few lines, and it's one of those neat things that was either impossible or a horrendous hassle before XNA Game Studio 2.0. We'll go into more details about rumble input in Chapter 8. For now, we'll just get it working.

Rumble is state-based, so if we set the gamepad rumble to 1 and forget about it, the thing will never stop vibrating. We'll create a class-level variable (in Game1.cs again) to track rumble:

```
float[] force = new float[] { 0.0f, 0.0f };
float[] paddleLoc = new float[] { 300.0f, 300.0f };
```

Now we're getting into territory where it would be a better idea to keep all of these fields in a Player class or something, but trust us, we're not going to go much further. In Update(), add the following:

```
for (int i = 0; i < paddleLoc.Length; i++)
{
    GamePadState state = GamePad.GetState((PlayerIndex)i);
    .
    .
    .

    if (force[i] > 0.0f)
        force[i] -= (float)gameTime.ElapsedGameTime.Milliseconds;

    float t = (force[i] / 50.0f);
    if (t > 1.0f) t = 1.0f;
    if (t < 0.0f) t = 0.0f;
    GamePad.SetVibration((PlayerIndex)i, t, t);
}
```

This is straightforward. First, we decrement `force[i]` by `gameTime`. We calculate `t` to be a number between 0 and 1, and then set the `GamePad` vibration to `t` for both the left motor and the right motor. The function `setVibration()` looks like this:

```
GamePad.SetVibration(PlayerIndex playerIndex,
    float leftMotor,
    float rightMotor)
```

An Xbox 360 gamepad has two motors, which are weighted differently. Off-brand gamepads may yield slightly different results.

Finally, we'll have ball collisions cause force feedback. In `TestBallCollision()`, add this:

```
if (reverse)
    ballTraj.X = -ballTraj.X;
ballTraj.Y = (ballLoc.Y - paddleLoc[i]) * 0.01f;
force[i] = 100.0f;
```

This will cause `force[i]` to be at 100% for both motors at impact and reduce to zero over one-tenth of a second. Actually, the gamepad's motors won't hit 100% speed, because that takes a bit of time—much longer than one-tenth of a second. We'll still get a nice bit of tactile feedback, and you can always tweak it to your liking.

Run it, and enjoy a mainstay of modern console gaming on your Windows box!

Last But Not Least: Audio with XACT

Love it or hate it, the way to go for XNA audio is the Cross-Platform Audio Creation Tool (XACT). Essentially, an XACT project organizes wave files and a healthy amount of metadata, allowing users to model game audio—specifying things like volume and pitch variation, digital signal processing (DSP) effects, and more—outside the game codebase. It's as if Microsoft decided what an excellent audio engine should look like, built it for you, and isn't charging for it. On the downside, if you're used to making your own audio engine, you initially probably won't like having to do things the XACT way, but we think that overall the benefits of XACT far outweigh any negatives.

Creating Wave Banks and Sound Banks

Open XACT by selecting Start ➤ MS XNA GS 2.0 ➤ Tools TRA Microsoft Cross-Platform Audio Creation Tool (XACT). XACT organizes sounds through wave banks and sound banks. Wave banks consist of raw audio files with minimal metadata. Sound banks reference waves and contain a lot of metadata—wave variations, pitch variation, and more. (We'll cover XACT in detail in Chapter 8.)

To create a new wave bank, right-click Wave Banks and select New Wave Bank. Open the new wave bank, and from the Wave Bank window, right-click and select Insert Wave File(s). Navigate to an audio file to use. We used zap.wav, which we put in a directory named sfx. As you may have guessed, sfx sits next to gfx in the project directory. The Wave Bank window, with our new zap wave added, is shown in Figure 2-11.

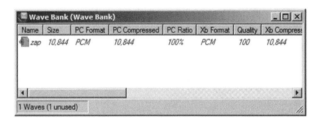

Figure 2-11. *Wave Bank window in XACT*

The zap wave is red, which means that the wave is not used in the sound bank. Let's remedy this! Right-click Sound Banks and select New Sound Bank. Open your new sound bank. Here, you can define sounds and cues. There's a bit of hierarchy here that we'll explain more fully in Chapter 8. For now, we'll just create a new cue. Drag zap from the Wave Bank window to the Cue pane in the Sound Bank window to create a new cue with associated sound, as shown in Figure 2-12.

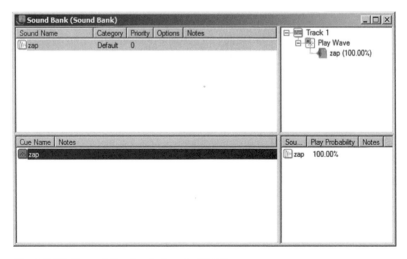

Figure 2-12. *Sound Bank window in XACT*

Now we have a zap cue. This is the object we'll be playing from XNAPong. Essentially, we'll tell the audio engine to play the zap cue, which will play the zap sound, which will play the zap wave with associated metadata. Notice that back in the Wave Bank window, zap is no longer red.

You'll need to set the build paths for the wave bank and sound bank, but before that, you need to save the project. Select File ➤ Save Project As and save the file in your sfx directory.

Next, in the Properties window, select Wave Bank, and set the values for Windows Build Path and Xbox 360 Build Path to snd.xwb. Then select Sound Bank and set the values for Windows Build Path and Xbox 360 Build Path to snd.xsb. The paths are shown in Figure 2-13.

Figure 2-13. *Properties set for the sound bank*

Save the project again. Now, in the Content project in XNAPong, add an sfx folder. The sfx.xap XACT project file should show up, and its Build Action in the Properties window should be Compile. If everything checks out, we're ready to start coding!

Coding the Audio

At the class level (yes, still in Game1.cs), declare the three objects we'll need for audio: AudioEngine, WaveBank, and SoundBank. When the Content Pipeline processes our XACT project, it spits out three files: the project file, wave file, and sound file with the paths that we specified from XACT:

```
AudioEngine engine;
WaveBank wave;
SoundBank sound;
```

To initialize the engine, wave bank, and sound bank, add some constructors in Initialize():

```
engine = new AudioEngine(@"sfx/sfx.xgs");
wave = new WaveBank(engine, @"sfx/snd.xwb");
sound = new SoundBank(engine, @"sfx/snd.xsb");

base.Initialize();
```

Sound is now locked and loaded! We'll have the sound play whenever the ball hits a paddle, so we'll add a line to play the cue in `testBallCollision()`:

```
force[i] = 100.0f;
sound.PlayCue("zap");
```

There's one more minor detail that we almost forgot, and have forgotten in the past, much to our chagrin. If you do not give `engine` some frequent attention, bad things will happen: sounds will start sounding choppy, refuse to play, and worse. Calling `Update()` allows the audio engine a chance to breathe—that is, to dispose of old sounds, manage streaming audio, and the like. In `Update()`, add the following:

```
engine.Update();
base.Update(gameTime);
```

XNAPong now has audio capabilities! Run it and see (or hear) for yourself. Shall we call this XNAPong 2.0?

Conclusion

In this short chapter, we've gone over loading and drawing imagery, gamepad input, force feedback, and audio. We've created a game that blows away every single video game from before 1985 or so. Granted, the game is missing a lot of polish, but that's not the point. Our intentions were to briefly touch on all of the concepts and features of XNA we will be using further down the road, in the upcoming chapters.

■ ■ ■

CHAPTER 3

Planning Your Game
A Nonscientific Take on the
Science of Game Planning

The goal of this book is to teach you, the aspiring independent game developer, how to create a sweet game from start to finish. Seeing as we're a bit closer to "start" than we are to "finish," we should dwell a bit on a debatably important, often unpleasant aspect: *planning*.

In large development projects, planning is crucial; projects fail because of ill-conceived plans. Loose or incomplete design documentation leads to rambling development and mushrooming budgets, outright failure, and far worse. Can a project do worse than failing? There are some games on the market that suggest the answer is "yes."

Depending on your experience with software development, you may know that the industry places a heavy emphasis on planning and design methodologies. The theory is that when a project spirals out of control (no, not *those* spirals—we're talking about the bad kind of spiraling), bad planning and inappropriate methodologies are to blame. We believe that the truth lies somewhere between incompetent planning and incompetent management. Thankfully, all of this discussion is moot, as we are not discussing a large development project, by-the-books design methodologies, or any sort of extensive planning.

Because the topic at hand here is indie game design, we're looking at a slightly different beast. Planning is important, but if you're a hobbyist or one-man team, development can be so agile that it's often more conducive to the quality of the overall game experience to create a loose plan and let it evolve naturally than it is to employ a rigid design document. In the case of an independent game developer, it becomes much more important to not go beyond what can conceivably be done. Starting with a small and loose design document allows for a game to grow past anyone's expectations. Of course, these things have their limits.

Because we don't have any hard numbers to back any of this up, we're going to use one of James's games, The Dishwasher: Dead Samurai, as a case study.

The Dishwasher: Dead Samurai Case Study

The initial plan of The Dishwasher: Dead Samurai game involved a handful of concepts:

- The protagonist would be a dishwasher out for revenge for some reason (or ex-dishwasher, considering his new occupation would be "revenge").

- He would look something like the character in Figure 3-1.

Figure 3-1. *A dishwasher out for revenge*

- He would be able to warp quickly by using the right analog stick.

- He would use a combo system similar to that used in popular action platformer titles.

- The graphical style would be mostly grayscale with red blood, with a gritty, hand-drawn look.

- The bad guys would be cyborgs.

- The game would be a 2D platformer.

- The character model format would be a hierarchical system consisting of animations, keyframes, frames, and parts and script commands (more on this in Chapter 5).

- The map model format would consist of nongridded images and a gridded and nongridded collision map (more on this in Chapter 4).

- The world would consist of interlinked maps.

   And there you have it—a design document! Anyone who lives by software design documents, engineering design documents, and Unified Modeling Language (UML) will probably be breaking into a cold sweat right about now, but that's the point, isn't it? We're trying to make game development fun, and sorry, no matter how hard we try, we cannot figure out how to extract fun from class diagrams.

   Let's get back to the task at hand. Armed with some basic concepts, James created some map imagery, character imagery, a map and character editor, and the beginnings of a game engine. He made the hero, The Dishwasher, and an enemy, the Goon. He added some fighting code, which, if you've seen the videos, is the essence of the game in a nutshell.

With a demo in place, the game became a great platform for trying out new ideas, so the revised plan began to include such gems as these:

- The Dishwasher should get an alternate weapon that would not allow warping, but would allow running up walls. This required a plot device in which the default weapon, a katana, was imbued with some magical power that allowed its user to warp.

- The Dishwasher should get some bullet-time magical power, using some magic orb stock supply system.

Now, wait just a minute here! These are two items that have nothing to do with the original focus of the game and run the risk of breaking game play. At the very least, they will lead to all sorts of tweaking and testing in both the game-play department and the art department. But therein lies the beauty of irresponsible development: as the driving force of a microscopic team, you can do things like that *all you want*.

As for the last two items, here's a quick epilogue:

- The alternate weapon became three, with quick weapon switching becoming a vital aspect of combat.

- The magical power likewise became three. The magic orb stock supply system was nixed in favor of a system that relied on players drawing energy from felled enemies and instantly activating magic, rather than hoarding magic for a big encounter.

The point here is that The Dishwasher: Dead Samurai game was started with pretty minimal planning—just a simple vision that was tweaked and tweaked until it just felt right. The vision evolved and mutated, and much like natural selection, the parts that didn't survive got the axe.

Of course, nothing revolutionary is being discussed here. We're just trying to make the point that with a realistic vision, it can be perfectly acceptable to jump into coding with minimal planning. The key to a realistic vision is, as you'll discover, in understanding your limits.

A Realistically Limited Vision—Bane of the Teenage Game Tycoon

Realistically limiting your vision is one of the most important keys to a successful project. In our various adventures in indie game development, we've come across the type of person who has terrible issues with this concept quite frequently. So frequently, in fact, that we've coined a term for them: Teenage Game Tycoon, or TGT.

Not all TGTs are teenagers, and not all teenagers are TGTs, but the teenager mentality is evident. The key attributes of TGTs are unrelenting optimism, unjustified arrogance, and difficulty connecting imagination to reality. (And we must admit that we were probably TGTs at some point.)

Once The Dishwasher: Dead Samurai started picking up momentum in the XNA community, people became aware that there was something special about the game. This is where the TGTs became more apparent. For every respectable developer who understood the blood, sweat, and tears that The Dishwasher must have exacted, there would be a TGT who believed, beyond a doubt, that he could produce a vastly superior title, and didn't hesitate to make this known. Please take note of the message in Figure 3-2.

Figure 3-2. *We could get behind this campaign.*

The essence of the problem with the TGT is in the glaring disconnect between imagination and reality. TGTs have seen loads of footage from the gaming industry's finest AAA titles, and have combined the cutting-edge visuals they have been exposed to with some novel game-play scenarios to create an imaginary *best game ever*. For example, a TGT with absolutely no experience with 3D modeling may be *convinced* that his modeling skills are superior to those of a developer who has actually created 3D games. We think that speaks a great deal of the power of imagination, for better or worse.

Prescribing to a TGT mentality of limitless ability is a sure recipe for disaster. Soaring ambitions eventually meet with the cold, hard reality of an empty template project, and *the best game ever* becomes a folder in Visual Studio whose sole function is to remind you of the time you tried game programming, but gave up because it was "too hard." The solution, of course, is to dial back your imagination a bit. Figure 3-3 illustrates this concept.

Figure 3-3. *Know your limits.*

As you saw in the previous chapter, designing something as simple as Pong can be fairly straightforward. But as you will see in the rest of the book, development and design complexity ramp up quickly for even a slightly complex 2D game. It's no wonder that the vast majority of development houses don't make their own engines—the engine complexity for AAA titles is utterly insane. In fact, the teams that have developed games like Epic Games' Gears of War and Polyphony Digital's Gran Turismo series are made up of a few dozen people working together on a single project. Big-budget titles like these also have the financial backing to acquire the necessary art and sound content that brings their games to life.

For the independent developer, here are a few key ideas to keep in mind when developing a realistic vision:

- 3D is a great deal more complicated, both with the underlying math and with content creation.

- You will spend a good 90% of your time with content.

- You'll probably end up ditching more complex ideas when you get to coding.

- Your vision should focus on game play first, art style second, and story last.

Don't worry about inventing the greatest way to do something. A game should just work, and its code should be manageable.

The most important concept is for you to understand your strengths and weaknesses. And if you've already given that some thought, you also probably already know the other four key concepts we just listed.

Planning the Zombie-Smashing Game

We've looked briefly at The Dishwasher: Dead Samurai as a case study on planning (or absence thereof) and discussed common pitfalls in hobbyist independent game development. So, it's about time to get to some actual planning! Now we'll turn to the sample game we'll be developing in this book.

3D or 2D?

Looking at our previous comments, you may get the impression that we are saying that 3D is nigh impossible for a small, inexperienced team, which isn't quite the case. 3D is very possible and, while not being overly easy, is quite doable. However, the major issue with 3D is *scope*.

It's a bit like fish in big ponds and small ponds. 2D is a small pond, so as a game developer with little in the way of resources and game-developing experience, you can still end up as a pretty big fish. 3D is a much bigger pond, and the same amount of resources just won't carry you as far. 3D brings new considerations: level of detail, lighting, animation, and a lot more. The math behind 3D games is also very complex relative to what is necessary for even the best 2D game. The amount of work you would have to put into polishing a 2D game to a glossy shine will get you only a dull glow in the 3D world.

The game we'll be creating will be 2D for these reasons.

Initial Design

Now that we've established that we're going the 2D route, let's make some art. We made a concept image for the protagonist, shown in Figure 3-4. We often do this on paper or whiteboards, but this one we made with a mouse and an old version of Paint Shop Pro.

Figure 3-4. *Concept art: the hero*

Here is our hero! He's evidently a late 1990s-era skater punk, armed with a revolver and a large pipe wrench. And that means, assuming everything in the movies is true, he'll certainly end up smashing some zombies to protect his brains by the end of the day.

The game (which at this point does not have a name) will be a fast-action plat-former—heavy on combos and relentless action. We'll be taking a great deal of inspiration from other games, including The Dishwasher: Dead Samurai.

Our protagonist has a wrench and a gun, and will be trying to use both liberally in any given combo. To paint a clearer picture of what we're imagining, we've created a stick-figure mockup of a basic air combo, as shown in Figure 3-5. The hero smacks the enemy with the wrench three times, uppercuts him, shoots him once in the air, and then finishes up with a nasty wrench slam.

Figure 3-5. *Concept art: combat*

We have some very rough mockups of a hero and some combat. Let's round this out with a level mockup.

We inadvertently created a protagonist who looks just *made* for a zombie-smashing epic. This means that zombies are bound to be the antagonists, and high-octane wrench-and-revolver smashing will become the game play. The setting, keeping in line with a game that is just making itself at this point, will have to be a cemetery, as shown in Figure 3-6.

Figure 3-6. *Concept art: maps*

There we have it! We think we've pretty much nailed the look and feel of this game with minimal effort. We haven't gotten into power-ups, enemy design, specific maps, health, death and dying, or any of that fun stuff, but we've made tremendous headway. The details will fall into place eventually.

Tool Planning

So far, we've made some basic decisions about how the game will look and feel, but in order to get one step closer to actually building the game, we need to broach the concept of tools. Tools will help us be more efficient at developing new level and character designs, and implanting them into the game without the need to change source code. Creating tools can be essential in the later stages of a game's development cycle, since they allow you to focus on what really matters: the drooling, brain-eating, out-to-get-you zombies!

The next couple of chapters will be specifically on creating the tools we'll be using, and even beyond that, we'll be tweaking them as new needs arise. In the meantime, we'll need to be pretty clear on the data formats for the two areas where we'll be creating all of the content: characters and maps.

Map Editor

Because we are building a tool, we can go back to a more event-based model, where the application waits for the user to do something before proceeding. Since we are designing a tool that can handle the generation of maps, it makes sense to model it after a jigsaw puzzle. Much like with a jigsaw puzzle, we'll drag pieces from a bin area to the map area, fitting them in just where they need to be.

In the mockup of the map editor, shown in Figure 3-7, you can see the map, minus the bounding boxes, as it should be rendered on the left side, and the map segment palette on the right side. The map is composed of map segments that are dragged and dropped, allowing us to give the map a more organic feel than if we used a 16-bit-era grid.

Figure 3-7. *Concept art: map editor*

Character Editor

The character tool format will use a concept similar to the map editor. We'll divide the characters into parts, like arms, torsos, legs, and so on, and then create frames of animation by combining parts. Figure 3-8 shows the character editor mockup.

We'll allow ourselves to rotate parts and move them around. This technique allows for some pretty flexible animation and is what was used in The Dishwasher: Dead Samurai game. Animations will be made up of frames, and we'll throw in a scripting system for combos and animation control. We'll dwell much more on this in Chapter 5, where we build the character editor, but this should suffice for planning purposes.

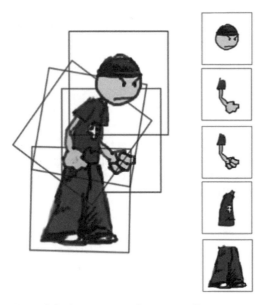

Figure 3-8. *Concept art: character editor*

Naming the Game

Game naming is an aspect of planning that barely deserves its own section. For one thing, you don't even have to give your game a name yet.

■**Note** When James created the solution for The Dishwasher: Dead Samurai, it was simply named ProjectDish1. Prior to The Dishwasher, there was ZSX3: Ninjastarmageddon (later renamed Manic Space), which was originally called ProjectNova.

Long story short: it doesn't matter what you call your game, but giving it a ProjectX code name is always fun. Regardless, let' go ahead and christen this project Zombie Smashers XNA.

A Game Plan

It's probably a good idea to formulate some approximate plan of attack before you blindly jump into any development. Doing so will help organize your thoughts and prevent you from feeling overwhelmed. Here's a rough rundown of the game plan for our Zombie Smashers XNA project:

- Create a map editor.

- Create a character editor.

- Create some map and character art.

- Create some maps and characters.

- Create the game.

- Bring the map and character functionality into the game.

- Add character movement and collision functionality.

- Add combat functionality.

- And take it from there!

Now we have some structure. It is a little disheartening that we don't get to the actual game development until halfway down the list. The fact is that the game is made up of the content; without anything to create the content, there will be no game. The more time we spend on the editors and content, the easier it will be to whip together a demo.

Conclusion

We've taken a look at planning concepts, or lack thereof, through a case study of James's own The Dishwasher: Dead Samurai and our newly christened Zombie Smashers XNA. We've examined some common pitfalls of overambitious indie development along with the unfortunate Teenage Game Tycoon (TGT) moniker, and settled on a just-ambitious-enough 2D side-scrolling action platformer. We sketched out some character, map, and game-play concept art, and made some initial tool plans. Everything may seem a bit vague at this point, but all will be revealed through implementation!

■■■

CHAPTER 4

The Map Editor
Making a World Maker

Depending on your exposure with the games industry, it may come as a surprise to learn that that vast majority of game development time is spent on level design, which leads to this question: would you rather spend the vast majority of game development time happy or miserable? Of course, if you have someone else doing level design, it now becomes a matter of keeping that person happy, which is probably important as well.

Since so much time in designing the game will be spent in the map editor, it's pretty critical to have a map editor that is robust and intuitive. Unfortunately, the map editor in our case study game, The Dishwasher: Dead Samurai (introduced in the previous chapter) was none of those things. This starts the chapter off in an awkward light and perhaps sets the tone for the book. A tech book should always reveal the best, cleanest practices. However, this tech book is setting out to reveal some rather ugly and hacky practices in the name of quick prototyping.

We'll be using The Dishwasher game as a model for our map editor. A few things will be cleaner in our version; a few things won't be. Consider yourself warned.

A map editor that isn't clean or polished is OK though, because it just needs to serve its purpose for the level designer. When creating a tool like a map editor, it is important to realize that the consumer—the person using this product—will be either yourself or a level designer; in other words, someone who is used to these products. In that light, you do not need to create the slickest interface or include the best features. The map editor, above all else, just needs to work by being able to create levels consistently.

Creating a New Project: Zombie Smashers

The first item on the to-do list is to set up our development environment. Before we can get to creating the actual map editor, we need to create a solution for the game we're building in this book, Zombie Smashers XNA.

Begin by opening Visual Studio (as we mentioned in Chapter 2, for the examples in this book, we are using Visual C# 2005 Express Edition). In Visual Studio, select File ➤ New Project, select the Windows Game (2.0) template, and type in the project name ZombieSmashers, as shown in Figure 4-1. Be sure the "Create directory for solution" check box is selected, and then click OK.

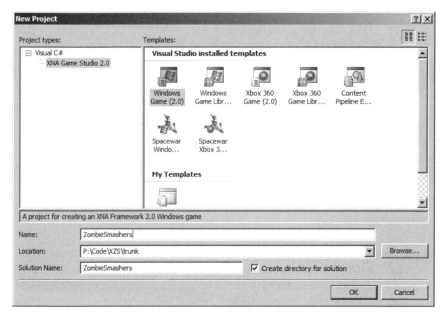

Figure 4-1. *Creating the ZombieSmashers project*

The next step is to add a MapEditor project, and make sure it is the project that runs when you start up. In Solution Explorer, right-click ZombieSmashers and select Add ➤ New Project. After making sure the Windows Game (2.0) template is selected again, enter the name MapEditor, as shown in Figure 4-2, and click OK.

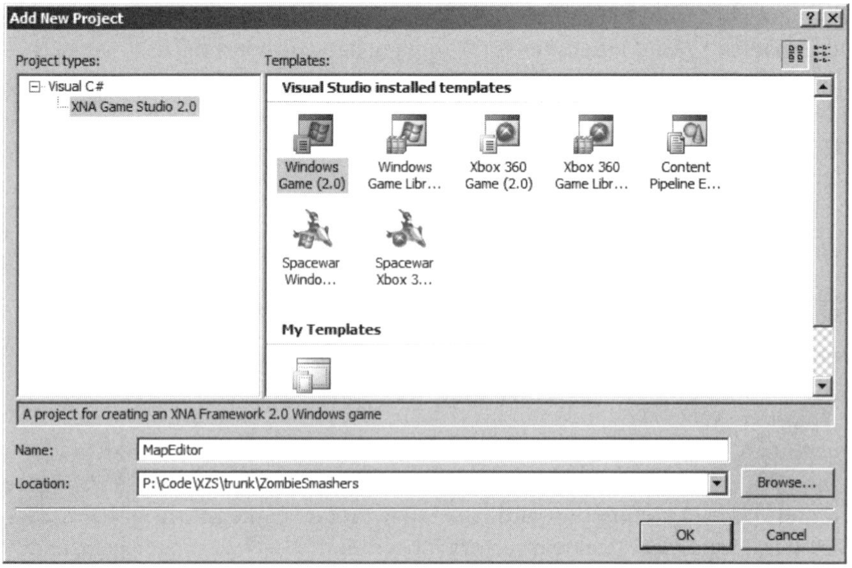

Figure 4-2. *Adding the MapEditor project*

Now, right-click the MapEditor project item in Solution Explorer and select Set As StartUp Project. This ensures the MapEditor project will run, and not the ZombieSmashers project. Solution Explorer now includes the MapEditor project, as shown in Figure 4-3.

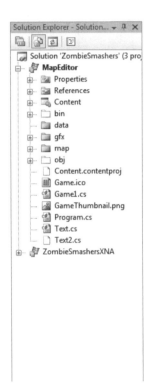

Figure 4-3. *The MapEditor project added to ZombieSmashers*

Before we can get to the map bits, we'll need some basic interface functionality—text rendering and interaction, mouse cursor rendering and input, scroll arrows, buttons, and that sort of thing.

Drawing Text

Text rendering is something that the XNA Framework didn't implement out of the box originally, so the early adopters had to create their own tools and techniques for implementing bitmap-based text drawing. Fortunately, we are now living in the 2.0 era, so we have a very handy tool called Sprite Font. We can add a Sprite Font to our Content project, and the Content Pipeline will automatically create a bitmap image from it. Then we can load the bitmap and draw it using our SpriteBatch.

First, add Sprite Font to your project. Add a Fonts folder to your Content project, and then right-click that folder and select Add ➤ New Item. Select Sprite Font and name the item Arial.spriteFont, as shown in Figure 4-4. Then click Add.

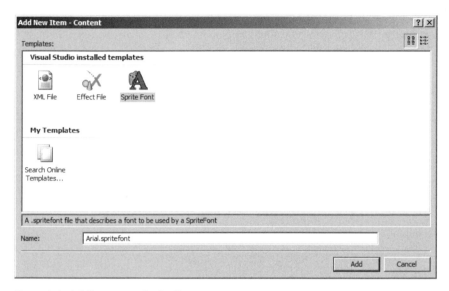

Figure 4-4. *Adding a new Sprite Font*

Now we'll make a Text class to encapsulate some functionality, like state-based color and size and "cheap" buttons. Select Project ➤ Add Class, name the class Text, as shown in Figure 4-5, and then click Add.

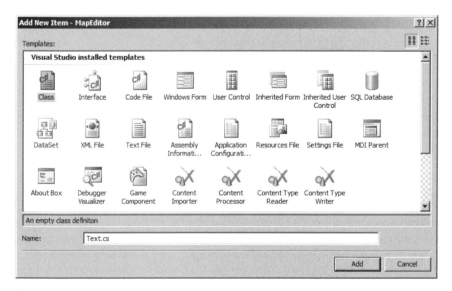

Figure 4-5. *Adding a Text class*

Time to start coding! We want the Text class to hold references to a SpriteBatch and Arial SpriteFont, as well as class-level fields for size and color. We'll declare this at the class level:

```
private float size = 1f;
private Color color = Color.white;
SpriteFont font;
SpriteBatch sprite;
```

Given these fields, and the fact that these fields should have something in them, the constructor is pretty straightforward:

```
public Text(SpriteBatch _sprite, SpriteFont _font)
{
    font = _font;
    sprite = _sprite;
}
```

We'll create some properties to set the text color and size. This is the state-based approach. In our program, we'll be able to set the text color and size once, and then do all of the drawing.

```
public Color Color
{
    get { return color; }
    set { color = value; }
}
```

```
public float Size
{
    get { return size; }
    set { size = value ; }
}
```

Moving on, the drawing method is fairly straightforward. We'll send it integer coordinates and a string, and then the method will cast the coordinates into a Vector2 and draw the string.

```
public void DrawText(int x, int y, String s)
{
    sprite.Begin(SpriteBlendMode.AlphaBlend);
    sprite.DrawString(font, s, new Vector2(
        (float)x, (float)y), color, 0f, new Vector2(),
        size, SpriteEffects.None, 1f);
    sprite.End();
}
```

As for the "cheap" buttons we talked about earlier, we're going to create a function to draw "clickable" text. This way, we'll be able to create buttons from our main project easily, as we'll be drawing text. The function defaults the draw color to white. If the mouse location is within the measured text dimensions (hover), the color will be yellow. If the mouse is hovering *and* clicked, the function returns true. Of course, this won't exactly mimic Windows button behavior, but it will be good enough.

```
public bool DrawClickText(int x, int y, String s,
    int mosX, int mosY, bool mouseClick)
{
    color = Color.White;

    bool r = false;

    if (mosX > x && mosY > y &&
        mosX < x + font.MeasureString(s).X * size &&
        mosY < y + font.MeasureString(s).Y * size)
    {
        color = Color.Yellow;
        if (mouseClick)
            r = true;
    }

    DrawText(x, y, s);

    return r;
}
```

Let's head back to Game1 to test this out! At the class level, we'll throw in the following:

```
Text text;
SpriteFont font;
```

In LoadContent(), we'll need to instantiate text and load our bitmap:

```
font = Content.Load<SpriteFont>(@"Fonts/Arial");
text = new Text(spriteBatch, font);
```

Finally, in Draw(), let's throw some test strings at it.

```
text.Size = 3.0f;
text.Color = new Color(0, 0, 0, 125);
for (int i = 0; i < 3; i++)
{
    if (i == 2)
        text.Color = Color.White;

    text.DrawText(25 - i * 2, 250 - i * 2,
    "Zombie Smashers XNA FTW!");
}

base.Draw(gameTime);
```

Run it. You'll get a nice drop-shadow effect, as shown in Figure 4-6.

Figure 4-6. *Text success!*

FTW, for the uninitiated, means "For The Win," which is exactly how we should be feeling about Zombie Smashers XNA at this point. Text is ready to go, so it's time to design our map editor now.

Creating the Map Editor

Our map editor should allow us to manage everything contained in the game's world and maps. To begin creating it, we need to establish a map model format. Our game world will use the hierarchy laid out in Figure 4-7.

As you can see in the diagram in Figure 4-7, the format has a simple hierarchy, with the top level representing everything, or the *world*. The world is composed of interlinking *maps*. Each map is composed of *map segments*, a *script*, and a *collision map*. The building block of the map is the map segment, so let's start there.

Figure 4-7. *Game world format hierarchy*

Map Segments

A map segment is a nongridded sprite that you can drag and drop, as well as rotate, to build your map. The graphics for map segments will be stored on large sprite sheets, where each map segment definition refers to a rectangle on the sprite sheet for its image source data. Overall, the following data is contained in a map segment definition:

- Name

- Source sprite sheet index

- Source rectangle

- Flags

Flags will hold any metadata we may want to use later for identifying specific behaviors, like emitting smoke or spinning. Being the lazy developers that we are, we can hard-code these.

We'll need to create a class to hold the map segment definitions, a method to load the data, a graphic containing map segments, and a text file containing the metadata that we'll be loading.

First, we'll take care of the class. We add a MapClasses folder in the project, and within that we add SegmentDefinitions.cs. Here's the relevant code, minus a few public properties for each private member:

```
class SegmentDefinition
{
    private string name;
    private int sourceIndex;
    private Rectangle srcRect;
    private int flags;

    public SegmentDefinition(string _name,
        int _sourceIndex,
        Rectangle _srcRect,
        int _flags)
    {
        Name = _name;
        SourceIndex = _sourceIndex;
        SourceRect = _srcRect;
        Flags = _flags;
    }
```

```
... getters and setters ...

}
```

The actual file format that we'll be using for our segment definition metadata will look like this:

```
#src n
Name
Source Rectangle: left top right bottom
Flags
```

The first line refers to the source image. Because we'll be using large sprite sheets containing numerous map segments, when we refer to a segment in the metadata, the loading function needs to know on which sprite sheet each segment belongs. We'll be using it as a state, so the line is necessary before Name only if the current segment is on a different sprite sheet as the previous segment.

We can store the metadata in an ordinary text file, which we call maps.zdx. Before we look at the metadata itself, let's take a peek at the actual sprite sheet we'll be working with. Our sprite sheet is shown in Figure 4-8.

■**Note** The .zdx extension means something along the lines of "Zombie Data XNA." If you're just using text files, you can give them whatever extension you like.

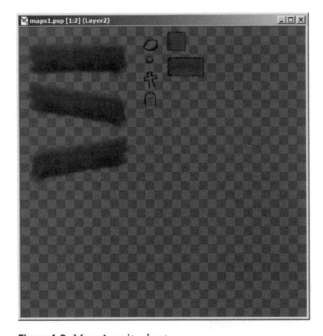

Figure 4-8. *Maps1 sprite sheet*

You can see that we have segments of grass, some stones, and some graves. We'll add trees later, but we're off to a good start. The metadata for this sprite sheet looks like this:

```
Map Defs
#src 1
grass1
0 26 410 178
0
grass2
0 178 404 369
0

.

.

.

block2
514 93 676 187
0
#end
```

When reading it, we'll just skip over the first line, which is sort of a comment.

We create a Map.cs class in the MapClasses folder. For now, we'll add functionality only to read and store segment definitions.

```
using System.IO;
...
class Map
{
    SegmentDefinition[] segDef;

    public Map()
    {
        segDef = new SegmentDefinition[512];
        ReadSegmentDefinitions();
    }

    private void ReadSegmentDefinitions()
    {
        StreamReader s = new StreamReader(@"Content/maps.zdx");
        string t = "";
        int n;
        int currentTex = 0;
        int curDef = -1;
        Rectangle tRect = new Rectangle();
        string[] split;

        t = s.ReadLine();
```

```
while (!s.EndOfStream)
{
    t = s.ReadLine();
    if (t.StartsWith("#"))
    {
        if (t.StartsWith("#src"))
        {
            split = t.Split(' ');
            if (split.Length > 1)
            {
                n = Convert.ToInt32(split[1]);
                currentTex = n - 1;
            }
        }
    }
    else
    {
        curDef++;
        string name = t;

        t = s.ReadLine();
        split = t.Split(' ');
        if (split.Length > 3)
        {
            tRect.X = Convert.ToInt32(split[0]);
            tRect.Y = Convert.ToInt32(split[1]);
            tRect.Width =
                Convert.ToInt32(split[2]) - tRect.X;
            tRect.Height =
                Convert.ToInt32(split[3]) - tRect.Y;
        }
        else
            Console.WriteLine("read fail: " + name);


        int tex = currentTex;

        t = s.ReadLine();
        int flags = Convert.ToInt32(t);

        segDef[curDef] = new
            SegmentDefinition(name, tex, tRect, flags);
    }
}
```

```
    public SegmentDefinition[] SegmentDefinitions
    {
        get { return segDef; }
    }
}
```

Basically, the process unfolds as follows:

1. Open the metadata file.

2. Skip a line.

3. While not end of file, read a line. If it's a `#src` line, change the source sprite sheet. Otherwise do the following:

  • Increment the current segment.

  • Read three lines: `name`, `srcRect`, and `flags`.

  • Instantiate the current segment with `name`, the source sprite sheet, `srcRect`, and `flags`.

4. Close the file.

In order to get `maps.zdx` into the project, select Show All Files for the `MapEditor` project. Right-click the Content folder, and select Include In Project. Then select all the files inside that Content folder and select Exclude From Project. Next, add the `maps.zdx` file to the Content folder and include it in the project. Then, from the Properties window, set the property Copy to Output Directory to Copy If Newer.

All we need to do to allow our map editor to load segment definitions now is to declare a new `Map` object at the class level of `Game1` and instantiate it with new in `Initialize()`. First, add `MapEditor.MapClasses` to your reference list at the top, and then add the following to the `Game1` class:

```
SpriteBatch sprite;
Map map;
And:
protected override void Initialize()
{
    map = new Map();
    base.Initialize();
}
```

As always, it's nice to have some visual confirmation of everything working correctly, so we're going to add some functionality to display our segment definitions in a palette.

First, we need to load our sprite sheet, maps1.png. We also added a bitmap that is essentially a solitary white pixel. Unfortunately, SpriteBatch does not allow us to use blank textures. If we want to create a solid-color rectangle, we must have a bitmap for it. So we're going to throw 1x1.bmp, a white image of dimensions 1 × 1, into the mix. At the class level of Game1, add the following:

```
Texture2D[] mapsTex;
Texture2D nullTex;
```

There is a reason behind calling our 1 × 1 texture nullTex. If we were working directly with the graphics device and not using SpriteBatch, we would have been able to use null as a texture to draw solid color. SpriteBatch does not accept null as a Texture2D parameter, so we'll do the next best thing: pretend we're sending a null texture.

Load the items in Game1.LoadGraphicsContent(), with these lines:

```
text = new Text(textTex, sprite);
nullTex = Content.Load<Texture2D>(@"gfx/1x1");
mapsTex = new Texture2D[1];
for (int i = 0; i < mapsTex.Length; i++)
    mapsTex[i] = Content.Load<Texture2D>(@"gfx/maps" +
            (i + 1).ToString());
```

We're creating mapsTex[] with a size of 1, because we have only one sprite sheet so far. Then we iterate through all members of mapsTex[], loading the images one by one. Notice how we turn 0 into 1 with (i + 1).ToString(). We must turn nonstring values into strings when we're putting together path names.

Now, in Game1.Draw(), take out the text-drawing tests, and then add the following method:

```
private void DrawMapSegments()
{
    Rectangle sRect = new Rectangle();
    Rectangle dRect = new Rectangle();

    text.Size = 0.8f;

    spriteBatch.Begin(SpriteBlendMode.AlphaBlend);
    spriteBatch.Draw(nullTex, new Rectangle(500, 20, 280, 550),
        new Color(0, 0, 0, 100));
    spriteBatch.End();

    for (int i = 0; i < 9; i++)
    {
        SegmentDefinition segDef = map.SegmentDefinitions[i];
        if (segDef == null)
            continue;
```

```
        spriteBatch.Begin(SpriteBlendMode.AlphaBlend);

        dRect.X = 500;
        dRect.Y = 50 + i * 60;

        sRect = segDef.SourceRect;

        if (sRect.Width > sRect.Height)
        {
            dRect.Width = 45;
            dRect.Height = (int)(((float)sRect.Height /
                    (float)sRect.Width) * 45.0f);
        }
        else
        {
            dRect.Height = 45;
            dRect.Width = (int)(((float)sRect.Width /
                    (float)sRect.Height) * 45.0f);
        }

        spriteBatch.Draw(
            mapsTex[segDef.SourceIndex], dRect, sRect, Color.White);

        spriteBatch.End();

        text.Color = Color.White;
        text.DrawText(dRect.X + 50, dRect.Y, segDef.Name);
    }
}
```

First, we're using our `nullTex` to draw a translucent, black rectangle behind our segment palette. Then we're iterating through our segment definitions, grabbing a local reference for each one and drawing each one in the palette. The `if` clause in the middle is a nifty little function that causes the destination rectangle to maintain scale while never exceeding 45 pixels on either dimension. After drawing each segment, we use our `text` class instance to draw the segment's name.

The last thing we need to do is place a call to `DrawMapSegments()` in our `Game1.Draw()` method before `base.Draw()` is called.

Now run what you have so far, and witness the segment palette in all its glory, as shown in Figure 4-9.

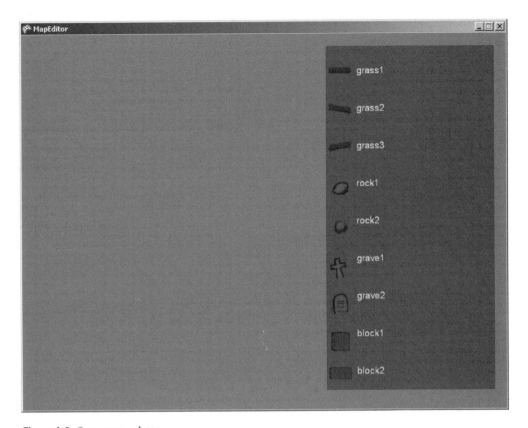

Figure 4-9. *Segment palette*

Simple Interaction

Let's add some simple interaction. You've probably noticed that the mouse cursor disappears whenever the cursor is in the MapEditor window. This is the first thing we need to remedy. We'll start by making our own mouse cursor. We've made an image with some simple interface icons, as shown in Figure 4-10.

Figure 4-10. *Icons image*

We'll need some class-level fields to keep track of our mouse:

```
Texture2D iconsTex;
int mosX, mosY;
bool rightMouseDown;
bool mouseClick;
```

Make sure to load `iconsTex` in `LoadContent()`. Then in `Game1.Update()`, add the following:

```
MouseState mState = Mouse.GetState();
mosX = mState.X;
mosY = mState.Y;
bool pMouseDown = rightMouseDown;
if (mState.LeftButton == ButtonState.Pressed)
    rightMouseDown = true;
else
    rightMouseDown = false;
if (pMouseDown && !rightMouseDown) mouseClick = true;
```

This slightly unwieldy bit of code stores the current mouse state in our local fields and catches mouse clicks—transitions between pressed and released—by comparing the current button state with the previous button state. This isn't a true mouse click, in that the user could conceivably mouse-down outside a button, move to within a button, and mouse-up to cause a click—an invalid scenario under Windows. However, we think we can let it slide.

To draw the cursor, we'll create a simple function in `Game1`:

```
private void DrawCursor()
{
    spriteBatch.Begin(SpriteBlendMode.AlphaBlend);

    spriteBatch.Draw(iconsTex, new Vector2(mosX, mosY),
        new Rectangle(0, 0, 32, 32),
        Color.White, 0.0f,
        new Vector2(0, 0), 1.0f, SpriteEffects.None, 0.0f);

    spriteBatch.End();
}
```

Put a call to `Game1.DrawCursor()` at the end of your `Game1.Draw()` function. Be sure to add it at the end, so that it is the last thing to be drawn on the screen. Figure 4-11 shows the map editor with our new cursor.

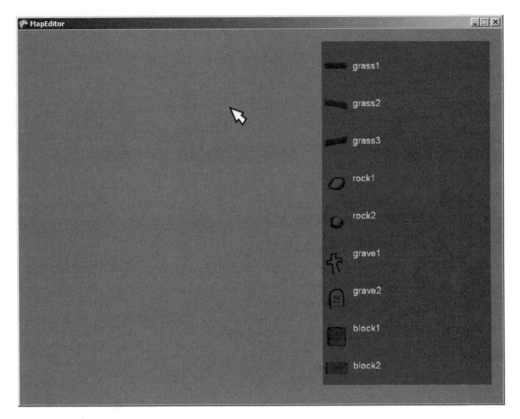

Figure 4-11. *Map editor with the cursor*

This is beginning to look a bit more natural. The next step will be to allow the user to drag map segments on to the map. This involves adding drawing functionality to the Map class and adding dragging functionality to the editor.

Drawing the Map

Our map will have a foreground layer and background layer sandwiching the main layer. We'll iterate through each layer, drawing all map segments on that layer, and translate and scale each layer a certain way to give that good-old parallax effect.

We need to add a MapSegment class for storing the data of each map segment as it appears on the map. It will contain only a segment definition index and a location.

```
class MapSegment
{
    public Vector2 Location;
    int segmentIndex;

    public int Index
    {
        get { return segmentIndex; }
        set { segmentIndex = value; }
    }
}
```

We need to make the Vector2 member, Location, public here because of how structs work in .NET languages. Structures like Vector2 are passed by value, and thus if you create a property (as we do for the segment index), you cannot edit the fields of the Vector2 without creating a new instance. This may be OK for small-scaled games, but creating hundreds of thousands of Vector2 objects per frame will never be good for anyone. By creating the Location member as a public field, we avoid any related issues.

We can put an array of map segments into the Map class now. Since we're going to be using parallax scrolling, we'll have three layers of map segments with up to 64 segments per layer, hence a two-dimensional array dimensioned 3 by 64.

```
SegmentDefinition[] segDef;
MapSegment[,] mapSeg;

public Map()
{
    segDef = new SegmentDefinition[512];
    mapSeg = new MapSegment[3, 64];
    ReadSegmentDefinitions();
}
```

Drawing Functionality

We'll need some functionality to manipulate and draw map segments from the Map class. We'll be doing all of our editing from Game1, so we need to expose some functionality in Map for moving and adding map segments.

```
public MapSegment[,] Segments
{
    get { return mapSeg; }
}

public int AddSeg(int layer, int index)
{
    for (int i = 0; i < 64; i++)
    {
```

```
        if (mapSeg[layer, i] == null)
        {
            mapSeg[layer, i] = new MapSegment();
            mapSeg[layer, i].Index = index;
            return i;
        }
    }
    return -1;
}
```

Let's make a Draw() function for Map. We're sending it the SpriteBatch object and our map sprite sheets, as well as a Vector2 that is the current scroll value. The scroll value will be used to allow the user to scroll around the map. When we draw, we'll always draw relative to the scroll value.

For the actual drawing, we'll iterate through mapSeg[] layer by layer, drawing all segments on each layer in order of first to last. We'll color each layer a little bit differently and use a different scalar, so the foreground will scroll faster and the background will scroll more slowly, giving us that nice parallax effect.

```
public void Draw(SpriteBatch sprite,
    Texture2D[] mapsTex,
    Vector2 scroll)
{
    Rectangle sRect = new Rectangle();
    Rectangle dRect = new Rectangle();

    sprite.Begin(SpriteBlendMode.AlphaBlend);

    for (int l = 0; l < 3; l++)
    {
        float scale = 1.0f;
        Color color = Color.White;
        if (l == 0)
        {
            color = Color.Gray;
            scale = 0.75f;
        }
        else if (l == 2)
        {
            color = Color.DarkGray;
            scale = 1.25f;
        }

        scale *= 0.5f;

        for (int i = 0; i < 64; i++)
        {
```

```
            if (mapSeg[1, i] != null)
            {
                sRect = segDef[mapSeg[1, i].Index].SourceRect;
                dRect.X = (int)(mapSeg[1, i].Location.X
                    - scroll.X * scale);
                dRect.Y = (int)(mapSeg[1, i].GetLoc().Y
                    - scroll.X * scale);
                dRect.Width = (int)(sRect.Width * scale);
                dRect.Height = (int)(sRect.Height * scale);

                sprite.Draw(
                    mapsTex[segDef[mapSeg[1, i].Index].SourceIndex],
                    dRect,
                    sRect,
                    color);
            }
        }
    }
    sprite.End();
}
```

Because SpriteBatch likes rectangles, there's a lot of ugly type casting at work here. The resultant rectangle's width and height dimensions are computed by multiplying the source rectangle's width and height (integers) by the scalar (a float) and casting the products as integers again.

Drag-and-Drop Functionality

Back in Game1, we need to implement some sort of dragging functionality to allow us to move map segments from our palette onto the map. We also need to know on which map layer we're drawing, and the previous cursor location. At the Game1 class level, add the following:

```
int mouseDragSeg = -1;
int curLayer = 1;
int pMosX, pMosY;
```

Then we add some dragging functionality to Update().

```
if (pMouseDown && !rightMouseDown) mouseClick = true;

if (mouseDragSeg > -1)
{
    if (!rightMouseDown)
        mouseDragSeg = -1;
```

```
    else
    {
        Vector2 loc = map.Segments[curLayer, mouseDragSeg].Location;
        loc.X += (mosX - pMosX);
        loc.Y += (mosY - pMosY);
        map.Segments[curLayer, mouseDragSeg].Location = loc;
    }
}
pMosX = mosX;
pMosY = mosY;
```

When dragging begins, we'll store the index of the dragged segment in mouseDragSeg. Then every time Update() is called, we can update the segment's location by the amount the mouse has moved since the last update.

We'll start the dragging from DrawMapSegments(). This is typically a tremendous taboo, as we don't want to put update logic in a drawing function, but we think as long as we acknowledge that it's a bad practice, we're nearly making up for doing it.

```
text.DrawText(dRect.X + 50, dRect.Y, segDef.GetName());

if (rightMouseDown)
{
    if (mosX > dRect.X && mosX < 780 &&
  mosY > dRect.Y && mosY < dRect.Y + 45)
    {
        if (mouseDragSeg == -1)
        {
            int f = map.AddSeg(curLayer, i);
            if (f <= -1)
                continue;

            map.Segments[curLayer, f].Location.X =
                (mosX - sRect.Width / 4);
            map.Segments[curLayer, f].Location.Y =
                (mosY - sRect.Height / 4);
            mouseDragSeg = f;
        }
    }
}
```

We decided to put the logic in the drawing routine because we already have some nice destination rectangles to work with here. We simply check that the mouse location is within a slightly wider, shorter version of the destination rectangle. If it is, and the mouse is down, we try to create a new segment. If this is successful, we put the segment in the correct location and set it as the currently dragged segment.

Don't forget to draw the map!

```
graphics.GraphicsDevice.Clear(Color.CornflowerBlue);
```

```
map.Draw(spriteBatch, mapsTex, new Vector2());
```

We should now have drag-and-drop functionality working, as shown in Figure 4-12.

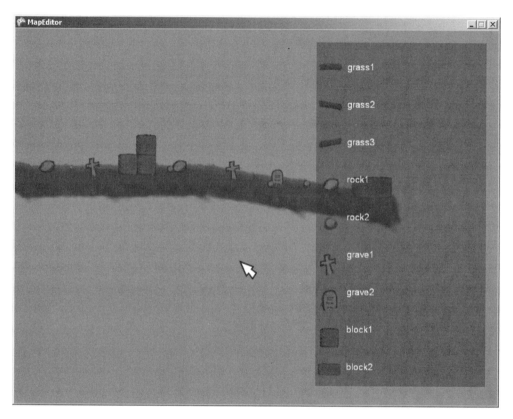

Figure 4-12. *Initial drag and drop*

Interactive Text

Remember our `DrawClickText()` function in `Text`? Let's use it to make our first button. We want to be able to place our map segments on different layers (to show off that parallax goodness), so we'll make a button that will switch among layers when pressed.

In a new method named `Game1.DrawText()`, which we will call from `Game1.Draw()`, "place" the button:

```
string layerName = "map";
switch (curLayer)
{
    case 0:
        layerName = "back";
        break;
    case 1:
        layerName = "mid";
        break;
    case 2:
        layerName = "fore";
        break;
}
if (text.DrawClickText(5, 5,
    "layer: " + layerName, mosX, mosY, mouseClick))
    curLayer = (curLayer + 1) % 3;
```

There's one little detail we can't forget. Since mouseClick is turned on from Update() when the mouse goes from pressed to released, we need to set mouseClick back to false again after we're finished checking to see if anything was clicked. At the end of DrawText(), put this:

```
mouseClick = false;
```

Just to give you an idea of where the Draw() method stands, the following is the order of calls contained within the method body. The order is important, since the last item drawn will be on top.

```
protected override void Draw(GameTime gameTime)
{
    graphics.GraphicsDevice.Clear(Color.CornflowerBlue);

    // TODO: Add your drawing code here
    map.Draw(spriteBatch, mapsTex, new Vector2());

    DrawMapSegments();
    DrawText();
    DrawCursor();

    base.Draw(gameTime);
}
```

The code we just added will give us a button that, when pressed, will toggle the current layer, changing its display name to reflect the layer change. It's all very low-tech, but just look at what we can do, as shown in Figure 4-13.

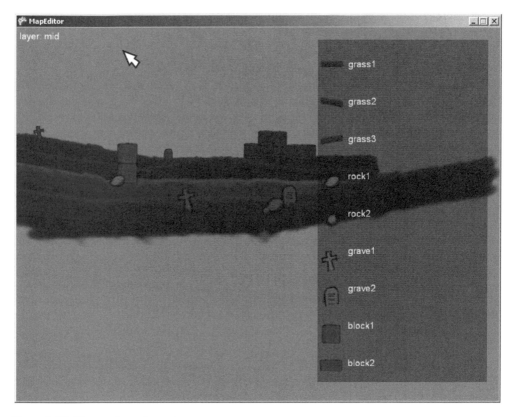

Figure 4-13. *Now we have layers!*

Scrolling the Map

We need some sort of functionality to let us move around in the map, as well as to really get a picture of how this parallax scrolling nonsense looks. We'll set it up so the user clicks and drags with the middle mouse button to scroll. First, at the class level of Game1, we need to add the following:

```
bool midMouseDown;
Vector2 scroll;
```

We're using a Vector2 for scroll. Everything will be drawn relative to scroll, so as scroll's x value increases, the map will appear to move left, and the viewer will seem to be "looking" right—well, panning right anyway.

In Game1.Update(), we need to check if the middle mouse button is newly clicked. If so, we set the previous location. If the middle mouse button is down, we'll update the scroll value by the change between the previous location and current location per frame.

```
midMouseDown = (mState.MiddleButton == ButtonState.Pressed);
.
.
.
```

```
if (midMouseDown)
{
    scroll.X -= (mosX - pMosX) * 2.0f;
    scroll.Y -= (mosY - pMosY) * 2.0f;
}
```

Lastly, we need to make sure we send scroll in our Game1.map.Draw() call:

```
map.Draw(sprite, mapsTex, scroll);
```

This should work fine, but if you try to add a new segment, you'll notice that it starts off in a bizarre location. We'll need to factor in the scroll and layer components when creating a new segment.

In Game1.DrawMapSegments(), find where we set the location of the new segment, and modify the code as follows:

```
if (f <= -1)
    continue;

float layerScalar = 0.5f;
if (curLayer == 0)
    layerScalar = 0.375f;
else if (curLayer == 2)
    layerScalar = 0.625f;

map.Segments[curLayer, f].Location.X =
    (mosX - sRect.Width / 4 + scroll.X * layerScalar);
map.Segments[curLayer, f].Location.Y =
    (mosY - sRect.Height / 4 + scroll.Y * layerScalar);
mouseDragSeg = f;
```

Now we won't have any bizarre floating-drag situations. And while we're tying up loose ends with segment-dragging functionality, we should implement segment dragging for segments that are already placed.

All we need to do here is implement some sort of functionality to determine if the cursor is within a segment on the current layer and the mouse button has just been pressed.

In the Map class, we can reuse some of the drawing code to make a new function, GetHoveredSegment(), which will return the index of a segment that the x,y coordinate passed to it is over, or -1 if no segment matches that description. We work from the end of the list toward the front, so that items added last (to the top of the map) are selected first.

```
public int GetHoveredSegment(int x, int y, int l, Vector2 scroll)
{
    float scale = 1.0f;
    if (l == 0)
        scale = 0.75f;
    else if (l == 2)
        scale = 1.25f;
    scale *= 0.5f;
```

```
    for (int i = 63; i >= 0; i--)
    {
        if (mapSeg[1, i] != null)
        {
            Rectangle sRect =
     segDef[mapSeg[1, i].Index].SourceRect;
            Rectangle dRect = new Rectangle(
                (int)(mapSeg[1, i].Location.X - scroll.X * scale),
                (int)(mapSeg[1, i].Location.Y - scroll.Y * scale),
                (int)(sRect.Width * scale),
                (int)(sRect.Height * scale));
            if (dRect.Contains(x, y))
                return i;
        }
    }
    return -1;
}
```

Then, in Game1, we change Update() just a bit:

```
if (mState.LeftButton == ButtonState.Pressed)
{
    if (!rightMouseDown && mosX < 500)
    {
        int f = map.GetHoveredSegment(mosX, mosY, curLayer, scroll);

        if (f != -1)
            mouseDragSeg = f;
    }
    rightMouseDown = true;
}
else
    rightMouseDown = false;
```

There's a bit of a hack in here, which we can always clean up later. We're checking for dragging only if the mouse x location is less than 500, which is where our palette starts. If we didn't do this, we would risk grabbing an already existing map segment while trying to bring in a new one from the palette. Now when the mouse button is pressed down, we'll be checking to see if it is within a valid segment. If it is, we'll set that as the currently dragged segment.

A Collision Map

We'll define the collision map as metadata containing a collision grid and ledges. A grid will give us the ability to quickly define rough but straight edges to detect collisions against. A ledge will give us some flexibility by defining where the ground is using line segments. First, we'll concentrate on the grid.

The Grid

We'll define the grid in the Map class, and then add functionality for viewing and editing it in Game1.

```
MapSegment[,] mapSeg;
int[,] col;
```

In the constructor, initialize col[,] to be a 20-by-20 array:

```
mapSeg = new MapSegment[3, 64];
col = new int[20, 20];
ReadSegmentDefinitions();
```

As usual, we add a property to gain access from the outside:

```
public int[,] Grid
{
    get { return col; }
}
```

Back in Game1, we make a function to draw the grid and collisions:

```
private void DrawGrid()
{
    spriteBatch.Begin(SpriteBlendMode.AlphaBlend);

    for (int y = 0; y < 20; y++)
    {
        for (int x = 0; x < 20; x++)
        {
            Rectangle dRect = new Rectangle(
                x * 32 - (int)(scroll.X / 2),
                y * 32 - (int)(scroll.Y / 2),
                32,
                32
                );

            if (x < 19)
                spriteBatch.Draw(nullTex, new Rectangle(
                    dRect.X, dRect.Y,
                    32,
                    1
                    ), new Color(255, 0, 0, 100));

            if (y < 19)
                spriteBatch.Draw(nullTex, new Rectangle(
                    dRect.X, dRect.Y,
                    1,
                    32
                    ), new Color(255, 0, 0, 100));
```

```
            if (x < 19 && y < 19)
            {
                if (map.Grid[x, y] == 1)
                {
                    spriteBatch.Draw(nullTex, dRect,
                        new Color(255, 0, 0, 100));
                }
            }
        }
    }

    spriteBatch.End();
}
```

We're using our 1 × 1 white texture again to draw a grid here, filling in grid spaces where the value of col is 1.

To allow the user to edit the collision map, we'll need to let the user change the drawing mode. Currently, the drawing mode allows us to place map segments; we want to be able to switch to a collision map drawing mode.

Add a new class to the MapEditor project called DrawingMode. When the editor opens, change it from a class to an enumerator, adding the following values:

```
enum DrawingMode
{
    SegmentSelection,
    CollisionMap
}
```

Then in the Game1 class, add the following field:

```
DrawingMode drawType = DrawingMode.SegmentSelection;
```

We'll make a drawing button sort of like our layer-selection button—ugly yet functional. In Game1.DrawText(), right next to the layer button, add the following:

```
switch (drawType)
{
    case DrawingMode.SegmentSelection:
        layerName = "select";
        break;
    case DrawingMode.CollisionMap:
        layerName = "col";
        break;
}
if (text.DrawClickText(5, 25, "draw: " + layerName,
  mosX, mosY, mouseClick))
    drawType = (DrawingMode)((int)(drawType + 1) % 2);
```

Because we don't want to see our map segment palette while we're in collision map editing mode, modify the Game1.Draw() method to look like the following:

```
map.Draw(spriteBatch, mapsTex, scroll);

switch(drawType)
{
    case DrawingMode.SegmentSelection:
        DrawMapSegments();
        break;
}
DrawGrid();
DrawText();
DrawCursor();
```

Back in Game1.Update(), we'll change the block that checks to see if you're trying to drag a new segment so that it happens only when the user is in select mode.

```
if (drawType == DrawingMode.SegmentSelection)
{
    int f = map.GetHoveredSegment(mosX, mosY, curLayer, scroll);
    if (f != -1)
        mouseDragSeg = f;
}
```

Then, to allow users to edit the collision map, add this:

```
else if (drawType == DRAW_COL)
{
    int x = (mosX + (int)(scroll.X / 2)) / 32;
    int y = (mosY + (int)(scroll.Y / 2)) / 32;
    if (x >= 0 && y >= 0 && x < 20 && y < 20)
    {
        if (mState.LeftButton == ButtonState.Pressed)
            map.Grid[x, y] = 1;
        else if (mState.RightButton == ButtonState.Pressed)
            map.Grid[x, y] = 0;
    }
}
```

We're computing the x and y coordinates by getting the mouse coordinates relative to scroll, and then dividing them by the grid size to get the proper collision map cells. If the left button is down, we'll set the collision map value to 1. If the right button is down, we'll set the value to 0.

If you try playing with our current build, you'll see that clicking the draw button will also draw a collision square below the button. We'll need to make a more standard method for determining whether the user is drawing in a safe draw zone and not below buttons. We can define this method in Game1:

```
private bool GetCanEdit()
{
    if (mosX > 100 && mosX < 500 && mosY > 100 && mosY < 550)
        return true;
    return false;
}
```

In Game1.Update(), we change every occurrence of (mosX < 500) to GetCanEdit(). We should also draw a rectangle to show users the drawing area.

In Game1.DrawGrid(), add the following code segment after the drawing of the collision grid:

```
Color oColor = new Color(255, 255, 255, 100);
spriteBatch.Draw(nullTex, new Rectangle(100, 50, 400, 1), oColor);
spriteBatch.Draw(nullTex, new Rectangle(100, 50, 1, 500), oColor);
spriteBatch.Draw(nullTex, new Rectangle(500, 50, 1, 500), oColor);
spriteBatch.Draw(nullTex, new Rectangle(100, 550, 400, 1), oColor);
```

The current state of our build is shown in Figure 4-14.

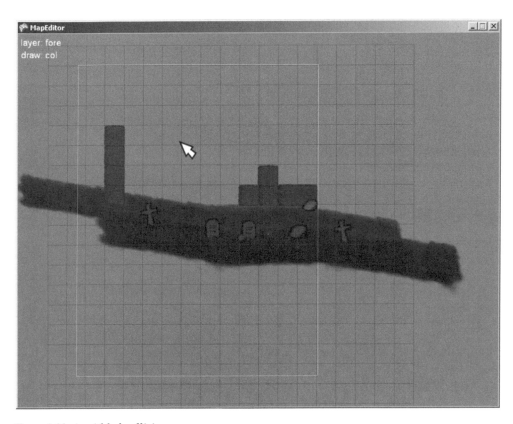

Figure 4-14. *A gridded collision map*

Ledges

The gridded collision map will work really well for all things blocky (like our blocks), but sloping sections like grass will need a different type of collision definition. We'll use line strips, which we'll call *ledges*.

We'll define a new Ledge class in the MapClasses folder as such:

```
class Ledge
{
    Vector2[] nodes = new Vector2[16];
    public int totalNodes = 0;
    public int flags = 0;

    public Vector2[] Nodes
    {
        get { return nodes; }
    }
}
```

A ledge is a series of points. For simplicity, we'll assume these points always go from left to right. Each point is a *node*. We're also throwing in a flags variable for good measure. For now, we'll say that with flags, 0 is a "soft" ledge and 1 is a "hard" ledge, meaning that the player cannot drop below it.

Now add ledges to our Map class:

```
Ledge[] ledges;

public Map()
{
    ...
    ledges = new Ledge[16];
    for (int i = 0; i < 16; i++)
        ledges[i] = new Ledge();
}
```

As usual, we include a property to expose ledge functionality to Game1:

```
public Ledge[] Ledges
{
    get { return ledges; }
}
```

Now we need to add a new draw type to Game1 to go along with CollisionGrid and SegmentSelection. This can be done by adding another item, named Ledges, to the DrawingMode enumeration in Game1.

We'll also be using a state-based ledge drawing system, where every time the user clicks, a node will be added to the current ledge. To set this up, add the following to the Game1 class level:

```
int curLedge = 0;
int curNode = 0;
```

We'll need to make sure our new draw type gets drawn and can be selected by clicking on our fantastically minimal draw button. In Game1.DrawText(), we evaluate drawType and then draw a button that the user can click to change drawType. Let's add a new case for ledges and change the DrawClickText() line as follows:

```
        case DrawingMode.Ledge:
        layerName = "ledge";
        break;
}
if (text.DrawClickText(5, 25, "draw: " + layerName,
    mosX, mosY, mouseClick))
        drawType = (drawType + 1) % 3;
```

Now we can switch the draw type between selection, collision, and ledge. Note that we've changed the DrawClickText() call modulus value to 3, because there are now three draw types.

Let's create a function in Game1 to draw all ledges.

```
private void DrawLedges()
{
    Rectangle rect = new Rectangle();
    spriteBatch.Begin(SpriteBlendMode.AlphaBlend);
    Color tColor = new Color();

    rect.X = 32;
    rect.Y = 0;
    rect.Width = 32;
    rect.Height = 32;

    for (int i = 0; i < 16; i++)
    {
        if (map.Ledges[i] != null && map.Ledges[i].TotalNodes > 0)
        {
            for (int n = 0; n < map.Ledges[i].TotalNodes; n++)
            {
                Vector2 tVec;
                tVec = map.Ledges[i].Nodes[n];
                tVec -= scroll / 2.0f;
                tVec.X -= 5.0f;
                if (curLedge == i)
                    tColor = Color.Yellow;
                else
                    tColor = Color.White;
                spriteBatch.Draw(iconsTex, tVec, rect,
                    tColor, 0.0f, Vector2.Zero,
                    0.35f, SpriteEffects.None, 0.0f);
```

```
            if (n < map.Ledges[i].TotalNodes - 1)
            {
                Vector2 nVec;
                nVec = map.Ledges[i].Nodes[n + 1];
                nVec -= scroll / 2.0f;
                nVec.X -= 4.0f;
                for (int x = 1; x < 20; x++)
                {
                    Vector2 iVec = (nVec - tVec)
                        * ((float)x / 20.0f) + tVec;

                    Color nColor = new Color(255, 255, 255, 75);
                    if (map.Ledges[i].Flags == 1) nColor =
                        new Color(255, 0, 0, 75);
                    spriteBatch.Draw(iconsTex, iVec, rect,
                        nColor,
                        0.0f, Vector2.Zero, 0.25f,
                        SpriteEffects.None, 0.0f);
                }
            }
        }
    }
}

    spriteBatch.End();
}
```

Here, we have three nested for loops:

- The outermost iterates through all ledges.

- The middle loop iterates through all nodes within the current ledge, drawing each node.

- The innermost loop iterates through a series of midpoints between every adjacent pair of nodes in the current ledge, drawing a makeshift line.

We added some little color niceties as well. We draw the main nodes in yellow if the ledge is currently selected. We draw the midpoints in red if the ledge's flag value is 1.

Don't forget to add a call to DrawLedges() in Game1.Draw(). After the DrawGrid() call, add the following:

```
DrawLedges();
```

In Game1.Update(), in the block where we check for hovered segments, we put our functionality for adding ledge nodes:

```
else if (drawType == DrawingMode.Ledges)
{
    if(map.Ledges[curLedge] == null)
        map.Ledges[curLedge] = new Ledge();
```

```
    if (map.Ledges[curLedge].TotalNodes < 15)
    {
        map.Ledges[curLedge].Nodes[map.Ledges[curLedge].TotalNodes] =
            new Vector2(mosX, mosY) + scroll / 2.0f;

        map.Ledges[curLedge].TotalNodes++;
    }
}
```

All we're doing is setting the node at index TotalNodes to the current location we'll give it (we're factoring in scroll), and then incrementing TotalNodes by one.

Let's add a ledge palette for selecting ledges and changing ledge flag values by creating a new method, Game1.DrawLedgePalette(), which we call from the Game1.Draw() method.

```
private void DrawLedgePalette()
{
    for (int i = 0; i < 16; i++)
    {
        if(map.Ledges[i] == null)
            continue;

        int y = 50 + i * 20;
        if (curLedge == i)
        {
            text.Color = Color.Lime;
            text.DrawText(520, y, "ledge " + i.ToString());
        }
        else
        {
            if (text.DrawClickText(520, y,
    "ledge " + i.ToString(),
                mosX, mosY, mouseClick))
                    curLedge = i;
        }
        text.Color = Color.White;
        text.DrawText(620, y,
      "n" + map.Ledges[i].TotalNodes.ToString());

        if (text.DrawClickText(680, y, "f" +
            map.Ledges[i].Flags.ToString(), mosX, mosY, mouseClick))
                map.Ledges[i].Flags = (map.Ledges[i].Flags + 1) % 2;
    }
}
```

The currently selected ledge is drawn in lime green; unselected ledges are drawn as clickable text. After each ledge button, the number of nodes is drawn, followed by a clickable display of the ledge's flag value. It's all so very ugly, yet functional. Our ledge-editing functionality is shown in action in Figure 4-15.

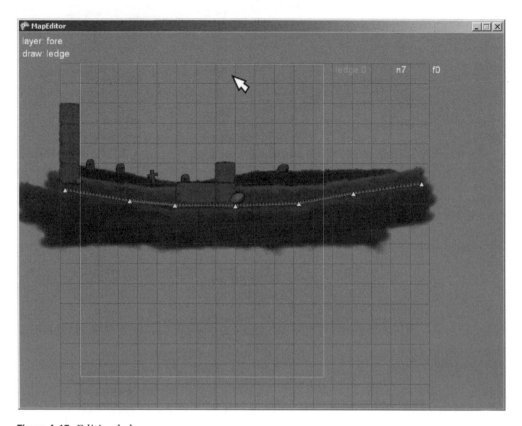

Figure 4-15. *Editing ledges*

Text Editing

Now we need to add a way to name our map. Editing text is another bit of functionality that's ugly to implement due to the fact that XNA does not strictly follow an event-based model, especially for keyboard, gamepad, and mouse input. We need to track keyboard state changes, handle pressed keys, and handle special cases, like the Backspace and Enter keys.

Much as we did with drawing, we can simplify the current editing mode with an enumeration in Game1. This time, we have called the enumeration EditingMode. Go ahead and create this enumeration with the following states:

```
enum EditingMode
{
    None,
    Path
}
```

At the class level of Game1, we'll add some fields to keep track of previous keyboard state (so we know when it changes), as well as to keep track of what text is currently being edited.

```
KeyboardState oldKeyState;
EditingMode editMode = EditingMode.None;
```

Before we go any further, we also need to add a string in the Map class that represents its path:

```
private string path = "maps.zdx";
public string Path
{
    get { return path; }
    set { path = value; }
}
```

Back in the Game1 class, add two functions for handling keyboard input: UpdateKeys() to compare the current keyboard state to the previous to check for new key presses, and PressKey() to handle the key presses.

```
private void UpdateKeys()
{
    KeyboardState keyState = Keyboard.GetState();

    Keys[] currentKeys = keyState.GetPressedKeys();
    Keys[] lastKeys = oldKeyState.GetPressedKeys();
    bool found = false;

    for (int i = 0; i < currentKeys.Length; i++)
    {
        found = false;

        for (int y = 0; y < lastKeys.Length; y++)
        {
            if (currentKeys[i] == lastKeys[y]) found = true;
            break;
        }
        if (!found)
        {
            PressKey(currentKeys[i]);
        }
    }

    oldKeyState = keyState;
}

private void PressKey(Keys key)
{
    string t = String.Empty;
    switch (editMode)
    {
```

```
        case EditingMode.Path:
            t = map.Path;
            break;
        default:
            return;
    }

    if (key == Keys.Back)
    {
        if (t.Length > 0) t = t.Substring(0, t.Length - 1);
    }
    else if (key == Keys.Enter)
    {
        editMode = EditingMode.None;
    }
    else
    {
        t = (t + (char)key).ToLower();
    }

    switch (editMode)
    {
        case EditingMode.Path:
            map.path = t;
            break;
    }
}
```

The PressKey() function isn't great, but it will suffice for our current needs. It will handle only *a–z* and 0–9; any other key will add bizarre characters to the string we are working on. If the Backspace key is pressed, the length of the string is reduced by 1. If the Enter key is pressed, editingMode will be set to None.

Back in our Game1.DrawText() method, we'll make another button:

```
text.Color = Color.White;
if (editMode == EditingMode.Path)
    text.DrawText(5, 45, map.Path + "*");
else
{
    if (text.DrawClickText(5, 45, map.Path, mosX, mosY, mouseClick))
        editMode = EditingMode.Path;
}
```

Be sure to put a call to Game1.UpdateKeys() in Game1.Update(), and we should be all set. Immediately at the start of Game1.Update(), add the following:

```
UpdateKeys();
```

Saving and Loading

The map editor, admittedly, is at a very ugly, semifunctional state. But creating it should have taken only about an hour, and the sooner we have a semifunctional map editor, the sooner we can start work on the tech demo. Our primary goal at this point is to be able to create rudimentary maps and characters as quickly as possible so we can start playing with the actual game development.

Now we're ready to add the saving and loading functionality. We'll start by creating a function to draw those load and save icons from our icons file (Figure 4-10, shown earlier).

```
private bool DrawButton(int x, int y,
    int index, int mosX, int mosY, bool mouseClick)
{
    bool r = false;

    Rectangle sRect = new Rectangle(32 * (index % 8),
        32 * (index / 8), 32, 32);
    Rectangle dRect = new Rectangle(x, y, 32, 32);

    if (dRect.Contains(mosX, mosY))
    {
        dRect.X -= 1;
        dRect.Y -= 1;
        dRect.Width += 2;
        dRect.Height += 2;
        if (mouseClick)
            r = true;
    }
    spriteBatch.Begin(SpriteBlendMode.AlphaBlend);
    spriteBatch.Draw(iconsTex, dRect, sRect, Color.White);
    spriteBatch.End();

    return r;
}
```

Next, add some method calls in the Game1.Draw() function so we can read and save some files:

```
if (DrawButton(5, 65, 3, mosX, mosY, mouseClick))
    map.Write();

if (DrawButton(40, 65, 4, mosX, mosY, mouseClick))
    map.Read();
```

Let's make load and save functions in the Map class. We'll call them Read() and Write(), and save them as binary files. The BinaryWriter allows us to spew out a series of values, which we can easily take back in again with the (you guessed it) BinaryReader. There are a few odd special considerations here. For instance, we write -1 for null map segments (which we'll need to take into consideration when we read).

```
public void Write()
{
    BinaryWriter file = new BinaryWriter(File.Open(@"data/"
  + path + ".zmx",
        FileMode.Create));

    for (int i = 0; i < ledges.Length; i++)
    {
        file.Write(ledges[i].TotalNodes);
        for (int n = 0; n < ledges[i].TotalNodes; n++)
        {
            file.Write(ledges[i].Nodes[n].X);
            file.Write(ledges[i].Nodes[n].Y);
        }
        file.Write(ledges[i].Flags);
    }
    for (int l = 0; l < 3; l++)
    {
        for (int i = 0; i < 64; i++)
        {
            if (mapSeg[l, i] == null)
                file.Write(-1);
            else
            {
                file.Write(mapSeg[l, i].Index);
                file.Write(mapSeg[l, i].Location.X);
                file.Write(mapSeg[l, i].Location.Y);
            }
        }
    }
    for (int x = 0; x < 20; x++)
    {
        for (int y = 0; y < 20; y++)
        {
            file.Write(col[x, y]);
        }
    }
    file.Close();
}
```

Read() is essentially the opposite. We process the file linearly in exactly the same order in which we wrote it.

```
public void Read()
{
    BinaryReader file = new BinaryReader(File.Open(@"data/"
  + path + ".zmx",
        FileMode.Open));
```

```
        for (int i = 0; i < ledges.Length; i++)
        {
            Ledges[i] = new Ledge();
            ledges[i].TotalNodes = file.ReadInt32();
            for (int n = 0; n < ledges[i].TotalNodes; n++)
            {
                ledges[i].Nodes[n] = new Vector2(
                    file.ReadSingle(), file.ReadSingle());
            }
            ledges[i].Flags = file.ReadInt32();
        }
        for (int l = 0; l < 3; l++)
        {
            for (int i = 0; i < 64; i++)
            {
                int t = file.ReadInt32();
                if (t == -1)
                    mapSeg[l, i] = null;
                else
                {
                    mapSeg[l, i] = new MapSegment();
                    mapSeg[l, i].Index = t;
                    mapSeg[l, i].Location = new Vector2(
                        file.ReadSingle(),
                        file.ReadSingle());
                }
            }
        }
        for (int x = 0; x < 20; x++)
        {
            for (int y = 0; y < 20; y++)
            {
                col[x, y] = file.ReadInt32();
            }
        }
        file.Close();
}
```

One interesting detail that we can't neglect is to create the data folder you see in the file path. Navigate to MapEditor/MapEditor/bin/x86/Debug and create a data folder. Another way to do this is to add the data folder to the project, and then add a text file called placeholder to that folder. Remove the file extension, and set it to be copied to the build folder when it is newer than the one there. This adds an extra file to the bin folder, but also allows us to create the data folder automatically.

With reading and writing in place, we can now create a map to work with. Such a map is shown in Figure 4-16.

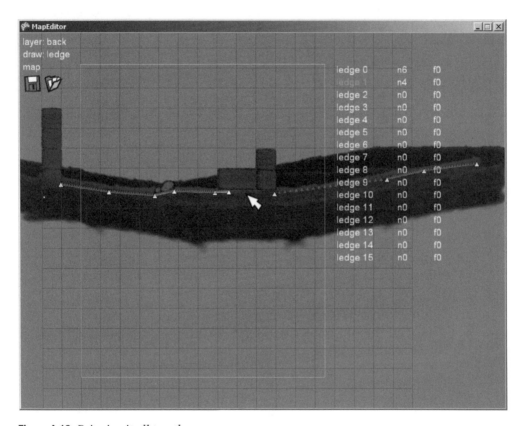

Figure 4-16. *Bringing it all together*

Figure 4-16 shows a simple map we've created and named map, which we will be using for testing initially. This was our goal: to create a simple map. As the game engine grows more complex and requires more detail, we'll put more work into the map editor, but its current state will suffice for now.

A quick list of some of the improvements that must be added to the map editor is as follows:

- Segment-ordering functionality

- Segment-deleting functionality

- Ledge-deleting functionality

- Script editor

- Map script definition

Conclusion

The map editor we've created is not particularly nice-looking or overly user-friendly, but the focus here is on creating a functional tool in as little time as possible, and to that end, we think we've succeeded with flying colors. We've created simple interface elements, a map segment definition format, drag-and-drop functionality, ledge-creation functionality, collision-map painting, and reading and writing functionality. We've also taken our first step toward the creation of Zombie Smashers XNA! We hope it wasn't *too* exhausting.

The next step will be to build a similarly rudimentary character editor, create a hero and an enemy, and then start right in on our game engine. Of course, when we create our game engine, we'll already have a lot of functionality (map loading and drawing; character loading, animating, and drawing) in place from our editors, so the amount of work to do will be relatively minimal.

■ ■ ■

CHAPTER 5

The Character Editor
The Meat and Bones

The characters in our game will be, quite literally, the most animated aspect of our final product. Creating a robust character format will allow us to roll out expressive and reactive heroes and monsters with fluid animations and immersive interactivity. Imagine, for a moment, a first-person shooter with a lot of explosions, trees, houses, tanks, aliens, and soldiers. Now imagine that instead of the aliens and soldiers running around, they glide—their limbs not moving a bit, no matter how fast they run. Without animation, the life of a game is quickly cut short, because it is one of the most essential aspects of immersing a player.

Much like the map editor, our character editor will be extremely lacking in polish, but should make up for it in utility. We need to be able to move, rotate, and scale pieces to assemble frames of animation, edit keyframe parameters, and compose animations.

In this chapter, we'll do the necessary setup for the new project. Then we'll take a look at the design of our character format. It's a pretty intuitive format that works very well for good-looking 2D characters. After discussing the planned character format, we'll look at the structure it will have to take, and then implement the heck out of it. Once we have all of our character format definition classes in place, we'll build a character editor around it, much as we did with the map editor in the previous chapter.

Creating a New Project: Character Editor

We've already started the MapEditor project. Now it's time to create CharacterEditor. Open your existing ZombieSmashers solution in Visual Studio and add a new project called CharacterEditor, as shown in Figure 5-1. As you did with the MapEditor project, set the new project to be the startup project for the solution.

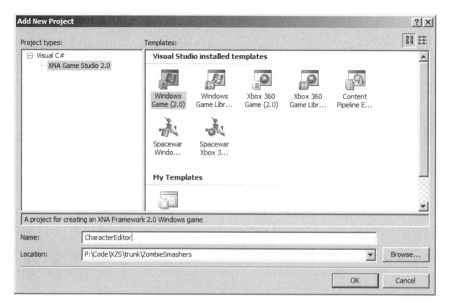

Figure 5-1. *Adding the CharacterEditor project*

We can reuse the Text class from MapEditor, but let's move it to a library so it will be easier to reuse.

Creating a Windows Game Library

So far, we have been creating Windows Game projects. Now, we will create a Windows Game Library project. However, what is created by the .NET platform for a library is not that different from what is produced for a game. The main difference between a game (*.exe) and a library (*.dll) is that you can double-click a game to run it. The game is an executable (EXE), and the library is a dynamic link library (DLL). This does not mean that you can't house a game project inside a DLL. It just means that Windows doesn't know how to run it like an EXE. In terms of referencing, a DLL and an EXE are considered assemblies, and can be referenced by any type of .NET project.

To create a library, right-click the ZombieSmashers solution in Solution Explorer and choose Add ➤ New Project. In the Add New Project dialog, select Windows Game Library (2.0). Name the project TextLib, as shown in Figure 5-2.

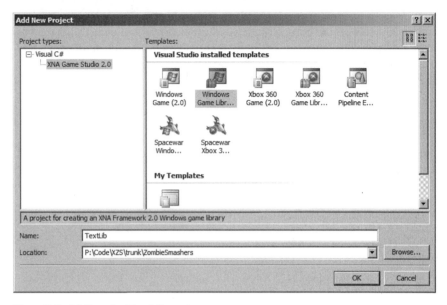

Figure 5-2. *Adding the TextLib project*

Visual Studio sets us up with a fresh library, complete with a Class1.cs class. We'll just need to do a bit of refactoring. In MapEditor, copy the class Text { ... } block from our Text class. Paste this over the public class Class1 line in Class1, and add the public modifier, because we'll need Text to be public now that it's in its own library. It should look like this:

```
    .
    .
    .
using Microsoft.Xna.Framework;

namespace TextLib
{
    public class Text
    {
        private float size;
        private Color color;
            .
            .
            .
```

This should be all we need to do to set up our text library. Now we need to put it in CharacterEditor. In Solution Explorer, right-click References in the CharacterEditor project and select Add Reference. In the Add Reference dialog, click the Projects tab. Select TextLib and click OK.

Finally, in Game1, we need to specify that we'll be using TextLib. Add the following:

```
using Microsoft.Xna.Framework.Storage;
using TextLib;
```

Remember this process; reusable code can be abstracted and put in a central library. When you have enough code in this central library, you have a framework of your own! Doing this can help you in the future when you want to make a new game, whether it's a side-scroller or a first-person shooter. Having easy access to code that you have tested and maintained greatly decreases the development time of new projects.

Drawing Text

Now we need to make some additions to `CharacterEditor` to draw text, much the same as the code changes we made in `Game1` in `MapEditor` to draw text.

First, add `Arial.spritefont` to your `Content/Fonts` folder. Then add a `gfx` folder to your Content project.

Next, declare and load our Arial texture and `text` object in `Game1`, with the following code:

```
SpriteBatch spriteBatch;
SpriteFont font;
Text text;
```

Then load our texture and use it in instantiating our `text` object:

```
protected override void LoadContent()
{
    spriteBatch = new SpriteBatch(GraphicsDevice);
    font = Content.Load<SpriteFont>(@"Fonts/Arial");
    text = new Text(spriteBatch, font);
}
```

We're good to go now.

At this point, it makes a lot of sense to refactor `MapEditor` to use `TextLib` instead of the `Text` class it uses. That way, if you need to make any changes to `Text`, you can do that in one place.

After you've made the necessary changes in `MapEditor`, it's time to start work on the character editor.

Creating the Character Editor

The character format is a fairly intuitive hierarchical format that we touched on briefly in Chapter 3. The breakdown, from the ground up, is as follows:

- A *part* is a piece of a character, like a head, arm, sword, and so on.

- A *frame* is a collection of parts arranged into a pose. Frame `attack1` could contain a head, arms, a torso, legs, and a wrench, all arranged into our hero ready to strike.

- A *keyframe* is a reference to a frame, plus metadata. A keyframe could point to `attack1`, indicate a duration of 5 ticks, and play a swooshing sound.

- An *animation* is made up of a series of keyframes, like `attack1 attack2 attack3 attack4`.

Figure 5-3 shows a far-too-adorable rendition of this hierarchy.

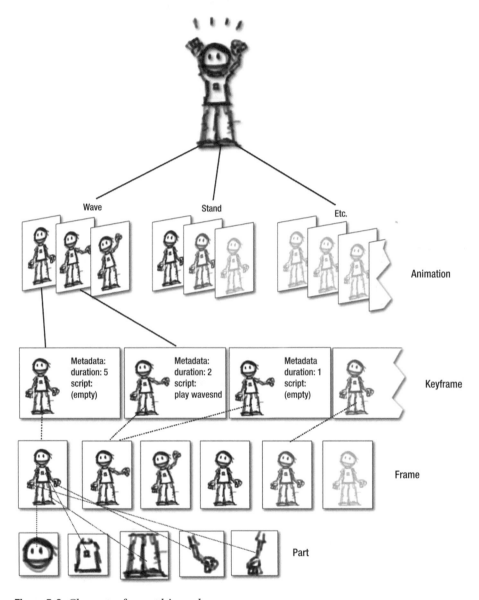

Figure 5-3. *Character format hierarchy*

This should be fairly straightforward. If not, all will become clear as we work through building the character editor.

The Character Definition

Now it's time to start some coding. We'll organize all of our character-related class files into a Character folder. A quick glance at our planning reveals that we need five class files: CharDef, Animation, KeyFrame, Frame, and Part. Your solution should end up looking like Figure 5-4.

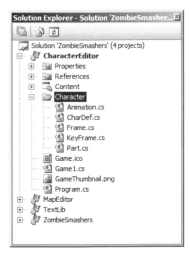

Figure 5-4. *The class files for the character definition*

We'll start from the ground up, with the Part class:

```
class Part
{
    public Vector2 Location;
    public float Rotation;
    public Vector2 Scaling;
    public int Index;
    public int Flip;

    public Part()
    {
        Index = -1;
        Scaling = new Vector2(1.0f, 1.0f);
    }
}
```

The first three fields—location, rotation, and scaling—have quite a bit of history in 3D graphics (where they're known as translation, rotation, and scaling). Location refers to where the part is. Rotation is the angle of the part in radians. Scaling is the horizontal and vertical scale of the part; for example (1, 1) is normal, and (5, 0.5) is very wide and flat.

We'll keep the fields public. The index field is instantiated to -1, meaning that the part does not exist—when we draw a character, we won't draw any parts where index < 0.

Moving up, we have Frame:

```
class Frame
{
    Part[] parts;
    public string name;
```

```
    public Frame()
    {
        parts = new Part[16];
        for (int i = 0; i < part.Length; i++)
            parts[i] = new Part();
        Name = String.Empty;
    }

    public Part[] Parts
    {
        get { return parts; }
    }
}
```

A Frame is made up of parts, so we're using an array to store them all, made accessible with a property. The way we're representing the data, Frame and Animation both will sit in CharDef, so we'll need to move laterally and work upward, meeting at CharDef. Let's start at the bottom again, with KeyFrame:

```
class KeyFrame
{
    public int FrameRef;
    public int Duration;
    string[] scripts;

    public KeyFrame()
    {
        FrameRef = -1;
        Duration = 0;
        scripts = new string[4];
        for (int i = 0; i < scripts.Length; i++)
            scripts[i] = String.Empty;
    }

    public string[] Scripts
    {
        get { return scripts; }
    }
}
```

As we've said, KeyFrame contains a frame reference and some metadata. Here, we use FrameRef to specify the index of the frame this KeyFrame refers to, Duration to specify how many ticks this KeyFrame occupies, and scripts[] to hold any scripting this KeyFrame may use. We're limiting it to four lines, which will probably be enough for any situation.

Moving up, we define Animation as follows:

```
class Animation
{
    public string name;
    KeyFrame[] keyFrames;

    public Animation()
    {
        Name = String.Empty;
        keyFrames = new KeyFrame[64];
        for (int i = 0; i < keyFrames.Length; i++)
            keyFrames[i] = new KeyFrame();
    }

    public KeyFrame[] KeyFrames
    {
        get { return keyFrames; }
    }
}
```

This class is very straightforward. An Animation consists of an array of up to 64 keyframes and a name. The animation names are very important. We'll be using them for scripting and (*gasp*) a bit of hard-coding, with names like idle, run, and jump.

Now we can put it all together in CharDef:

```
class CharDef
{
    Animation[] animations;
    Frame[] frames;
    public string Path;

    public int HeadIndex;
    public int TorsoIndex;
    public int LegsIndex;
    public int WeaponIndex;

    public CharDef()
    {
        animations = new Animation[64];
        for (int i = 0; i < animations.Length; i++)
            animations[i] = new Animation();
        frames = new Frame[512];
        for (int i = 0; i < frames.Length; i++)
            frames[i] = new Frame();

        Path = "char";
    }
```

```
public Animation[] Animations
{
    get { return animations; }
}

public Frame[] Frames
{
    get { return frames; }
}
}
```

Here, we have our frames and animations together, along with a few surprises. One is path, which doubles as the character definition name and file path. We also have headIdx, torsoIdx, legsIdx, and weaponIdx, which specify the textures that this character definition will be using.

We still have quite a bit of work to do before we can actually see any of the many fruits of our labors. We've defined the character format, and now we need to make a function to draw a character, but that's only the tip of the ever-increasing-in-size iceberg.

After we've created our draw function in our Game1 class, we'll need to build an editor, which, as you've probably noticed by now, is the title of this chapter.

Drawing the Character

Before we create the function to draw the character, we again need to set up the class to handle characters:

```
using CharacterEditor.Character;
namespace CharacterEditor
{
    class Game1 : Game
    {
        CharDef charDef;
    }
}
```

Next, we create a Game1.DrawCharacter() function. Don't worry if a few or many of the members are not declared just yet, as they will all be covered over the course of the chapter.

```
private void DrawCharacter(Vector2 loc, float scale,
int face, int frameIndex, bool preview, float alpha)
{
    Rectangle sRect = new Rectangle();

    Frame frame = charDef.Frames[frameIndex];

    spriteBatch.Begin(SpriteBlendMode.AlphaBlend);
```

```
for (int i = 0; i < frame.Parts.Length; i++)
{
    Part part = frame.Parts[i];
    if (part.Index > -1)
    {
        sRect.X = ((part.Index % 64) % 5) * 64;
        sRect.Y = ((part.Index % 64) / 5) * 64;
        sRect.Width = 64;
        sRect.Height = 64;
        if (part.Index >= 192)
        {
            sRect.X = ((part.Index % 64) % 3) * 80;
            sRect.Width = 80;
        }

        float rotation = part.Rotation;

        Vector2 location = part.Location * scale + loc;
        Vector2 scaling = part.Scaling * scale;
        if (part.Index >= 128) scaling *= 1.35f;

        if (face == FACE_LEFT)
        {
            rotation = -rotation;
            location.X -= part.Location.X * scale * 2.0f;
        }
```

So far, we are iterating through the Part array for the frame to draw, FrameIndex, getting set up to draw each Part.

We're using one of the sprite sheets in Figure 5-4. On these sprite sheets, each sprite is 64 × 64, except on the weapons sheet, where they are spaced 80 × 64 (weapons tend to be longer, so why waste space?).

In Part, we have only one field to indicate which image that part is using, but we need to specify an image index *and* a texture—head, torso, legs, or weapon—so we use a truly ugly method of keeping track of this value: modulus arithmetic. Essentially, the index is as follows:

- 0–63 uses the head texture.

- 64–127 uses the torso texture.

- 128–191 uses the legs texture.

- 192–256 uses the weapons texture.

To get the texture, we use Index / 64. To get the image index on that texture, we use index % 64. It's a little cumbersome at first, but soon enough, you'll be thinking in modulus!

There are a few special cases. The first special case occurs when we want to draw a weapon. Since weapons are spaced 80 × 64 (three rows) on their sheet, we'll need to compute their source rectangle slightly differently. To check to see if a part is using a weapons texture, we check if Index >= 192.

The second special case occurs when we want to draw legs or a weapon. Legs take up a bit more space in the game, so we shrunk them down in Paint Shop Pro before saving them. If index >= 128, we're looking at legs or weapons. Rather than manually scale them each frame, we just hard-code the default size of legs to be 35% larger than other part types.

The third special case is for a left-facing character. For this, we negate the rotation and translation values:

```
Texture2D texture = null;

int t = part.Index / 64;
switch (t)
{
    case 0:
        texture = headTex[charDef.HeadIndex];
        break;
    case 1:
        texture = torsoTex[charDef.TorsoIndex];
        break;
    case 2:
        texture = legsTex[charDef.LegsIndex];
        break;
    case 3:
        texture = weaponTex[charDef.WeaponIndex];
        break;
}
```

Here, we figure out which texture we're using based on the Index / 64 value. Finally, we draw the thing with our spriteBatch. The only special case worth nothing is the preview value. We'll be drawing two characters on screen: an editable one and an animation preview. On the editable one, we would like to highlight in red whichever part is selected.

```
Color color =
    new Color(255, 255, 255, (byte)(alpha * 255));

if (!preview && selPart == i) color = new
    Color(255, 0, 0, (byte)(alpha * 255));

bool flip = false;

if ((face == FACE_RIGHT && part.flip == 0) ||
    (face == FACE_LEFT && part.flip == 1)) flip = true;

if (texture != null)
{
    spriteBatch.Draw(texture, location, sRect,
        color, rotation, new Vector2(
        (float)sRect.Width / 2f, 32.0f),
        scaling, (flip ?
```

```
                    SpriteEffects.None :
                    SpriteEffects.FlipHorizontally),
                    1.0f);
            }
        }
    }

    spriteBatch.End();
}
```

And that should take care of drawing the character. Unfortunately, we have no way of creating a character to draw until we implement a proper editor. In the meantime, take a look at Figure 5-5.

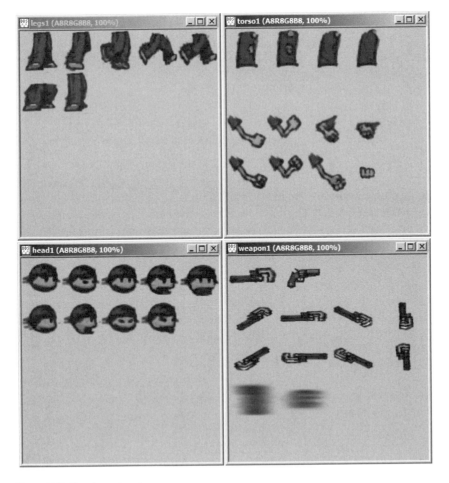

Figure 5-5. *Our hero in pieces*

We use headTex[], torsoTex[], legsTex[], and weaponsTex[] to store our textures. We'll load the images in LoadContent() as usual, with one exception. Due to the large number of

texture arrays, an extra method is helpful to reduce the amount of redundant code. Starting off
with the code in LoadContent:

```
legsTex = new Texture2D[1];
torsoTex = new Texture2D[1];
headTex = new Texture2D[1];
weaponTex = new Texture2D[1];

LoadTextures(legsTex, @"gfx/legs");
LoadTextures(torsoTex, @"gfx/torso");
LoadTextures(headTex, @"gfx/head");
LoadTextures(weaponTex, @"gfx/weapon");
```

And then we have the helper function:

```
private void LoadTextures(Texture2D[] textures, string path)
{
    for (int i = 0; i < textures.Length; i++)
        textures[i] = Content.Load<Texture2D>(
            path + (i + 1).ToString());
}
```

Also, we've taken the liberty of defining some class-level fields that we refer to in
DrawCharacter():

- Constants FACE_LEFT and FACE_RIGHT, which indicate a left-facing or right-facing character

- charDef, which is the instance of CharDef we'll be using from Game1

- selPart, which is the currently selected part

Now that we have what we need to draw characters, we'll do a bit of setup for the editor.

Some Editor Setup

We'll be snagging a few classes and graphics and such from MapEditor. We could make another
library, but we're copying just a few blocks of code.

We'll need Game1.DrawCursor() and Game1.DrawButtons(), so with those we'll also need to
bring in icons.dds and instantiate it as iconsTex. Also, we'll bring in 1x1.dds for nullTex for
good measure.

We'll be keeping track of the mouse location by using a class-level MouseState called
mouseState, as well as keeping track of the previous state using preState. Update that in
Game1.Update() with the following:

```
mouseState = Mouse.GetState();

if (mouseState.LeftButton == ButtonState.Pressed)
{
    ...
}
```

```
else
{
    if (preState.LeftButton == ButtonState.Pressed)
    {
        mouseClick = true;
    }
}

preState = mouseState;
```

Finally, it's time to start adding tools to our character editor, much as we did for our map editor.

The Icon Palette

The first thing we'll add is the icon palette, which will be a palette of texture images that we can use for parts.

Add a method, Game1.DrawPalette(), with the following body:

```
spriteBatch.Begin(SpriteBlendMode.AlphaBlend);
for (int l = 0; l < 4; l++)
{
    Texture2D texture = null;
    switch (l)
    {
        case 0:
            texture = headTex[charDef.HeadIndex];
            break;
        case 1:
            texture = torsoTex[charDef.TorsoIndex];
            break;
        case 2:
            texture = legsTex[charDef.LegsIndex];
            break;
        case 3:
            texture = weaponTex[charDef.WeaponIndex];
            break;
    }
    if (texture != null)
    {
        for (int i = 0; i < 25; i++)
        {
            Rectangle sRect = new Rectangle((i % 5) * 64,
                (i / 5) * 64, 64, 64);
            Rectangle dRect = new Rectangle(i * 23, 467
                + l * 32, 23, 32);
            spriteBatch.Draw(nullTex,
        dRect, new Color(0, 0, 0, 25));
```

So far, we're iterating through all images for each texture, getting the source and destination rectangles so that we can draw them in a neat row on the bottom of the screen. Of course, the special case with weapons is coming right up:

```
if (l == 3)
{
    sRect.X = (i % 4) * 80;
    sRect.Y = (i / 4) * 64;
    sRect.Width = 80;

    if (i < 15)
    {
        dRect.X = i * 30;
        dRect.Width = 30;
    }
}
```

With the correct source and destination rectangles, we draw the image. But since we have the destination rectangle, we might as well check if the mouse location is within the rectangle and clicking:

```
spriteBatch.Draw(texture, dRect,
    sRect, Color.White);

if (dRect.Contains(mouseState.X, mouseState.Y))
{
    if (mouseClick)
    {
        charDef.Frames[selFrame].Parts[selPart].Index
            = i + 64 * l;
    }
}
        }
    }
}
spriteBatch.End();
```

Assuming we add a call to DrawPalette() and DrawCursor() at the end of Game1.Draw() somewhere, we'll be treated to the result shown in Figure 5-6. Also, be sure to set mouseClick to false at the end of the Draw() method.

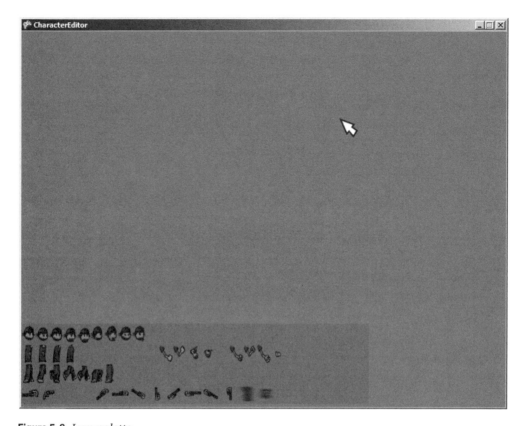

Figure 5-6. *Icon palette*

The Parts List

We'll use the icon palette to specify which image index each part uses. The parts list will allow us to manipulate our composited character in a way similar to a layer-heavy image-editing approach. We'll be able to select a part to manipulate, move parts up and down the list (like Send to Bottom and Bring to Top in layer ordering), and delete parts. We do this in a method called Game1.DrawPartsList(), as follows:

```
for (int i = 0; i <
    charDef.Frames[selFrame].Parts.Length; i++)
{
    int y = 5 + i * 15;
    text.Size = 0.75f;
    string line = "";
    int index = charDef.Frames[selFrame].Parts[i].Index;
    if (index < 0)
        line = "";
```

```
else if (index < 64)
    line = "head" + index.ToString();
else if (index < 74)
    line = "torso" + index.ToString();
else if (index < 128)
    line = "arms" + index.ToString();
else if (index < 192)
    line = "legs" + index.ToString();
else
    line = "weapon" + index.ToString();

if (selPart == i)
{
    text.Color = Color.Lime;
    text.DrawText(600, y, i.ToString() + ": " +
        line);
```

We'll put in two buttons to swap the current part with the one on the previous or next layer, using a function named Game1.SwapParts():

```
if (DrawButton(700, y, 1, mouseState.X, mouseState.Y, mouseClick))
{
    SwapParts(selPart, selPart - 1);
    if (selPart > 0) selPart--;
}
if (DrawButton(720, 5 y, 2, mouseState.X, mouseState.Y, mouseClick))
{
    SwapParts(selPart, selPart + 1);
    if (selPart <
        charDef.Frames[selFrame].Parts.Length - 1)
        selPart++;
}
```

We'll put some makeshift buttons next to the swap buttons to modify the parts. One of these is to mirror parts. For the mirror button, we'll use an (n) for normal and an (m) for mirrored.

```
Part part = charDef.Frames[selFrame].Parts[selPart];
if (text.DrawClickText(740, y,
    (part.Flip == 0 ? "(n)" : "(m)"),
    mouseState.X, mouseState.Y, mouseClick))
{
    part.Flip = 1 - part.Flip;
}
```

Because scaling leaves all sorts of openings for things to go terribly wrong in artistic consistency, we'll put in a button next to the selected part to reset the scale, denoted with an (r). We'll also add a part delete button, marked with an (x).

```
        if (text.DrawClickText(762, y, "(r)",
            mouseState.X, mouseState.Y, mouseClick))
        {
            part.Scaling =
                            new Vector2(1.0f, 1.0f);
        }
        if (text.DrawClickText(780, y, "(x)",
            mouseState.X, mouseState.Y, mouseClick))
        {
            part.Index = -1;
        }
    }
    else
    {
        if (text.DrawClickText(600, y, i.ToString() + ": " +
            line, mouseState.X, mouseState.Y, mouseClick))
        {
            selPart = i;
        }
    }
}
```

Earlier in Draw(), add a line to draw the character:

```
DrawCharacter(new Vector2(400f, 450f), 2f, FACE_RIGHT, selFrame,
    false, 1.0f);
```

Also, put in a line to draw the black box under the parts list (for contrast). You'll end up with what you see in Figure 5-7.

Define selPart at the class level to indicate which part is currently selected. We'll ultimately end up with class-level variables selFrame, selKeyFrame, and selAnim as well.

Remember Game1.SwapParts()? We use it while changing part layers. Here's the code:

```
private void SwapParts(int idx1, int idx2)
{
    if (idx1 < 0 || idx2 < 0 ||
        idx1 >= charDef.Frames[selFrame].Parts.Length ||
        idx2 >= charDef.Frames[selFrame].Parts.Length)
        return;

    Part i = charDef.Frames[selFrame].Parts[idx1];
    Part j = charDef.Frames[selFrame].Parts[idx2];

    charDef.Frames[selFrame].Parts[idx1] = j;
    charDef.Frames[selFrame].Parts[idx2] = i;
}
```

Notice that when this is called from Game1.Draw(), we don't check any bounds there. We escape in the first four lines if we're out of bounds here.

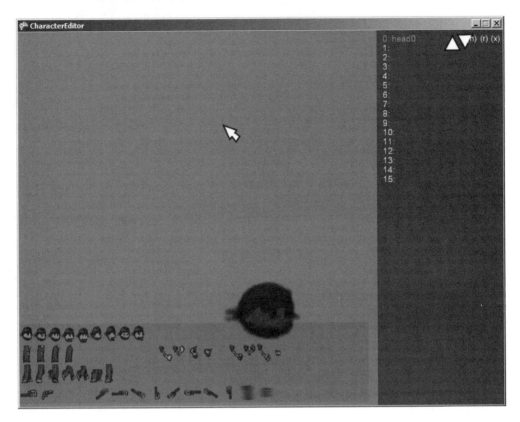

Figure 5-7. *Parts list*

It's the classic swap algorithm, $t = i$; $i = j$; $j = t$, but it's applied to two objects, so we store the references temporarily, rather than storing the values themselves.

Moving, Rotating, and Scaling Parts

Now we can specify part icons, but we can't move them, so we can only end up with a head, arms, and legs in a heap on the floor, which isn't what we're really going for. We need to be able to manipulate parts. We allow that with the following code:

```
int xM = mouseState.X - preState.X;
int yM = mouseState.Y - preState.Y;
if (mouseState.LeftButton == ButtonState.Pressed)
{
    if (preState.LeftButton == ButtonState.Pressed)
    {
        charDef.Frames[selFrame].Parts[selPart].Location +=
            new Vector2((float)xM / 2.0f, (float)yM / 2.0f);
    }
}
```

```
else
{
    if (preState.LeftButton == ButtonState.Pressed)
    {
        mouseClick = true;
    }
}

if (mouseState.RightButton == ButtonState.Pressed)
{
    if (preState.RightButton == ButtonState.Pressed)
    {
        charDef.Frames[selFrame].Parts[selPart].Rotation +=
            (float)yM / 100.0f;
    }
}

if (mouseState.MiddleButton == ButtonState.Pressed)
{
    if (preState.MiddleButton == ButtonState.Pressed)
    {
        charDef.Frames[selFrame].Parts[selPart].Scaling +=
            new Vector2((float)xM * 0.01f, (float)yM * 0.01f);
    }
}

preState = mouseState;
```

This should be fairly self-explanatory. For each click type, we figure out how far the mouse has moved since the last update, and then translate, rotate, or scale accordingly. We're using left-button dragging for moving, right-button dragging for rotating, and middle-button dragging for scaling.

We're now able to move, rotate, and scale parts, so we can finally get a look at what we're shooting for with this character format. Take a look at our guy in Figure 5-8, which should give you a much better idea of what we're creating.

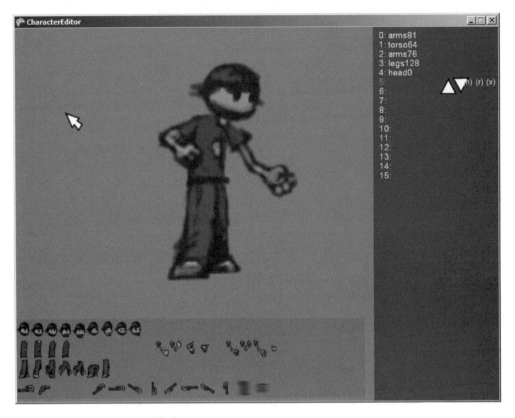

Figure 5-8. *Our hero (assembled)*

The Frames List

The character you see in Figure 5-8 is one frame. If we're going to have animation, we'll need a series of frames. Figure 5-8 could be idle1. Then we would need idle2, idle3, and so on.

Let's create a frames list in Game1.DrawFramesList():

```
for (int i = frameScroll; i < frameScroll + 20; i++)
{
    if (i < charDef.Frames.Length)
    {
        int y = (i - frameScroll) * 15 + 280;
        if (i == selFrame)
        {
            text.Color = Color.Lime;
            text.DrawText(600, y, i.ToString() + ": " +
                charDef.Frames[i].Name +
                (editMode == EditingMode.FrameName
                ? "*" : ""));
```

Remember how we edited text in the map editor? We're using a similar system here. We use the class-level variable editingMode to keep track of which field we're editing, and then from `Game1.Update()`, we call `UpdateKeys()`, which may call `PressKey()`. We can basically copy the code over from `MapEditor`, with a few changes, which we'll get to soon.

Next to the selected frame, we'll draw a little add frame button, denoted with an (a). Clicking this button will add a reference to this frame to the selected animation.

```
if (text.DrawClickText(720, y, "(a)",
    mouseState.X, mouseState.Y, mouseClick))
{
    Animation animation = charDef.Animations[selAnim];

    for (int j = 0; j < animation.KeyFrames.Length; j++)
    {

        KeyFrame keyFrame = animation.KeyFrames[j];

        if (keyFrame.FrameRef == -1)
        {
            keyFrame.FrameRef = i;
            keyFrame.Duration = 1;

            break;
        }
    }

}
}
else
{
    if (text.DrawClickText(600, y, i.ToString() + ": " +
        charDef.Frames[i].Name, mouseState.X,
        mouseState.Y, mouseClick))
    {
```

When selecting a frame, two things happen. If the frame's name was empty, we copy the previously selected frame to the current frame. This isn't very intuitive, but it works. Also, we make the currently selected frame's name editable.

```
if (selFrame != i)
{
    if (String.IsNullOrEmpty(charDef.Frames[i].Name))
        CopyFrame(selFrame, i);
    selFrame = i;
    editingText = EDITING_FRAME_NAME;
}
}
}
}
}
```

Finally, we allow our list to be scrolled.

```
if (DrawButton(770, 280, 1,
    mouseState.X, mouseState.Y,
    (mouseState.LeftButton == ButtonState.Pressed)) && frameScroll > 0)
    frameScroll--;
if (DrawButton(770, 570, 2,
    mouseState.X, mouseState.Y,
    (mouseState.LeftButton == ButtonState.Pressed))
    && frameScroll < charDef.Frames.Length - 20)
    frameScroll++;
```

We can now create several frames of animation, as shown in Figure 5-9.

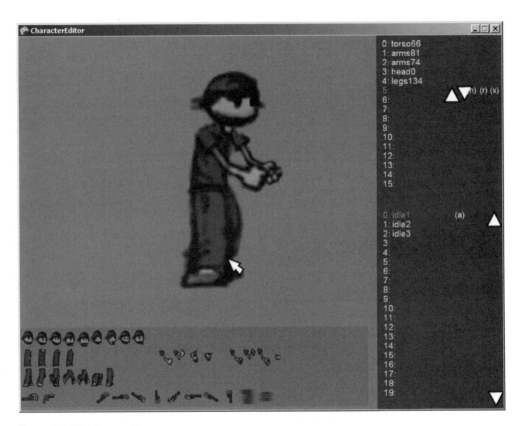

Figure 5-9. *The frames list*

Let's take a little look at Game1.PressKey(). In MapEditor, we would evaluate editMode, copy an appropriate string into a temporary string, work with that temporary string, and then copy the string back. All that we change here is where we're copying that string to and from:

```
string t = "";
switch (editMode)
{
    case EditingMode.FrameName:
        t = charDef.Frames[selFrame].Name;
        break;
    case EditingMode.AnimationName:
        t = charDef.Animations[selAnim].Name;
        break;
    case EditingMode.PathName:
        t = charDef.path;
        break;
    default:
        return;
}

...

switch (editMode)
{
    case EditingMode.FrameName:
        charDef.Frames[selFrame].Name = t;
        break;
    case EditingMode.AnimationName:
        charDef.Animations[selAnim].Name = t;
        break;
    case EditingMode.PathName:
        charDef.Path = t;
        break;
}
```

We'll be editing frame names, animation names, and paths, and we've defined some constants appropriately.

Also, we use a nonintuitive method for copying frames: if the user selects a frame that has a blank name (that is, a fresh, unused frame under typical circumstances), the previously selected frame will be copied onto the new one using the CopyFrame() method. Here's Game1.CopyFrame():

```
private void CopyFrame(int src, int dest)
{

    Frame keySrc = charDef.Frames[src];
    Frame keyDest = charDef.Frames[dest];

    keyDest.Name = keySrc.Name;
```

```
for (int i = 0; i < keyDest.Parts.Length; i++)
{
    Part srcPart = keySrc.Parts[i];
    Part destPart = keyDest.Parts[i];

    destPart.Index = srcPart.Index;
    destPart.Location = srcPart.Location;
    destPart.Rotation = srcPart.Rotation;
    destPart.Scaling = srcPart.Scaling;
}
}
```

We iterate through the source frame's part array, copying all part fields to the destination frame's part array.

Next, we'll implement our animations and keyframes lists.

The Animations List

The animations list will be fairly simple. We'll draw a list of all animations at the top-left side of the window. If the user clicks an animation, its name becomes editable and it becomes the selected animation. The list is scrollable as well, so we use the variable animScroll. There's not much more to it than that. As usual, we put this in its own function named Game1.DrawAnimationList().

```
for (int i = animScroll; i < animScroll + 15; i++)
{
    if (i < charDef.Animations.Length)
    {
        int y = (i - animScroll) * 15 + 5;
        if (i == selAnim)
        {
            text.Color = Color.Lime;
            text.DrawText(5, y, i.ToString() + ": " +
                charDef.Animations[i].Name +
                ((editMode == EditingMode.AnimationName)
                ? "*" : ""));
        }
        else
        {
            if (text.DrawClickText(5, y, i.ToString() + ": " +
                charDef.Animations[i].Name, mouseState.X,
                mouseState.Y, mouseClick))
            {
                selAnim = i;
                editMode = EditingMode.AnimationName;
            }
        }
    }
}
```

```
if (DrawButton(170, 5, 1, mouseState.X, mouseState.Y, (mouseState.LeftButton ==
    ButtonState.Pressed)) && animScroll > 0)
    animScroll--;
if (DrawButton(170, 200, 2, mouseState.X, mouseState.Y,   (mouseState.LeftButton ==
    ButtonState.Pressed)) && animScroll <
    charDef.Animations.Length - 15) animScroll++;
```

The Keyframes List

The keyframes list is more of the same, with a bit of a hassle thrown in for good measure. We'll implement functionality to allow the user to modify keyframe durations, allowing us to fine-tune animation pacing. We put this in a function called `Game1.DrawKeyFramesList()`.

```
for (int i = keyFrameScroll; i < keyFrameScroll + 13; i++)
{
    Animation animation = charDef.Animations[selAnim];

    if (i < animation.KeyFrames.Length)
    {
        int y = (i - keyFrameScroll) * 15 + 250;
        int frameRef = animation.KeyFrames[i].FrameRef;
        string name = "";
        if (frameRef > -1)
        {
            name = charDef.Frames[frameRef].Name;
        }
        if (i == selKeyFrame)
        {
            text.Color = Color.Lime;
            text.DrawText(5, y, i.ToString() + ": " +
                name);
        }
        else
        {
            if (text.DrawClickText(5, y, i.ToString() + ": " +
                name, mouseState.X,
                mouseState.Y, mouseClick))
            {
                selKeyFrame = i;
            }
        }
    }
```

Here's the fun part. For all visible keyframes that exist (`frameRef > -1`), we're going to draw the keyframe duration and minus and plus sign buttons. These buttons will allow us to change the keyframe duration. If a keyframe has a duration of 1 and we click the minus button, we want to kill the keyframe, which means moving all of the following keyframes up one.

```
        if (frameRef > -1)
        {
            if (text.DrawClickText(110, y, "-", mouseState.X,
                mouseState.Y, mouseClick))
            {
                animation.KeyFrames[i].Duration--;
                if (animation.KeyFrames[i].Duration <= 0)
                {
                    for (int j = i;
                        j < animation.KeyFrames.Length - 1; j++)
                    {
                        KeyFrame keyframe = animation.KeyFrames[j];
                        keyframe.frameRef =
                            animation.KeyFrames[j + 1].FrameRef;
                        keyframe.duration =
                            animation.KeyFrames[j + 1].Duration;
                    }
                    animation.KeyFrames[
                        animation.KeyFrames.Length - 1].FrameRef = -1;
                }

            }
            text.DrawText(125, y,
                animation.KeyFrames[i].Duration.ToString());

            if (text.DrawClickText(140, y, "+", mouseState.X,
                mouseState.Y, mouseClick))
                animation.KeyFrames[i].duration++;
        }
    }

}
if (DrawButton(170, 250, 1, mouseState.X, mouseState.Y, (mouseState.LeftButton ==
    ButtonState.Pressed)) && keyFrameScroll > 0)
    keyFrameScroll--;
if (DrawButton(170, 410, 2, mouseState.X, mouseState.Y, (mouseState.LeftButton ==
    ButtonState.Pressed)) && keyFrameScroll <
    charDef.Animations[selAnim].KeyFrames.Length - 13) keyFrameScroll++;
```

An Onionskin Effect

Moving back to our character-drawing call, we can implement a really simple onionskin effect with our editor. An onionskin effect is where you can see a translucent version of neighboring frames of animation layered over the current frame. However, ours won't be exactly correct, because the effect will operate only on neighboring frames as they appear in the frames list.

```
if (selFrame > 0)
    DrawCharacter(new Vector2(400f, 450f), 2f, FACE_RIGHT,
        selFrame - 1, false, 0.2f);
if (selFrame < charDef.GetFrameArray().Length - 1)
    DrawCharacter(new Vector2(400f, 450f), 2f, FACE_RIGHT,
        selFrame + 1, false, 0.2f);
DrawCharacter(new Vector2(400f, 450f), 2f, FACE_RIGHT, selFrame,
    false, 1.0f);
```

Figure 5-10 shows our animations list, keyframes list, and onionskin effect in action. Note how the onionskin effect looks correct here because the selected and neighboring frames are of running animations. If we had selected run1 or idle5, we would see neighboring frames from a separate animation. It's not the end of the world, but it is a shortcoming worth noting.

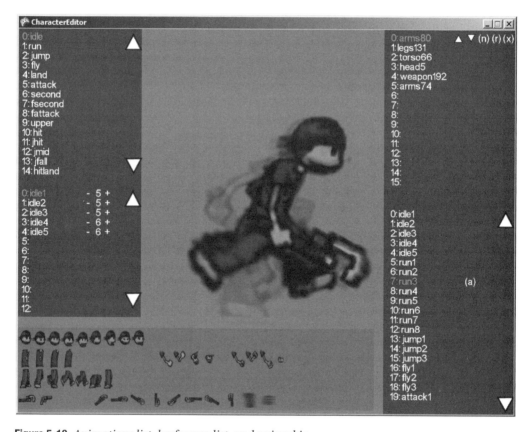

Figure 5-10. *Animations list, keyframes list, and onionskin*

Playback Preview

It's finally time to implement that preview character we've been talking about.

We're using a class-level integer, curKey, for the current keyframe. However, keyframes point to frame references from our frames list, and if keyframes are blank, their frame reference will be -1. We're going to try to account for all of this here.

```
int fref = charDef.Animations[selAnim].KeyFrames[curKey].FrameRef;
if (fref < 0)
    fref = 0;

DrawCharacter(new Vector2(500f, 100f), 0.5f, FACE_LEFT,
    fref,
    true, 1.0f);
```

We also have a class-level Boolean, playing, to toggle whether or not the animation is playing.

```
if (playing)
{
    if (text.DrawClickText(480, 100, "stop",
        mouseState.X, mouseState.Y, mouseClick))
        playing = false;
}
else
{
    if (text.DrawClickText(480, 100, "play",
        mouseState.X, mouseState.Y, mouseClick))
        playing = true;
}
```

We'll do the actual animation updating in Game1.Update():

```
UpdateKeys();

Animation animation = charDef.Animations[selAnim];
KeyFrame keyframe = animation.KeyFrames[curKey];

if (playing)
{
    curFrame += (float)gameTime.ElapsedGameTime.TotalSeconds * 30.0f;

    if (curFrame > (float)keyframe.duration)
    {
        curFrame -= (float)keyframe.duration;
        curKey++;

        if (curKey >= animation.KeyFrames.Length)
            curKey = 0;

        keyframe = animation.KeyFrame[curKey];
    }
}
```

```
else
    curKey = selKeyFrame;

if (keyframe.FrameRef < 0)
    curKey = 0;

mouseState = Mouse.GetState();
```

We're using an arbitrary time value for duration ticks, where one tick equals one-thirtieth of a second. This is because it's easier to work in small, standard units when every change of duration involves clicking a tiny + or −.

Figure 5-11 shows our preview in action.

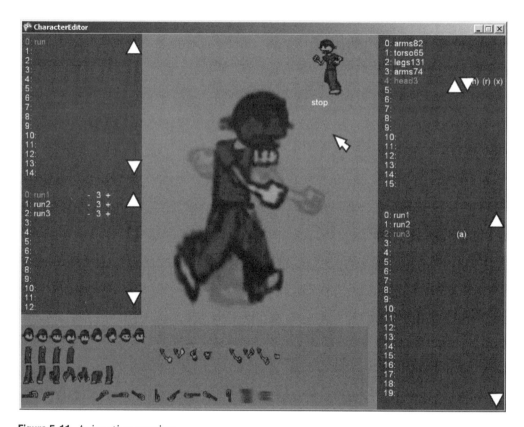

Figure 5-11. *Animation preview*

Loading and Saving

If you've been following along, you probably aren't too happy with the fact that each time you debug CharacterEditor, you must create a new character from scratch. That means it's time to implement loading and saving. We'll create a Read() and Write() function in CharDef. Here's the Write() function:

```
public void Write()
{
    BinaryWriter b = new
        BinaryWriter(File.Open(@"data/" + Path + ".zmx",
        FileMode.Create));

    b.Write(Path);
    b.Write(HeadIndex);
    b.Write(TorsoIndex);
    b.Write(LegsIndex);
    b.Write(WeaponIndex);

    for (int i = 0; i < animations.Length; i++)
    {
        b.Write(animations[i].Name);

        for (int j = 0; j <
            animations[i].KeyFrames.Length; j++)
        {
            KeyFrame keyframe = animations[i].KeyFrames[j];
            b.Write(keyframe.FrameRef);
            b.Write(keyframe.Duration);
            String[] scripts = keyframe.Scripts ;
            for (int s = 0; s < scripts.Length; s++)
                b.Write(scripts[s]);
        }
    }

    for (int i = 0; i < frames.Length; i++)
    {
        b.Write(frames[i].Name);

        for (int j = 0; j < frames[i].Parts.Length; j++)
        {
            Part p = frames[i].Parts[j];
            b.Write(p.Index);
            b.Write(p.Location.X);
            b.Write(p.Location.Y);
            b.Write(p.Rotation);
            b.Write(p.Scaling.X);
            b.Write(p.Scaling.Y);
            b.Write(p.Flip);
        }
    }

    b.Close();
```

```
        Console.WriteLine("Saved.");
}
```

This should look very familiar to the technique we used in MapEditor. We iterate through all arrays and subarrays, writing. For Read(), we do the opposite:

```
public void Read()
{
    BinaryReader b = new
        BinaryReader(File.Open(@"data/" + Path + ".zmx",
        FileMode.Open, FileAccess.Read));

    Path = b.ReadString();
    HeadIndex = b.ReadInt32();
    TorsoIndex = b.ReadInt32();
    LegsIndex = b.ReadInt32();
    WeaponIndex = b.ReadInt32();


    for (int i = 0; i < animations.Length; i++)
    {
        animations[i].Name = b.ReadString();

        for (int j = 0; j <
            animations[i].KeyFrames.Length; j++)
        {
            KeyFrame keyframe = animations[i].KeyFrames[j];
            keyframe.FrameRef = b.ReadInt32();
            keyframe.Duration = b.ReadInt32();

            string[] scripts = keyframe.Scripts;
            for (int s = 0; s < scripts.Length; s++)
                scripts[s] = b.ReadString();
        }
    }

    for (int i = 0; i < frames.Length; i++)
    {
        frames[i].Name = b.ReadString();

        for (int j = 0; j < frames[i].Parts.Length; j++)
        {
```

```
            Part p = frames[i].Parts[j];
            p.Index = b.ReadInt32();
            p.Location.X = b.ReadSingle();
            p.Location.Y = b.ReadSingle();
            p.Rotation = b.ReadSingle();
            p.Scaling.X = b.ReadSingle();
            p.Scaling.Y = b.ReadSingle();
            p.Flip = b.ReadInt32();
        }
    }

    b.Close();

    Console.WriteLine("Loaded.");
}
```

Now we just need to make some buttons in Game1.Draw(). Fortunately, we brought DrawButton() over from MapEditor, so it's a pretty simple implementation:

```
if (DrawButton(200, 5, 3, mouseState.X, mouseState.Y, mouseClick))
    charDef.Write();
if (DrawButton(230, 5, 4, mouseState.X, mouseState.Y, mouseClick))
    charDef.Read();
```

We'll draw an editable path right next to the buttons:

```
if (editMode == EditingMode.PathName)
{
    text.Color = Color.Lime;
    text.DrawText(270, 15, charDef.Path + "*");
}
else
{
    if (text.DrawClickText(270, 15, charDef.Path, mouseState.X,
        mouseState.Y, mouseClick))
    {
        editMode = EditingMode.PathName;
    }
}
```

We now have saving and loading functionality in a Spartan-yet-functional interface, all shown in Figure 5-12. We haven't implemented keyframe script editing, but we'll get to that once we start fleshing out the rest of the game.

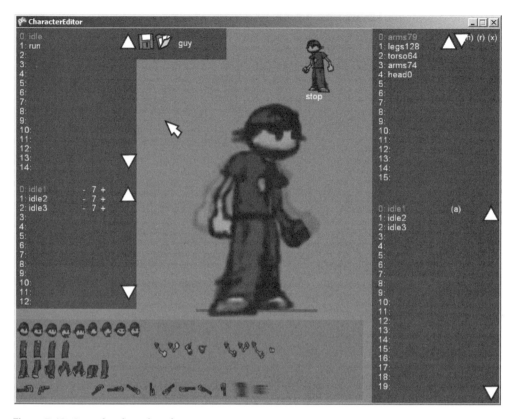

Figure 5-12. *Save, load, and path*

Conclusion

In this chapter, we put together a robust, ugly character editor in a hurry. We discussed our hierarchical character format, created some classes to implement the structure, and built an editor around it.

We now have a fairly functional character editor in place, to go with our fairly functional map editor, so we can finally start working on the actual game. And as we've said before, the nice aspect of these crazy tools is that there won't be too much to actually do to create the game now that we have them.

CHAPTER 6

■■■

Bringing It to the Game
The Payoff

Well, here we are. Six chapters in, and we're finally making something we can play. And isn't that the whole reason we got into this? (It certainly wasn't for the money!)

In this chapter, we'll get a rough idea of the game and also implement a scripting system to afford deeper animation interactivity.

We're taking this in two chunks: first create our rudimentary game engine, and then create scripting. By the time you're finished with this chapter, you'll have a very slick-looking start to Zombie Smashers XNA.

Building the Game

To put together our game, we'll need to set up our environment, and then get to coding. Specifically, we'll do the following:

- Create a new project in our game's solution.

- Copy over and change the map and character classes.

- Load our map and character.

- Create a new character class to control game functionality for an individual character.

- Implement simple movement and collision detection.

So, let's get started with a new ZombieSmashers project.

Creating a New Project: ZombieSmashers

Create a new Windows Game (2.0) called ZombieSmashers in our ever-growing ZombieSmashers solution. Again, by putting most of our code into a single solution, we can leverage the quick-access capabilities of Visual Studio to easily reference and use code in adjacent projects. (Although, in this case, we're going to make enough changes to our map and character classes to warrant copying them over to the project, rather than referencing them.)

■**Tip** Referencing, rather than copying, code makes your projects more flexible. One way you can do this is to link files across projects and solutions. To do this, right-click the project in Solution Explorer, select Add Existing Item, and browse to the file you wish to link to. Instead of clicking the Add button, select the down arrow next to it and select Add As Link. This way, the file will show up and compile in the project, but it won't actually be copied over. This is a great way to manage files for projects that are cross-platform, because it allows you to change code based on the platform for which it is being developed.

Copy the MapClasses folder from the MapEditor solution and the Character folder (renaming it CharClasses) from CharacterEditor to the ZombieSmashers solution folder. In ZombieSmashers in Solution Explorer, include the MapClasses and CharClasses folders.

Next, manually change the namespaces in all of the copied classes from MapEditor and CharEditor, respectively, to ZombieSmashers. Also, create a Character class in the CharClasses folder. We'll use this class to encapsulate all logic and drawing functionality for a game character. This is where we'll be doing the majority of the work for this chapter.

From here, copy all of the art assets into the Content project. From MapEditor, we're taking maps1.png. From CharacterEditor, we're taking legs1.png, torso1.png, head1.png, and weapon1.png. We'll also take 1x1.bmp, Arial.spritefont, and icons.dds for good measure.

We also need the data files we created: guy.zmx and map.zmx. Move those to the ZombieSmashers project, in the folders data/chars and data/maps, respectively. Make sure to include these files in your solution and specify Copy If Newer.

Finally, we need the map segment definition data. Copy maps.zdx from MapEditor into the data folder. You should end up with a project organized as shown in Figure 6-1.

From here, we can start coding by modifying our map classes to work with the new game. Unfortunately, we'll be doing quite a bit of jumping around; hopefully, nothing will get lost in the shuffle!

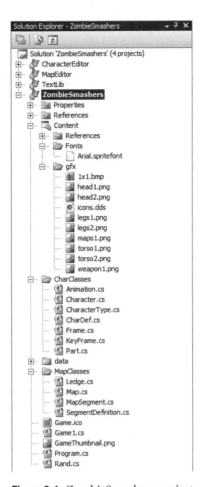

Figure 6-1. *ZombieSmashers project*

A Random Numbers Class

We're going to be using a ton of randomization from the game, so let's make a nice class, in the project root, to help us out. We need only a class-level static `Random` object, which we'll use from within various classes we create, and some methods that we can throw some number ranges at and expect random values in return.

```
public static class Rand
{
    private static Random random;
    public static Random Random{
        get { return random; }
        private set { random = value; }
    }
```

```
static Rand(){
    Random = new Random();
}

public static float GetRandomFloat(float fMin, float fMax)
{
    return (float)random.NextDouble() * (fMax - fMin) + fMin;
}

public static double GetRandomDouble(double dMin, double dMax)
{
    return random.NextDouble() * (dMax - dMin) + dMin;
}

public static Vector2 GetRandomVector2(float xMin, float xMax,
    float yMin, float yMax)
{
    return new Vector2(GetRandomFloat(xMin, xMax),
        GetRandomFloat(yMin, yMax));
}

public static int GetRandomInt(int iMin, int iMax)
{
    return random.Next(iMin, iMax);
}
}
```

By using a static constructor (which has no scope attribute), we can automatically instantiate objects within the class immediately before anything is called or used. This way, we do not need to instantiate the objects from within a separate class such as Game1. Looking toward the future, this will be really handy to have lying around for when we want to make some fluid particle effects. For now, however, it will sit unused for a bit while we gather all the other classes and functionality together.

Modifying the Map Functionality

We will now make some changes to the map functions, so the map is better suited for game play. We'll adjust its look and feel, and add some helper functions.

Map Look and Feel

We need to change some of how the map moves and renders, because in a game, a map looks and feels quite different than in an editor. In an editor, you want to see a quick, rough overview of how the game will look, with the ability to change as much on the map as possible. For instance, in the editor, we drew the map in a zoomed-out fashion to give a wide view on the map. We don't want to do this for the players, because we want to get them close in on the action. For now, we will draw the map at two times the zoom level of the map editor. This is simple enough. Just remove this line from the Map.Draw() function:

```
scale *= 0.5f;
```

We draw the map in layers for that good old parallax scrolling effect, but what happens when we start drawing zombies, explosions, and all that on the screen? We can't draw the whole map, and then draw some zombies, because then if there are any foreground sprites, they'll end up under zombies. When creating a game that has many layers as we are doing, it is always a good idea to sketch out a scene in either a drawing or a simple list to gain the understanding of the order in which the items need to be drawn. We'll be drawing in this order:

- Map background layer

- Map main layer

- Character, particles, and so on

- Map foreground layer

- Heads-up display (HUD)

We'll modify the Draw() function to allow us to select which layers we'll be drawing:

```
public void Draw(SpriteBatch sprite, Texture2D[] mapsTex,
    int startLayer, int endLayer)
{
    Rectangle sRect = new Rectangle();
    Rectangle dRect = new Rectangle();

    sprite.Begin(SpriteBlendMode.AlphaBlend);

    for (int l = startLayer; l < endLayer; l++)
    {
```

Note that we also removed the scroll vector from the parameters. We'll be using a static variable in Game1 instead, so we can access the scroll value from any class. Then, rather than iterate through all layers, we iterate through only what we've been told to draw.

Next, we need to update the draw rectangle for each map segment by multiplying it by two:

```
dRect.X = (int)(mapSeg[l, i].Location.X * 2f- Game1.Scroll.X * scale);
dRect.Y = (int)(mapSeg[l, i].Location.Y * 2f - Game1.Scroll.Y * scale);
```

And last but not least, we need to adjust the map's ledge segments to match moving the map segments themselves. In the Map.Read() function, modify the following line to include multiplying by two:

```
ledges[i].Nodes[n] = new Vector2(file.ReadSingle() * 2f, file.ReadSingle() * 2f);
```

Helper Functions

Because characters will soon be interacting with the map, it would be nice to have some basic collision-detection functionality built in to the map, particularly for our ledges.

We'll create a Map.GetLedgeSec() function to return the section of a ledge in which an entity's x value resides. If the x value is not within the horizontal span of the ledge, our function will return -1.

```
public int GetLedgeSec(int l, float x)
{
    for (int i = 0; i < ledges[l].TotalNodes - 1; i++)
    {

        if (x >= ledges[l].Nodes[i].X &&
            x <= ledges[l].Nodes[i + 1].X)
            return i;
    }
    return -1;
}
```

We'll be using GetLedgeSec() in conjunction with a function we'll define next: GetLedgeYLoc(), which will take a ledge index, a section index (which we'll get from GetLedgeSec()), and an x value, and return an interpolated y value.

```
public float GetLedgeYLoc(int l, int i, float x)
{
    return (ledges[l].Nodes[i + 1].Y - ledges[l].Nodes[i].Y) *
        ((x - ledges[l].Nodes[i].X) / (ledges[l].Nodes[i + 1].X
        - ledges[l].Nodes[i].X))
        + ledges[l].Nodes[i].Y;
}
```

Essentially, the functionality we're creating will allow us to determine if a character's location is within a ledge's bounds. At this point, we do not really need to test the y position of the character, because this function does not do collision detection. Rather, it simply finds the ledge that the character is currently within range of landing on. The purpose of these functions will become clearer once we start implementing them through the Character class.

Figure 6-2 shows interpolated y locations based on ledge dimensions and character locations.

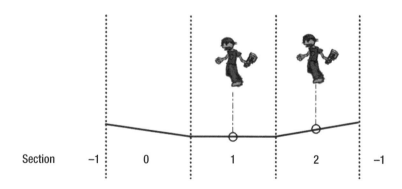

Figure 6-2. *Interpolated y locations based on ledge dimensions and character locations*

We'll also want a function to quickly tell us whether a location vector is on a collision cell or a blank cell, and return `true` if we're on a collision cell or out of bounds. Create the `Map.CheckCol()` function to handle this check.

```
public bool CheckCol(Vector2 loc)
{
    if (loc.X < 0f) return true;
    if (loc.Y < 0f) return true;

    int x = (int)(loc.X / 64f);
    int y = (int)(loc.Y / 64f);

    if (x >= 0 && y >= 0 && x < 20 && y < 20)
    {
        if (col[x, y] == 0) return false;
    }
    return true;
}
```

This is all we'll really need to do with the `Map` class for now. Let's move on to the `Character` class.

Creating the Character Class

In Chapter 5, we said that `CharDef` could easily be used in a real situation, and that putting all the character code in `Game1` was feasible but not the best solution? Well, a better solution is to create the `Character` class—a class that helps us manage characters no matter who controls them or what they represent.

Most of the functionality we'll be implementing in this chapter will be in the `Character` class. `Character` will store relevant fields, such as location, trajectory, animation state, and health, as well as character-relevant functions, like initialization, drawing, and updating.

Before we get started with the fields, we will need to create two enumerations that will help us change and maintain some states in our `Character` class. The first one, `CharState`, will guide us in knowing whether or not our character is in the air. The second, `CharDir`, will tell us which direction our character is facing.

```
public enum CharState
{
    Grounded = 0,
    Air = 1
}

public enum CharDir
{
    Left = 0,
    Right = 1
}
```

Now we can move on to the fields. We'll store character textures as public statics in the Character class.

```
public static Texture2D[] headTex = new Texture2D[1];
public static Texture2D[] torsoTex = new Texture2D[1];
public static Texture2D[] legsTex = new Texture2D[1];
public static Texture2D[] weaponTex = new Texture2D[1];
```

The character-specific fields are somewhat straightforward. loc and trajectory define the character's location and trajectory, respectively. For example, a location of (0, 100) and a trajectory of (5000, -5000) describe a character on the left side of the world flying up and to the right pretty quickly.

In other words, the trajectory of the character is not only the speed at which the character is traveling, but also the direction. This is commonly represented as a vector that maintains both direction and magnitude (speed). In our case, the trajectory will be multiplied by the elapsed time since the previous update and added to the character's location. We multiply it against the elapsed time to smooth out the visible animation of the character for each individual's computer.

When you consider the trajectory to be the amount of pixels moved each frame, the actual movement is dependent on how many frames a second can be processed. Thus, faster computers will run game play faster than slower computers. In our case, we want to eliminate that by turning the trajectory into the number of pixels moved per an unspecified unit of time (a second, a millisecond, or some other unit—it doesn't really matter). The end result is that although slower computers may experience a bit of a choppy animation, the game should play the same as on higher-end systems.

Among the animation state fields, anim holds the number of the current animation, animName holds its name (for example, run), and animFrame holds the active key frame of the current animation.

```
public Vector2 Location;
public Vector2 Trajectory;
public CharDir Face;
public float Scale;
public int AnimFrame;
public CharState State;
public int Anim;
public String AnimName;
```

We'll use bool fields to keep track of which keys a player has held down (the word *keys* is a bit of an abstraction, since we'll be using a gamepad for primary input). These fields form a sort of virtual keyboard, in that when we start working on artificial intelligence (AI), the AI object will only manipulate virtual keys directly. We're using only keyLeft, keyRight, and keyJump at this point; we'll get to the rest later.

```
public bool keyLeft;
public bool keyRight;
public bool keyUp;
public bool keyDown;
```

```
public bool keyJump;
public bool keyAttack;
public bool keySecondary;
CharDef charDef;
```

```
float frame = 0f;
```

When a character is standing on a ledge, we'll say he is attached to it, and we'll hold that ledge's index in ledgeAttach.

A common problem in physics engines for hobby games (and even some AAA titles) is that developers try to develop an engine that can handle everything well, including resting objects on other objects, but fall short. What ends up happening is that one or two of those objects resting on each other start to jitter uncontrollably. Sometimes they jitter so much and gain so much speed that they eventually just disappear from the game entirely! In our game, we are going to take the quick-and-dirty route to stop this. By storing the ledge the player is currently attached to, we can simply interpolate the position he should be at and set it once. It is simple, not extendable, and not an abstracted method, but it is extremely effective and realistic looking.

```
int ledgeAttach = -1;
```

We'll also want to hold the current gamepad state and previous gamepad state. That way, we'll be able to tell when buttons have been pressed.

```
GamePadState curState = new GamePadState();
GamePadState prevState = new GamePadState();
```

The constructor will take a location and character definition as parameters and set the character's facing, scale, state, and starting animation.

```
public Character(Vector2 newLoc, CharDef newCharDef)
{
    Location = newLoc;
    Trajectory = new Vector2();

    Face = CharDir.Right;
    Scale = 0.5f;
    charDef = newCharDef;

    SetAnim("fly");

    State = CharState.Air;
}
```

We set the animation with the function SetAnim(), which we define in the following section of code:

```
private void SetAnim(string newAnim)
{
    if (AnimName == newAnim)
        return;
```

```
for (int i = 0; i < charDef.Animations.Length; i++)
{
    if (charDef.Animations[i].Name == newAnim)
    {
        Anim = i;
        AnimFrame = 0;
        frame = 0;
        AnimName = newAnim;

        break;
    }
}
}
```

This function will allow us to start new animations on demand. We search through the different animations stored in the character, and when we find the correct one, we set the variables immediately. This has the potential to look bad and unprofessional when we switch to a new animation while the character is in the middle of another. We can fix that problem by providing an animation queue that starts animations only after the current one has finished, but for now, this will work fine.

The real meat is in the `Character.Update()` function, which we'll look at next.

Updating the Character

Updating even a single character requires quite a bit of logic, because of the multitude of actions that are involved. Remember that the more simultaneous things a character can be involved in, the more complex this routine will get. It is important to know not only what your character needs to do, but also in what order he must do it.

This is due to the idea that certain actions may affect how other actions are or are not carried out. For instance, you may wish to put collision detection at the end so that next time the draw method has been invoked, it has already been handled. Placing the collision detection before moving the player could cause a frame to be drawn with some overlap. In reality, the order is up to you and how you like to keep the separate functions organized. Here is the rundown for our Zombie Smashers XNA game:

- Update animation.

- Update location.

- Perform collision detection.

- Handle key input.

The order isn't all that sensitive right now, because of how independent each action is from the others. What is important in this case is that we hit all the main points. We'll put them all in the `Character.Update()` function, organized only with regions. One of the bonuses to working on the character in a single method is that we can act on local variables in order, and then check them and/or set them. This becomes very useful for optimization (a long, long way down the road), since in-line code can be optimized very quickly and easily.

> **Note** *In-line* code is code that is kept in one place, rather than componentized into methods and/or classes. It is not a great idea in terms of organization, but can be useful for optimizing memory usage.

Updating the Animation

We're basically copying and pasting the Update() code from Game1 in CharacterEditor to Character, with a few changes. We'll remove any functionality to determine whether the animation preview is playing. We'll also change some of the field names to make a bit more sense in the context. However, the core logic remains unchanged: update the frame index until we can't update it anymore, and then loop back to the beginning.

```
public void Update(GameTime gameTime)
{
    float et = (float)gameTime.ElapsedGameTime.TotalSeconds;

    #region Update Animation
    Animation animation = charDef.Animations[Anim];
    KeyFrame keyFrame = animation.KeyFrames[AnimFrame];

    frame += et * 30.0f;

    if (frame > (float)keyFrame.Duration)
    {
        frame -= (float)keyFrame.Duration;
        AnimFrame++;

        if (AnimFrame >= animation.KeyFrames.Length)
            AnimFrame = 0;

        keyFrame = animation.KeyFrames[AnimFrame];

        if(keyFrame.FrameRef < 0)
            AnimFrame = 0;
    }
    #endregion
```

Updating the Location

To update the location, we'll simply add the trajectory, multiplied by Game1.frameTime, to the character's current location. If the character's state is STATE_GROUNDED and the character's x trajectory is not zero, reduce the trajectory by Game1.friction. If the character is airborne, the y trajectory's value will be increased by Game1.gravity, giving him a nice airborne arc.

```
#region Update Location By Trajectory
Vector2 pLoc = new Vector2(Location.X, Location.Y);

if (State == CharState.Grounded)
{
    if (Trajectory.X > 0f)
    {
        Trajectory.X -= Game1.Friction * et;
        if (Trajectory.X < 0f) Trajectory.X = 0f;
    }

    if (Trajectory.X < 0f)
    {
        Trajectory.X += Game1.Friction * et;
        if (Trajectory.X > 0f) Trajectory.X = 0f;
    }
}

Location.X += Trajectory.X * et;

if (State == CharState.Air)
{
    Location.Y += Trajectory.Y * et;
    Trajectory.Y += et * Game1.Gravity;
}
#endregion
```

Collision Detection

Here comes a big chunk of code: collision detection. We'll split this further into regions for better organization. What basically must happen here is as follows:

- Airborne state collision:
  - Check horizontal collisions (moving left or right into walls)
  - Check vertical collisions:
    - Landing on ledge?
    - Landing on collision cell?
- Grounded state collision:
  - Check horizontal collisions
  - Check to make sure the character still has ground below him:
    - Falling off ledge?
    - Falling off collision cell?

Let's look at the code. We'll be using a few tiny functions, which will be defined in a few pages, but based on the preceding outline and their names, their purpose should be pretty obvious.

```
#region Collision detection
if (State == CharState.Air)
{
    #region Air State

    CheckXCol(map, pLoc);
```

To check whether our character has landed on a ledge, we'll do the following:

- Make sure our character is moving downward (trajectory.Y > 0.0f).

- Iterate through map ledges.

- Check map ledges where the number of nodes is > 1.

- Store the ledge section the character is over or under as s.

- Store the ledge section the character was over or under before his location was updated as ts.

- If s or ts is -1, the character isn't and wasn't over or under the ledge; otherwise, do this:

    - Store the interpolated y value for the character's current location as fY.

    - Store the interpolated y value for the character's previous location as tfY.

    - If the character's previous y location is <= tfY and the character's current location is >= fY, this means the character is attempting to pass through the ledge in this current Update(). Land him!

Figure 6-3 shows a few scenarios.

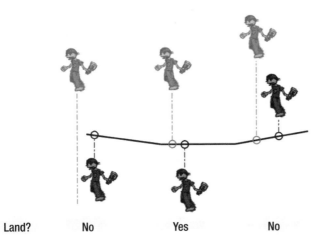

Figure 6-3. *Ledge landing scenario. The grayed figures represent the character's previous location for each scenario; the black figures represent the current locations.*

Here's the code for landing on a ledge:

```
#region Land on ledge
if (trajectory.Y > 0.0f)
{
    for (int i = 0; i < 16; i++)
    {
        if (map.GetLedgeTotalNodes(i) > 1)
        {
            int ts = map.GetLedgeSec(i, pLoc.X);
            int s = map.GetLedgeSec(i, Location.X);
            float fY;
            float tfY;
            if (s > -1 && ts > -1)
            {
                tfY = map.GetLedgeYLoc(i, s, pLoc.X);
                fY = map.GetLedgeYLoc(i, s, Location.X);
                if (pLoc.Y <= tfY && Location.Y >= fY)
                {
                    if (trajectory.Y > 0.0f)
                    {                           Location.Y = fY;
                        ledgeAttach = i;
                        Land();
                    }
                }
                else

                    if (map.GetLedgeFlags(i) ==
                            LedgeFlags.Solid
                        &&
                        Location.Y >= fY)
                    {
                        Location.Y = fY;
                        ledgeAttach = i;
                        Land();
                    }
            }

        }
    }
}
#endregion
```

We'll use a much simpler algorithm to detect whether a character has landed on a collision cell. If the location at the character's feet occupies a collision cell, we'll move the character's y location to the top of that cell and land him.

```
#region Land on col
if (State == CharState.Air)
{
    if (trajectory.Y > 0f)
    {
        if (map.checkCol(new Vector2(loc.X, loc.Y + 15f)))
        {
            loc.Y = (float)((int)((loc.Y + 15f) / 64f) * 64);
            Land();
        }
    }
}
#endregion

#endregion
}
else if (State == CharState.Grounded)
{
```

With the grounded character, instead of checking to see if he has landed on something, we check to see if he has fallen off something. If he is attached to a ledge, we check only if GetLedgeSec() returns -1, meaning there is no section for the character's current x location, or the character is not on a ledge. If the character is still on a ledge, we update his y location to the interpolated value we get from GetLedgeYLoc().

```
#region Grounded State

if (ledgeAttach > -1)
{
    if (map.GetLedgeSec(ledgeAttach, loc.X) == -1)
    {
        FallOff();
    }
    else
    {
        loc.Y = map.GetLedgeYLoc(ledgeAttach,
            map.GetLedgeSec(ledgeAttach, loc.X), loc.X);
    }
}
else
{
```

Likewise, if the character is not attached to a ledge, we'll check to see if he has a collision cell below him. If not, he falls off.

```
            if (!map.checkCol(new Vector2(loc.X, loc.Y + 15f)))
                FallOff();
        }

    CheckXCol(map, pLoc);



    #endregion
}
#endregion
```

Character Input

We'll handle our input with another code block in `Character.Update()`. We'll do some case-by-case logic, so that you can do certain things only while in certain animations.

The player can switch between idle and running animations based on which keys are pressed, and can jump while idle or running. Trajectory is also updated accordingly.

```
#region Key input
if (animName == "idle" || animName == "run")
{

    if (keyLeft)
    {
        SetAnim("run");
        trajectory.X = -200f;
        Face = CharDir.Left;
    }
    else if (keyRight)
    {
        SetAnim("run");
        trajectory.X = 200f;
        Face = CharDir.Right;
    }
    else
    {
        SetAnim("idle");
    }
    if (keyJump)
    {
        SetAnim("fly");
        trajectory.Y = -600f;
        State = CharState.Air;
        ledgeAttach = -1;
        if (keyRight) trajectory.X = 200f;
        if (keyLeft) trajectory.X = -200f;
    }
}
```

An airborne player can move either left or right for now—violating some physics in the name of game play. Pressing Left or Right on the gamepad while in midair nudges the trajectory slightly left or right.

```
if (animName == "fly")
{
    if (keyLeft)
    {
        Face = CharDir.Left;
        if (trajectory.X > -200f)
            trajectory.X -= 500f * Game1.frameTime;
    }
    if (keyRight)
    {
        Face = CharDir.Right;
        if (trajectory.X < 200f)
            trajectory.X += 500f * Game1.frameTime;
    }
}
```

```
#endregion
```

That concludes the massive Update() function. You might want to organize it differently, but regions work well enough for the time being.

New Character Functions

We've thrown a couple more functions into the mix, so let's define them before moving on.

CheckXCol()

To simplify movement, we check x movement collisions separately from y movement. We've defined a function for this. CheckXCol() checks whether the character location overlaps a collision cell on the left or right (with the location padded by 25f) and returns the character's x location to pLoc.X if so. We'll eventually use a padding value that's a function of the character's scale, so larger characters won't overlap collision cells.

```
private void CheckXCol(Map map, Vector2 pLoc)
{
    if (trajectory.X > 0f)
        if (map.checkCol(new Vector2(loc.X + 25f, loc.Y - 15f)))
            loc.X = pLoc.X;

    if (trajectory.X < 0f)
        if (map.checkCol(new Vector2(loc.X - 25f, loc.Y - 15f)))
            loc.X = pLoc.X;
}
```

FallOff()

The function FallOff() is called when a grounded character realizes that he no longer has ground below him, which could occur if he was on a collision cell or a ledge. He gets set to airborne state, has his animation set to fly, and has his y trajectory reset.

```
private void FallOff()
{
    State = CharState.Air;
    SetAnim("fly");
    trajectory.Y = 0f;
}
```

Land()

The character can land on collision cells or ledges, so we define a simple Land() function to set him to grounded state and idle animation.

```
private void Land()
{
    State = CharState.Grounded;
    SetAnim("idle");
}
```

Notice how we transition from airborne state to grounded state and vice versa. The character will simply launch into the air without crouching first, and will land on stiff legs. This won't look quite right, but it's the best implementation we can hope for before we get into scripting—and honestly, we just want to see something cool soon.

Now it's time to make a Draw() function.

Drawing the Character

We'll be reusing the drawing code from CharacterEditor. We'll just move it into Character and modify it slightly.

For starters, we don't need all of the parameters; the SpriteBatch is enough (everything else is now a class-level field).

```
public void Draw(SpriteBatch spriteBatch)
{
    Rectangle sRect = new Rectangle();

    int frameIdx =
        charDef.GetAnimation(anim).GetKeyFrame(animFrame).frameRef;

    Frame frame = charDef.GetFrame(frameIdx);

    spriteBatch.Begin(SpriteBlendMode.AlphaBlend);
    .
    .
    .
```

```
    float rotation = part.rotation;

    Vector2 location = part.location * scale + loc -
        Game1.scroll;
    Vector2 scaling = part.scaling * scale;
    .
    .
    .

    Color color = new Color(new
        Vector4(1.0f, 1.0f, 1.0f, 1f));
```

We can remove the line that changes the color for preview mode.

```
    bool flip = false;
    .
    .
    .
```

Everything else can be left the way it was. There are a few inherent changes going on where we didn't actually need to modify the code, such as loc and face now being class-level fields.

Texture Loading

Remember how we declared our character textures as statics? We can also make a static function to load them in Character, which we'll call from Game1.

```
internal static void LoadTextures(ContentManager content)
{
    for (int i = 0; i < headTex.Length; i++)
        headTex[i] = content.Load<Texture2D>(@"gfx/head" +
            (i + 1).ToString());

    for (int i = 0; i < torsoTex.Length; i++)
        torsoTex[i] = content.Load<Texture2D>(@"gfx/torso" +
            (i + 1).ToString());

    for (int i = 0; i < legsTex.Length; i++)
        legsTex[i] = content.Load<Texture2D>(@"gfx/legs" +
            (i + 1).ToString());

    for (int i = 0; i < weaponTex.Length; i++)
        weaponTex[i] = content.Load<Texture2D>(@"gfx/weapon" +
            (i + 1).ToString());
}
```

Lastly, we should handle some input.

Gamepad Input

At this point, we're going to let our character move only left and right and jump. Eventually, we'll add all sorts of nonsense.

We'll pass the controller index to the method, and then compare the state of the gamepad with the way it looked the last time we checked it. This way, we can test to see if a button has just been pressed.

```
public void DoInput(int index)
{
    curState = GamePad.GetState((PlayerIndex)index);
    keyLeft = false;
    keyRight = false;
    keyJump = false;
    keyAttack = false;
    keySecondary = false;
    keyUp = false;
    keyDown = false;

    if (curState.ThumbSticks.Left.X < -0.1f)
        keyLeft = true;

    if (curState.ThumbSticks.Left.X > 0.1f)
        keyRight = true;

    if (curState.ThumbSticks.Left.Y < -0.1f)
        keyDown = true;

    if (curState.ThumbSticks.Left.Y > 0.1f)
        keyUp = true;


    if (curState.Buttons.A == ButtonState.Pressed &&
        prevState.Buttons.A == ButtonState.Released)
        keyJump = true;

    if (curState.Buttons.Y == ButtonState.Pressed &&
        prevState.Buttons.Y == ButtonState.Released)
        keyAttack = true;

    if (curState.Buttons.X == ButtonState.Pressed &&
        prevState.Buttons.X == ButtonState.Released)
        keySecondary = true;

    prevState = curState;
}
```

Character Definition

Before we start bringing everything together in Game1, we'll declare a new enumerator for use in CharDef. For now, we'll just plan on using one for Guy and one for Zombie. Add a new file called CharacterType.cs with the following enumerator:

```
using System;

namespace ZombieSmashers.Character
{
    public enum CharacterType
    {
        Guy = 0,
        Zombie
    }
}
```

There will be more later on (what fun would our game be without bosses?), but this will serve our purposes for now. One of the nice things about using an enumeration like this is that we do not need to worry about redefining or defining different character types. By using a strong name in our code, we get around the actual values pertaining to each type.

Go ahead and add a new public field to the CharDef class that references this enumerator:

```
public CharacterType CharType = CharacterType.Guy;
```

Setting Things in Motion

We have set up our Character and Map classes. Now it's time to set them in motion. We'll be keeping a Map object and array of Character objects, which we'll update and draw from Game1.

We'll start with class-level objects:

```
Map map;

Texture2D[] mapsTex = new Texture2D[1];
Character[] character = new Character[16];
CharDef[] charDef = new CharDef[16];
```

There were a few fields that we used in Character and Map that we said we would have in Game1, such as frameTime, the amount of time elapsed since the last Update(), scroll, and the game camera location. We'll also add gravity and friction, which Character takes into account when updating the character's location.

```
public static float frameTime = 0f;
public static Vector2 scroll = new Vector2();

public const float gravity = 900f;
public const float friction = 1000f;

GraphicsDeviceManager graphics;
SpriteBatch spriteBatch;
```

To initialize, we'll do some hard-coding. We'll instantiate Map, read map, read our guy CharDef, and instantiate a new Character at location 100, 100. Notice how we're using CharacterType. Guy twice to refer to the guy CharDef.

```
protected override void Initialize()
{
    map = new Map();
    map.path = "maps/map";
    map.Read();

    charDef[(int)CharacterType.Guy] = new CharDef("chars/guy");

    character[0]
        = new Character(new Vector2(100f, 100f),
        charDef[(int)CharacterType.Guy]);
    character[0].Map = map;
    base.Initialize();
}
```

Next, we load the game content:

```
protected override void LoadContent()
{
    spriteBatch = new SpriteBatch(GraphicsDevice);

    for (int i = 0; i < mapsTex.Length; i++)
        mapsTex[i] = Content.Load<Texture2D>(@"gfx/maps" +
            (i + 1).ToString());

    Character.LoadTextures(Content);

}
```

Time to update! First, we'll grab frameTime, then we'll update scroll (bit of hard-coding again) and handle input, and finally, we'll do our general update of all characters.

```
protected override void Update(GameTime gameTime)
{
    // Allows the game to exit
    if (GamePad.GetState(PlayerIndex.One).Buttons.Back ==
        ButtonState.Pressed)
            this.Exit();

    frameTime = (float)gameTime.ElapsedGameTime.TotalSeconds;

    if (character[0] != null)
    {
```

We're updating scroll to loosely follow the player—we want the top-left corner of the camera to be at –400, –400 of the player's location. By updating scroll by the difference between the current scroll location and our goal location, we end up with a camera that sort of springs to its goal location.

```
        scroll += ((character[0].Location -
            new Vector2(400f, 400f)) - scroll) * frameTime * 20f;

        character[0].DoInput(0);
    }
    for (int i = 0; i < character.Length; i++)
    {
        if (character[i] != null)
        {
            character[i].Update(gameTime);
        }
    }

    base.Update(gameTime);
}
```

Last but not least, it's time to draw! As we said earlier, we won't draw the map all at once—we'll draw layers 0 and 1; then draw the characters, effects, and so on; then draw map layer 2; and, finally, draw the HUD. For now, we'll leave out the HUD (don't have one), particles, and stuff (don't have those either), and draw only one character.

```
protected override void Draw(GameTime gameTime)
{
    graphics.GraphicsDevice.Clear(Color.CornflowerBlue);

    map.Draw(spriteBatch, mapsTex, 0, 2);

    character[0].Draw(spriteBatch);

    map.Draw(spriteBatch, mapsTex, 2, 3);

    base.Draw(gameTime);
}
```

That should do it! Let's run it. Figure 6-4 shows where we are at this point.

We've done a bit of work so far, but this is the first time we have something we can actually play with. Of course, the amount of stuff we can do is pretty limited: move left, move right, jump, and run into invisible walls at each side.

Figure 6-4. *Zombie Smashers at last!*

Adding a Background Image

Now cornflower blue is great, but adding a background image will really make our game slicker and start setting the mood. We'll use a starry night on a blue gradient. Image back1.png is shown in Figure 6-5. Add this image to the solution's gfx folder. Next, add the following to the class level of Game1:

```
Texture2D[] mapBackTex = new Texture2D[1];
```

And then in LoadContent(), add this:

```
for (int i = 0; i < mapBackTex.Length; i++)
    mapBackTex[i] = Content.Load<Texture2D>(@"gfx/back" +
        (i + 1).ToString());
```

We'll need to change our Draw() method in Map to let us pass in the map background. We'll make it look like this:

```
public void Draw(SpriteBatch sprite, Texture2D[] mapsTex,
    Texture2D[] mapBackTex,
    int startLayer, int endLayer)
{
```

Figure 6-5. *Our background image*

And then in the beginning of the method, we'll draw the background with the following code. We also declare a new class-level constant, LAYER_BACK, and set it equal to zero.

```
sprite.Begin(SpriteBlendMode.AlphaBlend);

if (startLayer == LAYER_BACK)
{
    float xLim = GetXLim();
    float yLim = GetYLim();
    Vector2 targ = new Vector2(
        Game1.ScreenSize.X / 2f
        - ((Game1.scroll.X / xLim) - 0.5f) * 100f,
        Game1.ScreenSize.Y / 2f
        - ((Game1.scroll.Y / yLim) - 0.5f) * 100f
        );

    sprite.Draw(mapBackTex[0], targ, new
        Rectangle(0, 0, 1280, 720), Color.White, 0f,
        new Vector2(640f, 360f), 1f, SpriteEffects.None, 1f);
}

for (int l = startLayer; l < endLayer; l++)
```

We also need to add two more methods: GetXLim() and GetYLim(). We'll use these to get the horizontal and vertical limits for the scroll vector.

```
public float GetXLim()
{
    return 1280 - Game1.ScreenSize.X;
}

public float GetYLim()
{
    return 1280 Game1.ScreenSize.Y;
}
```

This brings us back again to Game1, where we create a class-level variable:

```
private static Vector2 screenSize = new Vector2();
public static Vector2 ScreenSize{
    get { return screenSize; }
    set { screenSize = value; }
}
```

In Initialize(), we'll hard-code in our screen size of 800, 600 with this:

```
screenSize.X = 800f;
screenSize.Y = 600f;
```

Now that we can get maximum value for scroll, let's lock it in so we don't have the camera flying off the edges of the map. In Update(), add the following:

```
Scroll += ((character[0].Location -
    new Vector2(400f, 400f)) - Scroll) * frameTime * 20f;

float xLim = map.GetXLim();
float yLim = map.GetYLim();

if (scroll.X < 0f) scroll.X = 0f;
if (scroll.X > xLim) scroll.X = xLim;
if (scroll.Y < 0f) scroll.Y = 0f;
if (scroll.Y > yLim) scroll.Y = yLim;
```

Now we should have a camera that doesn't slip off the edge of the map and a nice, starry night background. You should end up with what you see in Figure 6-6. If you don't, that means something went terribly wrong.

Figure 6-6. *Background image in action!*

Moody, right? We are now looking good, and we've officially completed the first part of the chapter. Wouldn't it be nice if our character could be just slightly more expressive?

Super Simple Scripting

What we want to add is the ability to define not only how the character can be animated, but how several different animations work together in conjunction. You can consider an animation to be a person running and another animation to be the stopping motion. Scripting will allow us to define that the stopping animation comes after the player has ended the running animation, thus giving the player a more realistic set of motions. In this case, we want to be able to have our character attack, fire his pistol, and string together attacks into complex combos. We're definitely not going to hard-code this; we need a scripting system.

To add the scripting, we will do the following:

- Design a scripting language.

- Implement script editing in CharacterEditor.

- Create some classes in ZombieSmashers to process and run scripts.

- Add scripts to our Guy character.

The Scripting Language

Our character-scripting system will be very basic. For each keyframe in an animation, there will be up to four associated script commands. We'll use commands for tasks such as the following:

- Navigating frames
- Switching animations
- Sliding and jumping

The syntax for scripting language is as simple as this:

```
command parameter
```

We'll have commands that look like **setanim** `attack2` and **goto** `3`.

Adding Script Editing to the Character Editor

We'll start by editing `CharacterEditor` to allow us to edit keyframe scripts. First, let's declare a class-level variable to know which script line we're editing. We'll also want to modify the `EditingMode` enumeration to know when we are modifying the script.

```
int selScriptLine = 0;
enum EditingMode
{
    None,
    FrameName,
    AnimationName,
    PathName,
    Script
}
```

In `Draw()`, we'll add our functionality to view and edit the script:

```
#region Script
for (int i = 0; i < 4; i++)
{
    if (editMode == EditingMode.Script && selScriptLine == i)
    {
        text.Color = Color.Lime;
        text.DrawText(210, 42 + i * 16, i.ToString() + ": " +
            charDef.Animations[selAnim].
            KeyFrames[selKeyFrame].Scripts[i]
            + "*");
    }
```

```
    else
    {
        if (text.DrawClickText(210, 42 + i * 16, i.ToString() + ": " +
            charDef.Animations[selAnim].
            KeyFrames[selKeyFrame].Scripts[i],
            mouseState.X, mouseState.Y, mouseClick))
        {
            selScriptLine = i;
            editMode = EditingMode.Script;
        }
    }
}
#endregion
```

Remember the functionality we used to allow text editing? We check the editing mode, grab the appropriate string, edit it, and restore it to the appropriate variable. We're adding a new editing mode, EditMode.Script. In PressKey(), add the following:

```
    break;
case EditMode.Script:
    t = charDef.Animations[selAnim].
        KeyFrames[selKeyFrame].Scripts[selScriptLine];
    break;
default:
```

And at the end, add this:

```
    break;
case EditMode.Script:
    charDef.Animations[selAnim].
        KeyFrames[selKeyFrame].Scripts[selScriptLine] = t;
    break;
```

One last detail is that we need to put a translucent black box under our new script editor. In Draw(), we'll need to extend the rectangle that we drew under our load/save/path area:

```
spriteBatch.Draw(nullTex, new Rectangle(590, 0, 300, 600), new
    Color(new Vector4(0.0f, 0.0f, 0.0f, 0.5f)));
spriteBatch.Draw(nullTex, new Rectangle(200, 0, 150, 110), new
    Color(new Vector4(0.0f, 0.0f, 0.0f, 0.5f)));
spriteBatch.End();
```

This was a bit roundabout! Figure 6-7 shows our new and improved character editor.

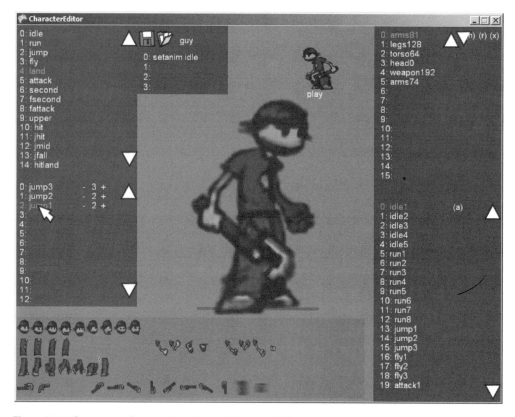

Figure 6-7. *Character editor with script-editing capabilties. Go nuts!*

Some Script Commands

Let's plan some commands. The following are some navigation commands:

- `setanim` *newanim*: Set current animation to *newanim* at frame 0.

- `goto` *frame*: Jump to frame *frame* of the current animation.

- `ifupgoto` *frame*: Jump to frame *frame* of the current animation if Up is pressed.

- `ifdowngoto` *frame*: Jump to frame *frame* of the current animation if Down is pressed.

  For movement, we'll use these commands:

- `float`: Cause an airborne character to begin hovering. We'll use this for air combos.

- `unfloat`: Cause an airborne, floating character to stop floating and drop to the ground at normal speed.

- `slide` *xval*: Slide the character forward by *xval*.

- `backup` *xval*: Back up the character by *xval*.

- `setjump` *yval*: Set the character airborne at speed *yval*.

- `joymove`: Cause the character to move left or right by the set speed if the joystick is pressed in that direction.

We'll be handling animation linking for combos with what we'll call a *key goto array*, which is basically an array of frame destinations associated with certain key presses. For instance, at the end of a wrench-swinging animation, we can set the uppercut, or `upper`, goto to take us to the start of a wrench-uppercutting animation. The following are the commands for these actions:

- `clearkeys`: Clear the key goto array.

- `setuppergoto` *frame*: Set the uppercut slot of the key goto array to link to frame *frame*.

- `setlowergoto` *frame*: Set the lower attack slot of the key goto array to link to frame *frame*.

- `setatkgoto` *frame*: Set the normal attack slot of the key goto array to link to frame *frame*.

- `setanygoto` *frame*: Set the normal attack, uppercut, and lower attack slots of the key goto array to link to frame *frame*.

We'll have commands for the secondary attack. Our protagonist wields a revolver. We'll want to check whether the player is holding Up or Down while pressing X. Here are the commands for the secondary attack actions:

- `setsecgoto` *frame*: Set the secondary attack slot of the goto array to link to frame *frame*.

- `setsecupgoto` *frame*: Set the upper secondary attack slot of the goto array to link to frame *frame*.

- `setsecdowngoto` *frame*: Set the lower secondary attack slot of the goto array to link to frame *frame*.

Maybe this is a bit confusing. Let's look at an example of how this will work in a realistic situation, for a section of animation `fattack` (named to indicate "flying attack," not something obesity-related). Behold the results in Figure 6-8!

Right off the bat, we're telling our character to start floating. We want a bit of hover for our air combos to really work. When the guy swings his wrench, we'll slide forward with a trajectory of 200. Toward the end of the animation, we'll clear the key goto array, and then set the goto slots for all attack animations to take us to frame 50. At the end of the animation, if the player hasn't pressed any attacking keys, we'll return to the `fly` animation.

Script Parsing

We'll be storing the script structure in two classes in the `CharClasses` folder: `ScriptLine`, which we'll use to parse and store a script line (command plus parameter), and `Script`, which we'll use to run the script.

float

slide 200

clearkeys

setanygoto 50

setanim fly

Figure 6-8. *The first ten frames of animation "fattack"*

The ScriptLine Class

The ScriptLine class starts like this:

```
class ScriptLine
{
    Commands command;
    String sParam;
    int iParam;
```

Our constructor will parse a script line in string form into a command and parameter. We're working on a case-by-case basis.

```
    public ScriptLine(String line)
    {
        String[] split = line.Split(' ');
        try
        {
            switch (split[0].Trim().ToLower())
```

```
{
    case "setanim":
        command = Commands.SetAnim;
        sParam = split[1];
        break;
    case "goto":
        command = Commands.Goto;
        iParam = Convert.ToInt32(split[1]);
        break;
    case "ifupgoto":
        command = Commands.IfUpGoto;
        iParam = Convert.ToInt32(split[1]);
        break;
    case "ifdowngoto":
        command = Commands.IfDownGoto;
        iParam = Convert.ToInt32(split[1]);
        break;

    case "float":
        command = Commands.Float;
        break;
    case "unfloat":
        command = Commands.UnFloat;
        break;
    case "slide":
        command = Commands.Slide;
        iParam = Convert.ToInt32(split[1]);
        break;
    case "backup":
        command = Commands.Backup;
        iParam = Convert.ToInt32(split[1]);
        break;
    case "setjump":
        command = Commands.SetJump;
        iParam = Convert.ToInt32(split[1]);
        break;
    case "joymove":
        command = Commands.JoyMove;
        break;

    case "clearkeys":
        command = Commands.ClearKeys;
        break;
    case "setuppergoto":
        command = Commands.SetUpperGoto;
        iParam = Convert.ToInt32(split[1]);
        break;
```

```
                case "setlowergoto":
                    command = Commands.SetLowerGoto;
                    iParam = Convert.ToInt32(split[1]);
                    break;
                case "setatkgoto":
                    command = Commands.SetAtKGoto;
                    iParam = Convert.ToInt32(split[1]);
                    break;
                case "setanygoto":
                    command = Commands.SetAnyGoto;
                    iParam = Convert.ToInt32(split[1]);
                    break;
                case "setsecgoto":
                    command = Commands.SetSecondaryGoto;
                    iParam = Convert.ToInt32(split[1]);
                    break;
                case "setsecupgoto":
                    command = Commands.SetSecUpGoto
                    iParam = Convert.ToInt32(split[1]);
                    break;
                case "setsecdowngoto":
                    command = Commands.SetSecDownGoto;
                    iParam = Convert.ToInt32(split[1]);
                    break;

            }
        }
        catch (Exception e)
        {
            Console.WriteLine(e.StackTrace);
        }

    }
```

Lastly, we'll throw in some properties to access our private fields:

```
public Commands Command
{
    get { return command; }
}

public int IParam
{
    get { return iParam; }
}
```

```
    public String SParam
    {
        get { return sParam; }
    }
}
```

The Script Class

To run our scripts, we'll create the Commands enumeration and the Script class.

```
enum Commands
{
    SetAnim,
    Goto,
    IfUpGoto,
    IfDownGoto,
    Float,
    UnFloat,
    Slide,
    Backup,
    SetJump,
    JoyMove,
    ClearKeys,
    SetUpperGoto,
    SetLowerGoto,
    SetAtKGoto,
    SetAnyGoto,
    SetSecondaryGoto,
    SetSecUpGoto,
    SetSecDownGoto
}
```

```
class Script
{
    Character character;
```

Each Script will have an associated Character on which it will operate. This Character will pass itself when it creates the Script.

```
    public Script(Character character)
    {
        this.character = _character;
    }
```

Our big DoScript() method will be called from Character every time the animation hits a new keyframe.

For the most part, the processing is very straightforward. The only bit that needs explaining is the done variable. When a goto is called, done is set to true and script reading ends. This way, a keyframe can call setanim *x* and then goto *y*, effectively setting the animation to *x*, frame *y*, but two gotos in a row cannot be called from the same keyframe.

```
public void DoScript(int animIdx, int keyFrameIdx)
{
    CharDef charDef = character.Definition
    Animation animation = charDef.Animations[animIdx];
    KeyFrame keyFrame = animation.KeyFrames[keyFrameIdx];

    bool done = false;

    for (int i = 0; i < keyFrame.GetScriptArray().Length; i++)
    {
        if (done)
            break;
        else
        {
            ScriptLine line = keyFrame.Scripts[i];
            if (line != null)
            {
                switch (line. Command)
                {
                    case Commands.SetAnim:
                        character.SetAnim(line.SParam);
                        break;
                    case Commands.Goto:
                        character.AnimFrame = line.IParam;
                        done = true;
                        break;
                    case Commands.IfUpGoto:
                        if (character.KeyUp)
                        {
                            character.AnimFrame = line.IParam;
                            done = true;
                        }
                        break;
                    case Commands.IfDownGoto:
                        if (character.KeyDown)
                        {
                            character.AnimFrame = line.IParam;
                            done = true;
                        }
                        break;
```

```
case Commands.Float:
    character.floating = true;
    break;
case Commands.UnFloat:
    character.floating = false;
    break;
case Commands.Slide:
    character.Slide(line.IParam);
    break;
case Commands.Backup:
    character.Slide(-line.IParam);
    break;
case Commands.SetJump:
    character.SetJump(line.IParam);
    break;
case Commands.JoyMove:
    if (character.KeyLeft)
        character.Trajectory.X =
            -character.Speed;
    else if (character.KeyRight)
        character.Trajectory.X =
            character.Speed;
    break;
case Commands.ClearKeys:
    character.PressedKey = PressedKeys.None;
    break;
case Commands.SetUpperGoto:
    character.GotoGoal[(int)PressedKeys.Upper] =
        line.IParam;
    break;
case Commands.SetLowerGoto:
    character.GotoGoal[(int)PressedKeys.Lower] =
        line.IParam;

    break;
case Commands.SetAtkGoto:
    character.GotoGoal[(int)PressedKeys.Attack] =
        line.IParam;

    break;
case Commands.SetAnyGoto:
    character.GotoGoal[(int)PressedKeys.Upper] =
        line.IParam;
    character.GotoGoal[(int)PressedKeys.Lower] =
        line.IParam;
```

```
                        character.GotoGoal[(int)PressedKeys.Attack] =
                            line.IParam;
                        break;
                    case Commands.SetSecondaryGoto:
                        character.GotoGoal[(int)PressedKeys.Secondary]
                            = line.IParam;
                        character.GotoGoal[(int)PressedKeys.SecUp] =
                            line.IParam;
                        character.GotoGoal[(int)PressedKeys.SecDown] =
                            line.IParam;
                        break;
                    case Commands.SetSecUpGoto:
                        character.GotoGoal[(int)PressedKeys.SecUp] =
                            line.IParam;

                        break;
                    case Commands.SetSecDownGoto:
                        character.GotoGoal[(int)PressedKeys.SecDown] =
                            line.IParam;

                        break;

                }
            }
        }
    }
}
```

Let's close the circle back in Character.

Character Class Updates

We've spent about a page of the script operation working with the key goto array. Now let's declare it at the class level in Character. Our key goto array is held in gotoGoal[]. We'll also need a new enumeration for pressed keys.

```
enum PressedKeys
{
    None,
    Upper,
    Lower,
    Attack,
    Secondary,
    SecUp,
    SecDown
}
```

```
class Character
{
    public float Speed = 200f;
    public PressedKeys PressedKey;

    public int[] GotoGoal = { -1, -1, -1, -1, -1, -1, -1, -1 };
```

In Update(), we'll turn various combinations of button presses and the analog stick into values for pressedKey.

```
pressedKey = PressedKeys.None;
if (KeyAttack)
{
    PressedKey = PressedKeys.Attack;
    if (KeyUp) PressedKey = PressedKeys.Lower;
    if (KeyDown) PressedKey = PressedKeys.Upper;
}
if (KeySecondary)
{
    PressedKey = PressedKeys.Secondary;
    if (KeyUp) pressedKey = PressedKeys.SecUp;
    if (KeyDown) pressedKey = PressedKeys.SecDown;
}
```

If PressedKey is not PressedKeys.None, we'll check the key goto array to see if we have any matches. If we do, we'll go to the goal frame, clear the array, and run the script for the new frame.

```
if (PressedKey != PressedKeys.None)
{
    if (GotoGoal[(int)PressedKey] > -1)
    {
        AnimFrame = GotoGoal[(int)PressedKey];

        if (keyLeft)
            face = CharDir.Left;
        if (keyRight)
            face = CharDir.Right;

        PressedKey = PressedKeys.None;

        for (int i = 0; i < GotoGoal.Length; i++)
            GotoGoal[i] = -1;

        frame = 0f;
        script.DoScript(Anim, AnimFrame);
    }
}
```

We'll also need to put in a line to call DoScript() in a few other places (basically whenever the keyframe is changed).

In Update(), we have a region where we update the character's animFrame. As soon as we progress from one animFrame to the next, we'll run the script on the previous frame. If our script includes a frame goto, we won't skip to the next frame.

```
if (frame > (float)keyFrame.Duration)
{
    int pframe = AnimFrame;
    script.DoScript(Anim, AnimFrame);

    frame -= (float)keyFrame.Duration;
    if (AnimFrame == pframe)
        AnimFrame++;
```

We decided to call the script at the end of a frame, rather than the beginning, because it's a more consistent approach and because it makes for easier planning when using a bunch of gotos between frames.

Finally, we need to parse the scripts when each CharDef is loaded. Before, we would just read in all the script lines as strings. Now, let's actually parse them with our ScriptLine constructor! In Read(), change our script-reading line to the following:

```
keyframe.FrameRef = b.ReadInt32();
keyframe.Duration = b.ReadInt32();

ScriptLine[] script = keyframe.GetScriptArray();
for (int s = 0; s < script.Length; s++)
    script[s] = new ScriptLine(b.ReadString());
```

This will get our scripts parsed and ready to go. If we kept them as strings, we would have needed to do some nasty string manipulation every time we ran a script, which would produce some terrible garbage on the Xbox 360.

Before we get to using this new feature, we also need to declare some new methods in the Character class for jumping and sliding. These are fairly straightforward and simply wrap up a few lines of code so we do not need to reproduce them whenever we need to jump or slide.

```
public void Slide(float distance)
{
    Trajectory.X = (float)Face * 2f * distance - distance;
}

public void SetJump(float jump)
{
    Trajectory.Y = -jump;
    State = CharState.Air;
    ledgeAttach = -1;
}
```

Putting Scripting into Practice

Let's look at how this scripting language actually works in a situation we could be using for Zombie Smashers XNA.

We've mapped out all of the important keyframes in the animation second (for secondary attack) and connected them with gotos in Figure 6-9. We've left out frame numbers, opting to use some attractive lines instead.

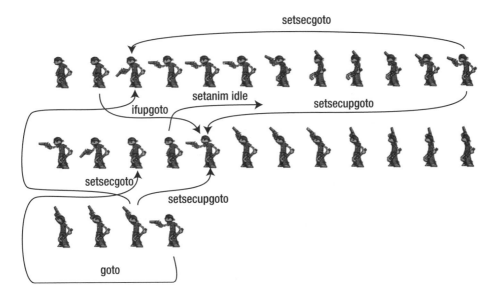

Figure 6-9. *Gotos in "second"*

It's all one animation, but it's split into two rows that just happen to coincide with the regular shoot and shoot up animations.

At the start of the animation, we'll check whether Up was pressed. If it was, we'll jump to the start of the shoot up segment. At the ends of both the regular shoot and shoot up animations, we'll check for input to send us to the start of the shooting animations. If we don't get input, we'll move to the end of the animation and finally idle.

Let's look at a more complicated example for the animation attack, shown in the same pseudo-format in Figure 6-10.

Now we're getting into the good stuff! We have got a four-hit combo: spanner-whack, spanner-whack, spanner-whack, flying kick. The player just needs to keep mashing those buttons. Of course, if the player doesn't keep mashing the buttons, each individual attack has a few back-to-idle frames, so we have a totally legit combo now.

The fun part is at the end. If the player does an uppercut (Down on the left analog + Y), we'll jump to the last row, launching skyward with a nice spanner-uppercut and finishing up in the fly animation.

See how powerful this stuff is? We can really go nuts with these combos—air juggles, complex ground combos, far-reaching mega slams. We've just opened up a really fun and exciting part of this whole design racket!

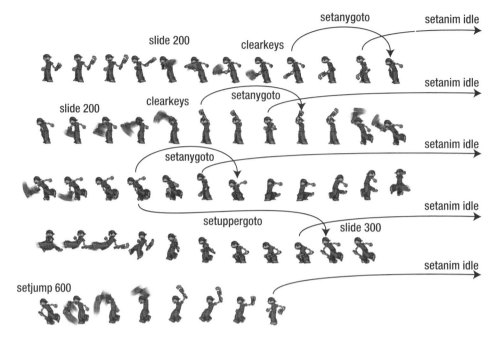

Figure 6-10. *Complex stuff: the "attack" animation*

Odds and Ends: Cleanup

Now that we have our script system in place (and gotten all hot and bothered in the process), we can clean up some placeholder animation code in Character—namely jumping and landing. Our character does look a little stiff-legged on the landing, doesn't he?

In Update(), we're going to change the key input part to this:

```
#region Key input
if (animName == "idle" || animName == "run")
{
    if (keyLeft)
    .
    .
    .
    if (keyAttack)
    {
        SetAnim("attack");
    }
    if (keySecondary)
    {
        SetAnim("second");
    }
```

```
    if (keyJump)
    {
        SetAnim("jump");
    }
}
```

And then we'll update `Land()` to look like this:

```
private void Land()
{
    State = CharState.Grounded;
    SetAnim("land");
}
```

This means that in our character definition file (`guy.zmx`), we need to create a `jump` anima-tion, which will have our guy crouching and end in a `joymove`, `setjump 600`, and `setanim fly`, and a `land` animation, which will end in a `setanim idle`. We've basically added an extra anima-tion between idle/running and flying through the air. These animations are then responsible for progressing the character's motion.

Conclusion

We've made some terrific headway into our game. We created our game solution, moved in all of the right classes, loaded our content, loaded our data, and set up what is shaping up to be a very complicated, very expressive `Character` class, complete with simple movement and colli-sion detection.

Next, we mapped out our scripting language, modified our character editor to allow script editing, and implemented script parsing and running from our `Character` class. We looked at how we can use our ultra-simple scripting language to add a lot of depth and expressiveness to our characters. We'll be building on this quite a bit as we flesh out our game.

Our next order of business is going to involve lots of particles: sparks, muzzle flashes, explosions, and more. We'll call it particle mayhem!

CHAPTER 7

∎∎∎

Particle Mayhem
Bring Out the Smashing!

Designing particle systems is probably one of the most exciting aspects of independent game development, yet it also happens to be an area where a lot of aspiring indie developers fall flat. This is another programmer art issue. While large teams with big budgets can rely on tools to better facilitate art direction for particle systems, independent developers must either work the entire thing out for themselves or try to collaborate with an artist to really nail the feel of it. Furthermore, many developers often take a side road and never come back once they hit particles. After building a basic system, it's easy to get caught up in adding features to the particle system and creating an editor, because particles are just so pretty. If possible, get someone else to build the particle system for you and integrate it into the game, so that you have time to work on more pressing matters. However, this book is written with the one-person team in mind, so we'll get it done.

It's always nice to have a bit of history under your belt when tackling something new. We're about to unleash some shiny, explosive particle mayhem, so to prepare ourselves, we'll take a brief look at the quintessential rocket contrail, starting in 1993.

A Brief History of Rocket Contrails in First-Person Shooters

Doom introduced rockets without contrails. Still, it had rockets, which we all thought was amazing. From the first inception of the rocket, players have been blowing each other up without actually hitting any rockets! But a rocket is nothing without a sweet trail of smoke and fire spewing out, attracting everyone's attention to the destruction that lies ahead and the person who created it, as you see in Figure 7-1.

Marathon (a Doom-like title that was a Mac exclusive for quite awhile) had rockets with billboarded smoke contrails. Unfortunately, something didn't quite sit right about the contrails. They were drawn "attached" to the rockets, such that each smoke billboard was rendered a fixed distance from the rocket. This created an illusion that the player wasn't firing a rocket, but instead launching a giant tube consisting mostly of fluffy gray stuff with a rocket-like protrusion at the business end.

Figure 7-1. *Rocket contrail*

Quake did it right, albeit cheaply. Because the technology was already so taxing on the systems of the day, the Quake developers settled for giant point particles, rather than billboarded quads. Each rocket left a trail of yellowish particles and gray particles; the yellow ones slowly fell, while the gray ones slowly rose. Still, we all thought it was amazing, and it looked right according to some basic level of physics.

Half-Life took another step backward in the name of progress. The technique is similar to sword slash effects. A contrail is made of a solid polygon with vertex pairs added at each point where a Quake rocket would have dropped some particles. The vertex pairs are rotated so that the viewer will get the widest view of each quad section. It seemed like a good idea, but in a number of cases, the technique just didn't look right.

Now that technology has caught up with the ubiquitous rocket contrail, it seems the industry has settled on billboarded quads. However, for those who look to the future, volumetric rendering could allow for some very gorgeous smoke trails. Coupled with a nice haze and fire effect, rockets of the future will look more realistic than ever. However, for our purposes (and for much of the industry), volumetric clouds are a bit of overkill.

In a nutshell, the modern rocket contrail is made up of billboarded quads, dropped from a fired rocket at regular intervals. These quads change colors, fade out, and die after a short life span. This modern rocket contrail just looks right. More important though, it is realistic enough without creating a huge performance hit.

Why is it important to pore over details like this? Much like many other aspects of game development, it is all too easy to get bogged down trying to make good-looking code rather than a good-looking game. It's important to be able to code, build, and run, and to be able to say not only, "this is doing what it's supposed to," but also "hey, this looks great!"

Setting Up a Particle System

We'll start of by setting up the programmatic structure for our particles, and then we'll make some mayhem. We personally think that the first task is the boring part and the second is the fun part, so the attention to detail on each will reflect that. Half the fun of particle systems is spent tweaking them to make explosions, splatters, and general effects look both on the money and dramatic enough to draw the player in for some more.

A Base Class

We'll start by defining a base `Particle` class. Particles have fairly limited functionality: they can be constructed, updated, and rendered. They have locations and trajectories, short life spans, and a few other flags that we can play with.

The Update() function will decrease the particle life (killing it if necessary) and move the particle along its trajectory. The trajectory works as it did in the Character class, acting as a consistent velocity to multiply by elapsed time and add onto the current location. Update() has a few parameters that we'll explain later.

```
public class Particle
{
    protected Vector2 location;
    protected Vector2 trajectory;

    protected float frame;
    protected float r, g, b, a;
    protected float size;
    protected float rotation;

    protected int flag;

    protected int owner;

    public bool Exists;
    public bool Background;

    public Vector2 GameLocation
    {
        get { return location - Game1.Scroll; }
    }

    public Particle()
    {
        Exists = false;
    }

    public virtual void Update(float gameTime,
            Map map,
            ParticleManager pMan,
            Character[] c)
    {
        location += trajectory * gameTime;
        frame -= gameTime;
        if (frame < 0.0f) KillMe();
    }

    public virtual void KillMe()
    {
        Exists = false;
    }
```

```
      public virtual void Draw(SpriteBatch sprite, Texture2D spritesTex)
      {
      }
}
```

We've included quite a few fields that we don't really need right now. Overextending the functionality in preparation for future revisions is a habit. Most of the fields are fairly self-explanatory, with a few exceptions:

- owner is typically used to indicate the index of the character that is responsible for this particle.

- flag is commonly used for special data, such as which image index a particle uses.

- background is used to determine whether the particle is drawn behind all characters or in front of them.

A Smoke Class

Now that we have a base class, let's make a particle. Appropriately enough, we'll make a particle that has quite a bit to do with particles in real life: smoke.

Creating decent-looking particles is typically an iterative process involving a lot of tweaking and refinement, but it helps to have a plan. The process of producing a realistic particle effect can be difficult because our brains cannot always detail in code what we imagine. The layers of interpretation between what we feel will look real and what actually works is muddied. Enough psychobabble though.

To get started, we need some imagery. We like to use sprite sheets full of all the miscellaneous particle imagery we'll need. Let's begin by making some fluffy white blobs, as shown in Figure 7-2.

Figure 7-2. *Fluffy white blobs (the particle sprite sheet)*

We'll create our Smoke class to extend the Particle base class.

```
class Smoke : Particle
{
    public Smoke(Vector2 location,
        Vector2 trajectory,
        float r,
        float g,
        float b,
        float a,
        float size,
        int icon)
    {
        this.location = location;
        this.trajectory = trajectory;
        this.r = r;
        this.g = g;
        this.b = b;
        this.a = a;
        this.size = size;
        this.flag = icon;
        this.owner = -1;
        this.Exists = true;
        this.frame = 1.0f;
    }

    public override void Update(float gameTime,
            Map map,
            ParticleManager pMan,
            Character[] c)
    {
        if (frame < 0.5f)
        {
            if (trajectory.Y < -10.0f) trajectory.Y += gameTime * 500.0f;
            if (trajectory.X < -10.0f) trajectory.X += gameTime * 150.0f;
            if (trajectory.X > 10.0f) trajectory.X -= gameTime * 150.0f;
        }
        base.Update(gameTime, map, pMan, c);
    }

    public override void Draw(SpriteBatch sprite, Texture2D spritesTex)
    {

        Rectangle sRect = new Rectangle(flag * 64, 0, 64, 64);

        float frameAlpha;
```

```
        if (frame > 0.9f)
            frameAlpha = (1.0f - frame) * 10.0f;
        else
            frameAlpha = (frame / 0.9f);

        sprite.Draw(spritesTex,
            GameLocation,
            sRect,
            new Color(
                new Vector4(frame * r,
                            frame * g,
                            frame * b,
                            a * frameAlpha)
            ),
            rotation,
            new Vector2(32.0f, 32.0f),
            size + (1.0f - frame),
            SpriteEffects.None,
            1.0f);
    }
}
```

The constructor is straightforward enough. The `Draw()` and `Update()` methods show a bit of life, and ironically enough, take it away!

The `Update()` method adds a bit of definition to the smoke particle by decelerating its trajectory as it nears death; that is, it will cause smoke to slow down as it fades out, giving it a more natural look (which is what this is all about, no?)

The `Draw()` method does a few things. It determines the source rectangle based on our `flag` field. Then it calculates a scalar, `frameAlpha`, as a linear function of `frame`—the particle will quickly fade in and slowly fade out. The `sprite.Draw()` call has a bit of substance to it. The color is calculated such that the RGB values steadily decrease, while the alpha value changes with `frameAlpha`. Also, the size steadily increases.

Particle Management

Now we need a class to manage all of these particles. Here's an area where we skimped a bit. Traditionally, particle systems are atomic entities, where one system governs its child particles, and each system has its own life cycle. We just used a big array, without an emitter-child hierarchy, where particles can act as particle emitters. This turns out to be very beneficial, because certain particles can act as particle emitters. For example, a spark-like particle that shoots through the air and explodes can be represented as a particle that explodes and emits particles. For now, however, we will focus on the more basic particle examples of blood, smoke, and fire.

```
class ParticleManager
{
    Particle[] particles = new Particle[1024];
    SpriteBatch sprite;
```

```
public ParticleManager(SpriteBatch sprite)
{
    this.sprite = sprite;
}

public void AddParticle(Particle newParticle)
{
    AddParticle(newParticle, false);
}

public void AddParticle(Particle newParticle, bool background)
{
    for (int i = 0; i < particles.Length; i++)
    {
        if (particles[i] == null)
        {
            particles[i] = newParticle;
            particles[i].Background = background;
            break;
        }
    }
}

public void UpdateParticles(float frameTime,
        Map map,
        Character[] c)
{

    for (int i = 0; i < particles.Length; i++)
    {
        if (particles[i] != null)
        {
            particles[i].Update(frameTime, map, this, c);
            if (!particles[i].Exists)
            {
                particles[i] = null;
            }
        }
    }
}

public void DrawParticles(Texture2D spritesTex, bool background)
{
    sprite.Begin(SpriteBlendMode.AlphaBlend);
    foreach (Particle p in particles)
    {
```

```
            if (p != null)
            {
                if (p.Background == background)
                    p.Draw(sprite, spritesTex);
            }
        }
        sprite.End();
    }
}
```

The particle manager is tasked with adding new particles, updating and destroying live particles, and drawing all particles. The UpdateParticles() method checks for any particles with Exists set to false, which is how we'll flag them for destruction. We can also put all the draw calls in the same batch for the sake of efficiency. One of the built-in strengths of this particle system is the static size of the particle array. Instead of using a dynamic sizing list, we can avoid some of the costs of generating many particles at a single time.

To see our smoke in action, we'll just set up our game so that smoke flies off of our hero's head, and then get to practical cases later. In the Character.Update() method, add the following:

```
#region Particle Test
for (int i = 0; i < 4; i++)
{
    Vector2 tloc = (Location - pLoc) * (float)i / 4.0f + pLoc;
    tloc.Y -= 100f;

    PManager.AddParticle(new Smoke(tloc,
        Rand.GetRandomVector2(-50.0f, 50.0f, -300.0f, -200.0f),
        1.0f, 0.8f, 0.6f, 1.0f, Rand.GetRandomFloat(0.25f, 0.5f),
        Rand.GetRandomInt(0, 4)));

}
#endregion
```

Here, we're adding smoke particles at four linearly interpolated locations between the current character location and the previous character location. The call to actually add the smoke particles is none too pleasant to behold. The parameter breakdown goes like this: add particle at tloc with x trajectory between –50 and 50; y trajectory between –300 and –200; RGBA value of 1, 0.8, 0.6, and 1; size between 0.25 and 0.5; and icon between 0 and 3. Good-looking particle systems are all about randomization, as this is what gives players the sense of a real environment. For our smoke system, randomization will give us the ability to fake the fluid dynamics of real smoke by introducing randomly moving particles.

Let's do some setup in Game1. At the class level, add this:

```
Texture2D spritesTex;
ParticleManager pManager;
```

In LoadContent(), we now can create our ParticleManager with spriteBatch and load our sprites texture:

```
protected override void LoadContent()
{
    spriteBatch = new SpriteBatch(GraphicsDevice);
    pManager = new ParticleManager(spriteBatch);
    spritesTex = Content.Load<Texture2D>
        (@"gfx/sprites");
character[0].PManager = pManager;
```

Update our particles in Update():

```
frameTime = (float)gameTime.ElapsedGameTime.TotalSeconds;

pManager.UpdateParticles(frameTime, map, character);
```

And finally, draw in (where else?) Draw():

```
pManager.DrawParticles(spritesTex, true);
character[0].Draw(spriteBatch);
pManager.DrawParticles(spritesTex, false);
```

Our hot-headed guy in action is shown in Figure 7-3. The picture doesn't do justice to the code in action, so give it a try.

Figure 7-3. *Smoke in action*

The parameters we used in AddParticle() were decided after a bit of tweaking. Not enough randomness would make the smoke look unnatural; too much randomness would make it look unnatural for other reasons. See for yourself the ravages of bad randomization in Figure 7-4.

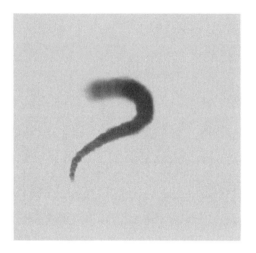 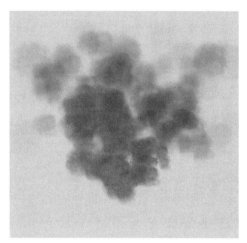

Figure 7-4. *Bad amounts of randomness: too little (left) and too much (right)*

Additive Blending: Fire

Additive blending is a cheap way to make flashy (literally) effects, and it's actually computationally cheaper than plain-old alpha blending. The idea of additive blending is that color values are added to what's currently on our backbuffer. (The *backbuffer* is what we draw on each time through the Draw() loop.) When we use vanilla alpha blending, we paint onto the backbuffer with the intensity of the alpha value, so drawing black with an alpha value of 0.5 will darken things a bit. Additive blending, on the other hand, adds only color values. Additive blending is great for bright, flashy effects—fire, electricity, muzzle flashes, lens flares, and laser blasts, to name a few.

We'll need to make a few structural changes to our ParticleManager and Particle classes to efficiently render additive particles. We want to draw all alpha-blended particles as one batch, and then additive particles as another, simply because we cannot mix the two methods of blending.

■**Note** There are other ways to blend what is currently on the backbuffer and what you are drawing. Those who wish to play around can look into modifying the render states on the graphics device.

In Particle at the class level, we add the following property with a public getter and a protected setter. We do this to make sure that objects outside the particle types cannot change how the particle is drawn.

```
private bool additive;

public bool Additive
{
    get { return additive; }
    protected set { additive = value; }
}
```

In `ParticleManager`, we modify the `Draw()` method so it does two draw loops: one for alpha-blended particles and one for additive particles. This is much faster than putting each sprite in its own batch, especially on the Xbox 360. This is due to how the `SpriteBatch` works and, in fact, how rendering in general works. It is more efficient to push as many graphics as possible through the pipeline at once, rather than pushing a small amount at fast intervals. You can liken it to trying to drink a thick milkshake through a straw—a thin straw isn't going to work as well as a wider straw.

```
sprite.Begin(SpriteBlendMode.AlphaBlend);
foreach (Particle p in particle)
{
    if (p != null)
    {
        if (!p.Additive && p.background == background)
            p.Draw(sprite, spritesTex);
    }
}
sprite.End();

sprite.Begin(SpriteBlendMode.Additive);
foreach (Particle p in particle)
{
    if (p != null)
    {
        if (p.Additive && p.background == background)
            p.Draw(sprite, spritesTex);
    }
}
sprite.End();
```

Now we'll make a `Fire` class, which can be fairly simple. Over time, the color of flames will transition from white to yellow to red to black. Because it will be rendered additively, black is synonymous with clear. The size may diminish slightly over time, and the flame wisps will rotate as well. It's simple in theory, but the settings and how the particles are morphed over time matter. Here's the code:

```
class Fire : Particle
{
    public Fire(Vector2 loc,
        Vector2 traj,
        float size,
        int icon)
```

```
    {
        this.location = location;
        this.trajectory = trajectory;
        this.size = size;
        Flag = icon;
        Exists = true;
        frame = 0.5f;
        Additive = true;
    }

    public override void Draw(SpriteBatch sprite, Texture2D spritesTex)
    {
        if(frame > 0.5f) return;

        Rectangle sRect = new Rectangle(flag * 64, 64, 64, 64);
        float bright = frame * 5.0f;
        float tsize;

        if (frame > 0.4)
        {
            r = 1.0f;
            g = 1.0f;
            b = (frame - 0.4f) * 10.0f;
            if (frame > 0.45f)
                tsize = (0.5f - frame) * size * 20.0f;
            else
                tsize = size;
        }
        else if (frame > 0.3f)
        {
            r = 1.0f;
            g = (frame - 0.3f) * 10.0f;
            b = 0.0f;
            tsize = size;
        }
        else
        {
            r = frame * 3.3f;
            g = 0.0f;
            b = 0.0f;
            tsize = (frame / 0.3f) * size;
        }

        if (flag % 2 == 0)
            rotation = (frame * 7.0f + size * 20.0f);
        else
            rotation = (-frame * 11.0f + size * 20.0f);
```

```
    sprite.Draw(spritesTex, GameLocation, sRect, new Color(
        new Vector4(r, g, b, 1.0f)
        ),
        rotation, new Vector2(32.0f, 32.0f), tsize,
        SpriteEffects.None, 1.0f);

    }
}
```

We've pared down the constructor a bit from the Smoke class. There are no longer parameters for color because we'll determine that on the fly. Likewise, we'll just use the parent Update() method.

The Draw() method plays with the appearance a bit, all as a function of frame. From 0.5 to 0.4, the blue channel will fade out and the fire will grow to full size. From 0.4 to 0.3, the green channel fades out. From 0.3 to 0, the red fades out and the size shrinks to zero. Also, the flame wisp rotates one way or the other as frame decreases.

For the flame wisp imagery, we update the source image. Now there's a row of flame wisps below the smoke clouds, as well as a glowy orb that we'll get to later, as shown in Figure 7-5.

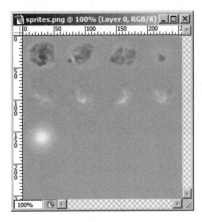

Figure 7-5. *The updated source image*

To add fire particles to go with our smoke, we'll throw another AddParticle() into our Update() block, at half the density of the smoke, with some tweaked location, trajectory, and size values.

```
if (i % 2 == 0)
{
    PManager.AddParticle(new Fire(
        tloc + Rand.GetRandomVector2(10.0f, 10.0f, -10.0f, 10.0f),
        Rand.GetRandomVector2(-30.0f, 30.0f, -250.0f, -200.0f),
        Rand.GetRandomFloat(0.25f, 0.75f),
        Rand.GetRandomInt(0, 4)));
}
```

Figure 7-6 shows the result.

Figure 7-6. *Smoke and fire*

It looks good, but something is not quite right. This is where the orb on the sprite sheet comes into play. The fire looks like it should be coming from some sort of source that emits more light than the wisps of flame. So, for the sake of completeness (and with very little to do with particle systems), let's add a visual fire source.

In Game1.Draw() of the main game, after drawing our particles, add the following:

```
character[0].Draw(spriteBatch);
pManager.drawParticles(spritesTex);

spriteBatch.Begin(SpriteBlendMode.Additive);
spriteBatch.Draw(
    spritesTex,
    character[0].Location - new Vector2(0f, 100f) - Scroll,
    new Rectangle(0, 128, 64, 64),
    Color.White, 0.0f,
    new Vector2(32.0f, 32.0f),
    Rand.getRandomFloat(0.5f, 1.0f),
    SpriteEffects.None, 1.0f);
spriteBatch.End();
```

This puts a flickering orb of light at our source location, giving the illusion that something intensely bright is generating fire and smoke. The brightness might be a bit of overkill, but it illustrates the technique. The final product, as shown in Figure 7-7, is a disembodied, flaming orb that will be the envy of every kid on the block.

Figure 7-7. *The final product*

Putting Fire on the Map

Let's put our fire to some use. Remember the torch map segment? We can use our friendly new particle system to light our torches on fire!

We'll add an `Update()` function to the `Map` class. For any map segment whose definition flag is 1, or `SegmentFlags.Torch`, we'll make some smoke and fire using the same calls we used to create the disembodied flaming orb. Of course, we no longer need the flaming orb over our hero's head.

First, we need to create another enumeration. If you haven't caught on already, enumerations are great for reducing the number of constants you declare in a class by moving them to their own centralized type. Not only does this clean up your class code, but it also reduces the dependency on that class and its constants. For now, we only need two in the `Map` class-level enumeration, and we will add as we go.

```
enum SegmentFlags
{
    None = 0,
    Torch
}
```

Within the Map class, we have the following:

```
public void Update(ParticleManager pMan)
{
    for (int i = 0; i < 64; i++)
    {
        if (mapSeg[LAYER_MAP, i] != null)
        {
            if (segDef[mapSeg[LAYER_MAP, i].Index].Flags == (int)SegmentFlags.Torch)
            {
                pMan.AddParticle(new Smoke(
                        mapSeg[LAYER_MAP, i].GetLoc() * 2f
                        + new Vector2(20f, 13f),
                        Rand.getRandomVector2
                        (-50.0f, 50.0f, -300.0f, -200.0f),
                        1.0f, 0.8f, 0.6f, 1.0f,
                        Rand.getRandomFloat(0.25f, 0.5f),
                        Rand.getRandomInt(0, 4)), true
                    );
                pMan.AddParticle(new Fire(
                        mapSeg[LAYER_MAP, i].GetLoc() * 2f
                        + new Vector2(20f, 37f),
                        Rand.getRandomVector2
                        (-30.0f, 30.0f, -250.0f, -200.0f),
                        Rand.getRandomFloat(0.25f, 0.75f),
                        Rand.getRandomInt(0, 4)), true
                    );
            }
        }
    }
}
```

Notice how the AddParticle() calls send new particles and true, designating them as background particles. Since our torches are in the background, it is only fitting for our fire and smoke to be in the background; otherwise, we would have our characters drawn between the torches and the fire they generate.

Now add a call to map.Update() from Game1. You should see some fiery torches, as shown in Figure 7-8.

Figure 7-8. *Fiery torches*

Adding Triggers

We have a nice little character format defined, but all of our shooting and spanner-whacking will be fruitless unless we create some sort of mechanism to allow our character to spawn particles—bullets, muzzle flashes, blood spurts, and the like. We'll call these things *triggers*.

Triggers will be types of parts. Just as we can add arms and legs to frames, we will be able to add triggers. Of course, this means we'll be jumping back into CharacterEditor for a spell.

Triggers in the Character Editor

Our character editor is an ugly beast, no doubt about it, and we're about to make it worse. Since we're going to run out of room if we add any more functionality to the screen, we'll introduce a low-budget version of tabs to the scene. The plan is to allow the user to switch between a keyframe script and the triggers list by clicking the appropriate tab.

We'll start out in script-editing mode. At the class level, we define constants for auxiliary window-editing mode and a scroll value for our triggers list:

```
const int AUX_SCRIPT = 0;
const int AUX_TRIGS = 1;

int auxMode = AUX_SCRIPT;
int trigScroll = 0;
```

We define all triggers as constants at the class level:

```
const int TRIG_PISTOL_ACROSS = 0;
const int TRIG_PISTOL_UP = 1;
const int TRIG_PISTOL_DOWN = 2;
```

In Draw(), we'll add a bit of functionality. First, create our tab buttons:

```
#region Script/Trigs Selector
if (auxMode == AUX_SCRIPT)
{
    text.Color = Color.Lime;
    text.DrawText(210, 110, "script");
}
else
{
    if (text.DrawClickText(210, 110, "script", mouseState.X,
        mouseState.Y, mouseClick))
        auxMode = AUX_SCRIPT;
}
if (auxMode == AUX_TRIGS)
{
    text.Color = Color.Lime;
    text.DrawText(260, 110, "trigs");
}
else
{
    if (text.DrawClickText(260, 110, "trigs", mouseState.X,
        mouseState.Y, mouseClick))
        auxMode = AUX_TRIGS;
}
#endregion
```

Around our script-drawing segment, we'll check to make sure we're in script-editing mode:

```
#region Script
if (auxMode == AUX_SCRIPT)
{
    for (int i = 0; i < 4; i++)
    {
        .
        .
        .
```

```
        }
    }
#endregion
```

Now we get to draw our triggers list. Since we have only four lines of text to work with, we'll put little scroll buttons next to our list. When a trigger is clicked, we set the appropriate part to the trigger index plus 1000. Remember how we used this same technique to differentiate between arms, legs, torsos, and weapons?

```
#region Trigs
if (auxMode == AUX_TRIGS)
{
    if (DrawButton(330, 42, 1, mouseState.X, mouseState.Y, mouseClick))
        if (trigScroll > 0) trigScroll--;

    if (DrawButton(330, 92, 2, mouseState.X, mouseState.Y, mouseClick))
        if (trigScroll < 100) trigScroll++;

    for (int i = 0; i < 4; i++)
    {
        int t = i + trigScroll;
        if (text.DrawClickText(210, 42 + i * 16,
            GetTrigName(t), mouseState.X,
            mouseState.Y, mouseClick))
        {
            charDef.Frames[selFrame].Parts[selPart].Index
                        = t + 1000;
        }
    }
}
#endregion
```

We'll define the GetTrigName() function, which will return a string to go with a constant name, as follows:

```
private string GetTrigName(int idx)
{
    switch (idx)
    {
        case TRIG_PISTOL_ACROSS:
            return "pistol across";
        case TRIG_PISTOL_DOWN:
            return "pistol down";
        case TRIG_PISTOL_UP:
            return "pistol up";
    }
    return "";
}
```

Now we'll add a couple of lines to the `DrawCharacter()` function to draw the name of the trigger onto the frame of the character we're drawing. For the animation preview of our character, we'll just draw a little lime green asterisk (so we don't end up too cluttered). Also, we check for `alpha` to be `>= 1f` to make sure we don't draw our text on any onionskins.

```
if (face == FACE_LEFT)
{
    rotation = -rotation;
    location.X -= part.Location.X * scale * 2.0f;
}


if (part.Index >= 1000 && alpha >= 1f)
{
```

Here's a tricky bit: since our text class calls a `SpriteBatch.Begin()` during text drawing, we'll need to end our current `SpriteBatch` before drawing our trigger name and then restart it after.

```
    spriteBatch.End();
    text.Color = Color.Lime;
    if (preview)
    {
        text.Size = 0.45f;
        text.DrawText((int)location.X,
            (int)location.Y,
            "*");
    }
    else
    {
        text.SetSize(1f);
        text.DrawText((int)location.X,
            (int)location.Y,
            "*" + GetTrigName(part.Index - 1000));
    }
    spriteBatch.Begin(SpriteBlendMode.AlphaBlend);
}
else
{
    Texture2D texture;
```

That should do it. With this functionality in place, we can go ahead and add the pistol triggers to the appropriate frames, as shown in Figure 7-9. (The frames we've named with an x suffix are the ones that get triggers on them; this is just a handy naming convention we've used to help with readability.)

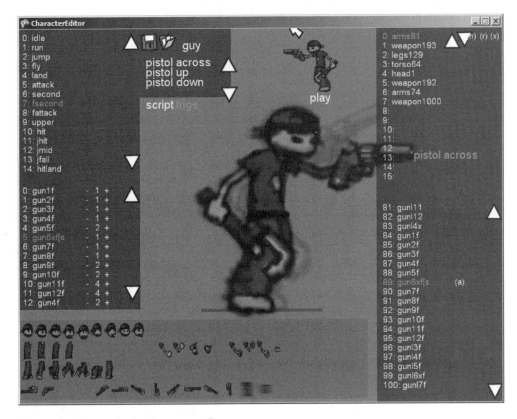

Figure 7-9. *Triggers in the character editor*

Bringing Triggers into the Game

Back in ZombieSmashers, we'll implement triggers. First, we need to take our three trigger constants from MapEditor and put them at the class level of our Character class.

Next, let's add some functionality to fire triggers. We'll be firing our triggers at the same time as we run our scripts: frame transitions. This is called from the Character.Update() method. First, we'll change the parameters we ask for in Update() to the following:

```
public void Update(GameTime gameTime, ParticleManager pMan, Character[] c)
```

Of course, this means that we need to change the call in Game1 to this:

```
character[i].Update(gameTime, pManager, character);
```

Back in Character.Update(), we add this call:

```
script.DoScript(anim, animFrame);
CheckTrig(pMan);
```

Next, we'll define the CheckTrig() method. We'll want a ParticleManager object so we can spawn whatever particles we need.

```
private void CheckTrig(ParticleManager pMan)
{
    int frameIndex = charDef.Animations[Anim].
                        KeyFrames[AnimFrame].FrameRef;

    Frame frame = charDef.Frame[frameIndex];

    for (int i = 0; i < frame.Parts.Length; i++)
    {
        Part part = frame.Parts[i];
        if (part.Index >= 1000)
        {
            Vector2 location = part.Location * Scale + Location;

            if (Face == CharDir.Left)
            {
                location.X -= part.Location.X * Scale * 2.0f;
            }

            FireTrig(part.Index - 1000, location, pMan);

        }
    }
}
```

The code we've put in here to find the location was taken right out of the Draw() function. Speaking of Draw(), we need to make sure we don't try to render any triggers! Near the top of the Draw() function, change a line to this:

```
Part part = frame.Parts[i];
if (part.Index > -1 && part.Index < 1000)
{
```

Now, getting back on track, let's define FireTrig(), which is called from CheckTrig() whenever we find a trigger to fire. We're calling a function, MakeBullet(), passing it a location, right-facing trajectory, facing, and owner ID (which is a new public integer).

```
private void FireTrig(int trig, Vector2 loc, ParticleManager pMan)
{
    switch (trig)
    {
        case TRIG_PISTOL_ACROSS:
            pMan.MakeBullet(loc, new Vector2(2000f, 0f), face, Id);
            break;
        case TRIG_PISTOL_DOWN:
            pMan.MakeBullet(loc, new Vector2(1400f, 1400f), face, Id);
            break;
        case TRIG_PISTOL_UP:
            pMan.MakeBullet(loc, new Vector2(1400f, -1400f), face, Id);
            break;
```

```
        }
}
```

This brings us to `ParticleManager`, where we'll define some functions to spawn a series of just the right particles, starting with `MakeBullet()`:

```
public void MakeBullet(Vector2 loc, Vector2 traj,
                       CharDir face, int owner)
{
    switch(face)
    {
        case CharDir.Left:
            AddParticle(new Bullet(loc, new Vector2(-traj.X, traj.Y)
                + Rand.GetRandomVector2(-90f, 90f, -90f, 90f),
                owner));

            MakeMuzzleFlash(loc, new Vector2(-traj.X, traj.Y));
            break;

        case CharDir.Right:
            AddParticle(new Bullet(loc, traj
                + Rand.GetRandomVector2(-90f, 90f, -90f, 90f),
                owner));

            MakeMuzzleFlash(loc, traj);
            Break;
    }
}
```

Now we're getting involved—we need to create a `Bullet` class *and* a `MakeMuzzleFlash()` method. Let's start with `MakeMuzzleFlash()`, and then round out this whole exercise with a few new particle classes.

```
public void MakeMuzzleFlash(Vector2 loc, Vector2 traj)
{
    for (int i = 0; i < 16; i++)
    {
        AddParticle(new MuzzleFlash(
            loc + (traj * (float)i) * 0.001f +
            Rand.GetRandomVector2(-5f, 5f, -5f, 5f),
            traj / 5f,
            (20f - (float)i) * 0.06f));
    }
    for (int i = 0; i < 4; i++)
        AddParticle(new Smoke(
            loc, Rand.GetRandomVector2(-30f, 30f, -100f, 0f),
            0f, 0f, 0f, 0.25f,
            Rand.GetRandomFloat(0.25f, 1.0f),
            Rand.GetRandomInt(0, 4)));
}
```

MakeMuzzleFlash() basically creates 16 MuzzleFlash particles trailing off in a direction defined by traj, with the particle size decreasing the farther the particles are from the source. It also creates a little puff of smoke.

Now we need to define two new particles: Bullet and MuzzleFlash. Let's start with MuzzleFlash:

```
class MuzzleFlash : Particle
{
    public MuzzleFlash(Vector2 loc,
        Vector2 traj,
        float size)
    {
        location = loc;
        trajectory = traj;
        this.size = size;
        Rotation = Rand.GetRandomFloat(0f, 6.28f);
        Exists = true;
        frame = 0.05f;
        Additive = true;
    }

    public override void Draw(SpriteBatch sprite,
                             Texture2D spritesTex)
    {

        sprite.Draw(spritesTex, GameLocation,
            new Rectangle(64, 128, 64, 64),
            new Color(
            new Vector4(1f, 0.8f, 0.6f, frame * 8f)
            ),
            rotation, new Vector2(32.0f, 32.0f),
            size - frame,
            SpriteEffects.None, 1.0f);

    }
}
```

We're creating this class with a very short life span and a random rotation. In the Draw() function, we're drawing it with a slight reddish tint, rapidly fading out as frame approaches 0.

Next, let's create Bullet:

```
class Bullet : Particle
{
    public Bullet(Vector2 loc, Vector2 traj, int owner)
    {

        location = loc;
        trajectory = traj;
```

```
        this.owner = owner;
        rotation = GlobalFunctions.GetAngle(Vector2.Zero, traj);
        Exists = true;
        frame = 0.5f;
        Additive = true;
    }

    public override void Draw(SpriteBatch sprite,
                              Texture2D spritesTex)
    {
        sprite.Draw(spritesTex, GameLoc(),
            new Rectangle(0, 128, 64, 64),
            new Color(new Vector4(1f, 0.8f, 0.6f, 0.2f)),
            rotation, new Vector2(32.0f, 32.0f),
            new Vector2(1f, 0.1f),
            SpriteEffects.None, 1.0f);
    }
}
```

For the bullet, we're just rendering the orb from the sprite sheet really long and thin. The third-to-last parameter we're using in Draw() is the scale vector, and we're sending it a Vector2 of 1f, 0.1f.

We snuck another function in there: GlobalFunctions.GetAngle(). When we create our Bullet particle, we'll want to set the rotation based on the initial trajectory we give it, so we'll define a function that gives us the angle between two Vector2 locations. We put it in a new class called GlobalFunctions, which will store all sorts of global helper functions, like this:

```
static class GlobalFunctions
{
    public static float GetAngle(Vector2 v1, Vector2 v2)
    {
        Vector2 d = new Vector2(v2.X - v1.X, v2.Y - v1.Y);
        if (d.X == 0.0f)
        {
            if (d.Y < 0.0f)
                return MathHelper.Pi * 0.5f;
            else if (d.Y > 0.0f)
                return MathHelper.Pi * 1.5f;
        }
        if (d.Y == 0.0f)
        {
            if (d.X < 0.0f)
                return 0.0f;
            else if (d.X > 0.0f)
                return MathHelper.Pi;
        }
```

```
    float a = (float)Math.Atan(Math.Abs(d.Y) / Math.Abs(d.X));

    if ((d.X < 0.0f) || (d.Y > 0.0f)) a = MathHelper.Pi - a;
    if ((d.X < 0.0f) || (d.Y < 0.0f)) a = MathHelper.Pi + a;
    if ((d.X > 0.0f) || (d.Y < 0.0f))
        a = MathHelper.Pi * 2.0f - a;

    if (a < 0) a = a + MathHelper.Pi * 2.0f;

    return a;
    }
}
```

You don't really need to understand how GetAngle() works. It's just basic trigonometry and does the job.

That should do it! If you run the game now, you'll have a fully firing gun (minus the sound, of course), as depicted in Figure 7-10.

Figure 7-10. *Triggers in action!*

Simple Particle Collision

Let's add some functionality to let particles collide with the map. We're going to have bullets hitting our collision map and leaving little dust clouds. We'll start with some simple functionality to determine if we've hit a grid collision or a solid ledge. We won't be doing any response yet, just killing off the offending particle.

In Map, let's add a CheckParticleCol() function to check on the position of a particle against our collision map:

```
public bool CheckParticleCol(Vector2 loc)
{
    if (CheckCol(loc))
        return true;
    for (int i = 0; i < 16; i++)
    {
        if (ledges[i].TotalNodes > 1)
        {
            if (ledges[i].Flags == (int)LedgeFlags.Solid)
            {
                int s = GetLedgeSec(i, loc.X);

                if (s > -1)
                    if (GetLedgeYLoc(i, s, loc.X) < loc.Y)
                        return true;
            }
        }
    }
    return false;
}
```

Now in Bullet, we can override Update() to check for map collisions. If one happens, we initiate some new particles that represent dust particles and smoke after the bullet hits.

```
public override void Update(float gameTime, Map map,
                            ParticleManager pMan, Character[] c)
{
    if (map.CheckParticleCol(location))
    {
        frame = 0f;
        pMan.MakeBulletDust(location, trajectory);
    }
    base.Update(gameTime, map, pMan);
}
```

We'll define MakeBulletDust() in ParticleManager as follows:

```
public void MakeBulletDust(Vector2 loc, Vector2 traj)
{
    for (int i = 0; i < 16; i++)
    {
```

```
        AddParticle(new Smoke(loc,
            Rand.GetRandomVector2(-50f, 50f, -50f, 10f)
            - traj * Rand.GetRandomFloat(0.001f, 0.1f),
            1f, 1f, 1f, 0.25f,
            Rand.GetRandomFloat(0.05f, 0.25f),
            Rand.GetRandomInt(0, 4)));

        AddParticle(new Smoke(loc,
            Rand.GetRandomVector2(-50f, 50f, -50f, 10f),
            0.5f, 0.5f, 0.5f, 0.25f,
            Rand.GetRandomFloat(0.1f, 0.5f),
            Rand.GetRandomInt(0, 4)));
    }
}
```

We're making a bunch of dust here! The first AddParticle() call sends a bit of light smoke back in the direction the bullet came from, albeit much slower (and at a random speed). The second AddParticle() creates a softer, darker bit of smoke. Since we're doing 16 of each, we get a soft spray of dust, as shown in Figure 7-11 (it looks better in motion, obviously).

Figure 7-11. *Bullet ricochet*

Adding Zombies

Shooting the earth is fun enough, but what we really need here are some undead punching bags, and not a moment too soon! We're all the way to Chapter 7 with nary a monster in sight, so, without further ado, let's make some zombies!

We need to start off with some graphics. We'll use a few new images: head2.png, torso2.png, and legs2.png, as shown in Figure 7-12.

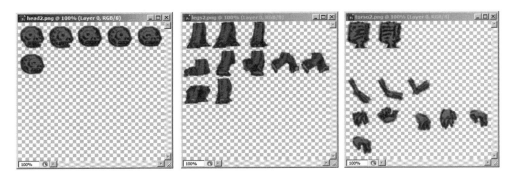

Figure 7-12. *Zombie parts*

We'll add these images to the Content project in two solutions: CharacterEditor and ZombieSmashers. We also need to upgrade CharacterEditor again to allow the user to specify which textures to use.

Zombies in the Character Editor

First, we'll change the arrays as created in Game1.LoadContent() to contain two indices. Fortunately, we don't need to change the loading, because we coded it to automatically load the textures based on the length of the array.

```
legsTex = new Texture2D[2];
torsoTex = new Texture2D[2];
headTex = new Texture2D[2];
weaponTex = new Texture2D[1];
```

Let's add a new tab to our low-budget triggers/script tab area, turning it into a triggers/script/textures tab area. We'll start by creating a new class-level constant:

```
const int AUX_SCRIPT = 0;
const int AUX_TRIGS = 1;
const int AUX_TEXTURES = 2;
```

Now we'll draw our texture-selection panel in Draw(). We'll just be iterating through the four texture indices, incrementing, decrementing, and drawing text.

```
#region Texture Switching
if (auxMode == AUX_TEXTURES)
{
```

```
for (int i = 0; i < 4; i++)
{
    if (DrawButton(210 + i * 21, 40, 1,
                    mouseState.X, mouseState.Y, mouseClick))
    {
        switch (i)
        {
            case 0:
                if (charDef.HeadIndex > 0) charDef.HeadIndex--;
                break;
            case 1:
                if (charDef.TorsoIndex > 0) charDef.TorsoIndex--;
                break;
            case 2:
                if (charDef.LegsIndex > 0) charDef.LegsIndex--;
                break;
            case 3:
                if (charDef.WeaponIndex > 0)
                    charDef.WeaponIndex--;
                break;
        }
    }
    string t = charDef.HeadIndex.ToString();
    switch (i)
    {
        case 1:
            t = charDef.TorsoIndex.ToString();
            break;
        case 2:
            t = charDef.LegsIndex.ToString();
            break;
        case 3:
            t = charDef.WeaponIndex.ToString();
            break;
    }
    text.Color = Color.White;
    text.DrawText(212 + i * 21, 60, t);
    if (DrawButton(210 + i * 21, 85, 2,
                    mouseState.X, mouseState.Y, mouseClick))
    {
        switch (i)
        {
```

```
                    case 0:
                        if (charDef.HeadIndex < headTex.Length - 1)
                            charDef.HeadIndex++;
                        break;
                    case 1:
                        if (charDef.TorsoIndex < torsoTex.Length - 1)
                            charDef.TorsoIndex++;
                        break;
                    case 2:
                        if (charDef.LegsIndex < legsTex.Length - 1)
                            charDef.LegsIndex++;
                        break;
                    case 3:
                        if (charDef.WeaponIndex < weaponTex.Length - 1)
                            charDef.WeaponIndex++;
                        break;
                }
            }
        }
}
#endregion
```

Finally, we add a third tab button to our triggers/script/texture area:

```
#region Script/Trigs Selector
.
.
.
if (auxMode == AUX_TEXTURES)
{
    text.Color = Color.Lime;
    text.DrawText(300, 110, "tex");
}
else
{
    if (text.DrawClickText(300, 110, "tex", mouseState.X,
        mouseState.Y, mouseClick))
        auxMode = AUX_TEXTURES;
}
#endregion
```

Our texture selection panel (and zombie) is shown in Figure 7-13.

We've set up the zombie with some simple animations: idle, fly, land, and run—which we've dealt with before—and hit, which will become a new reserved word animation that we'll set a character to when it has been hit.

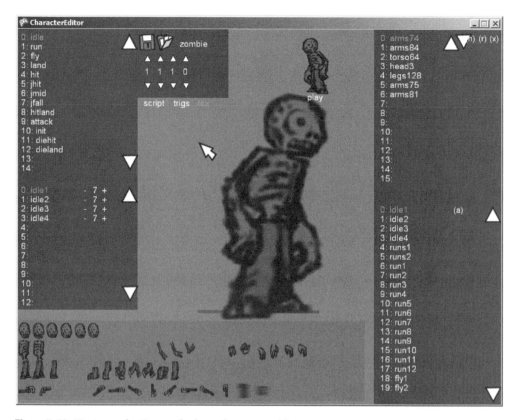

Figure 7-13. *Texture selection and a brand-new zombie*

Bringing Zombies into the Game

Now let's bring the zombie into ZombieSmashers. First, put the zombie.zmx file into data/chars, and make sure to include it in the project and select Copy If Newer. Now is probably a good time to add a new field to Character to specify which team that character is on (the good guys or the bad guys). At the class level in Character, add the following:

```
public const int TEAM_GOOD_GUYS = 0;
public const int TEAM_BAD_GUYS = 1;

public int Team;
```

Then change the constructor to this:

```
public Character(Vector2 newLoc,
    CharDef newCharDef, int newId, int newTeam)
{
    ...

    Id = newId;
    Team = newTeam;
```

Now that our Character class has a new team field and constructor, we need to update Game1.Initialize() to load the new zombie file and create characters using the new constructor.

```
charDef[(int)CharacterType.Guy] = new CharDef("chars/guy");
charDef[(int)CharacterType.Zombie] = new CharDef("chars/zombie");

character[0]
    = new Character(new Vector2(100f, 100f),
    charDef[(int)CharacterType.Zombie],
    0,
    Character.TEAM_GOOD_GUYS);
```

We deemed it prudent to make eight zombies, spaced at 100-pixel intervals across our map. They will just spawn in the sky, land, and stand there.

```
for (int i = 1; i < 9; i++){
    character[i] =
        new Character(new Vector2((float)i * 100f, 100f),
        charDef[(int)CharacterType.Zombie], i,
        Character.TEAM_BAD_GUYS);
     character[i].Map = map;
}
```

Now, in Draw(), we'll draw all existing characters instead of just the guy at index 0. Change the character[0].Draw() line as follows:

```
for (int i = 0; i < character.Length; i++)
    if (character[i] != null)
        character[i].Draw(spriteBatch);
```

There! We've added our zombie character definition file zombie.zmx to ZombieSmashers, parsed the file as CharacterType.Zombie, created eight zombies, and are now drawing all characters every frame. The result is shown in Figure 7-14. We don't have hit collision yet, but that's coming up soon.

Figure 7-14. *Zombies in a row*

Time for the fun part!

Smashing Zombies

We finally get to the whole point: smashing zombies. It's time to put our weapons to use.

Shooting Zombies

First, we need to put a function in Character that will determine if a vector is within our hit boundaries.

```
public bool InHitBounds(Vector2 hitLoc)
{
    if (hitLoc.X > Location.X - 50f * Scale &&
        hitLoc.X < Location.X + 50f * Scale &&
        hitLoc.Y > Location.Y - 190f * Scale &&
        hitLoc.Y < Location.Y + 10f * Scale)
        return true;
    return false;
}
```

Let's create a class to manage all things related to hitting characters; we'll call it HitManager. We'll use it to iterate through valid characters, determine if characters are fair game, and figure out what to do with characters that get hit. We are also going to do some refactoring in the Particle class, adding some properties for Owner, and making both Location and Trajectory into public fields.

```
class HitManager
{
    public static bool CheckHit(Particle p, Character[] c,
        ParticleManager pMan)
    {
        bool r = false;
        CharDir tFace = GetFaceFromTraj(p.Trajectory);

        for (int i = 0; i < c.Length; i++)
        {
```

We'll want to make sure characters can't hurt themselves with their own particles (otherwise, we could end up hitting ourselves with our own bullets):

```
            if (i != p.Owner)
            {
                if (c[i] != null)
                {
                    if (c[i].InHitBounds(p.Location))
                    {
                        if (p is Bullet)
                        {
                            if(tFace == CharDir.Left)
                                c[i].Face = CharDir.Right;
                            else
                                c[i].Face = CharDir.Left;

                            c[i].SetAnim("idle");
                            c[i].SetAnim("hit");
                            c[i].Slide(-100f);

                            pMan.MakeBulletBlood
                                (p.Location, p.Trajecotry / 2f);
                            pMan.MakeBulletBlood
                                (p.Location, -p.Trajectory);
                            pMan.MakeBulletDust
                                (p.Location, p.Trajectory);

                            r = true;
                        }
                    }
                }
            }
```

```
        }
      }
      return r;
    }
}
```

GetFaceFromTraj() is a short function that returns CharDir.Right for positive x trajectories, and CharDir.Left for negative and zero x trajectories.

```
public static CharDir GetFaceFromTraj(Vector2 trajectory)
{
    return (trajectory.X <= 0) ? CharDir.Left : CharDir.Right;
}
```

Now, in ParticleManager, we need to create a method for MakeBulletBlood(). It's a bit like MakeBulletDust(). We'll be calling it twice: once for the exit wound and once for a splatter in the direction of the bullet.

```
public void MakeBulletBlood(Vector2 loc, Vector2 traj)
{

    for (int t = 0; t < 32; t++)
        AddParticle(
            new Blood(loc,
            traj *
            -1f * Rand.GetRandomFloat(0.01f, 0.1f) +
            Rand.GetRandomVector2(-50f, 50f, -50f, 50f),
            1f, 0f, 0f, 1f,
            Rand.GetRandomFloat(0.1f, 0.3f),
            Rand.GetRandomInt(0, 4)));

}
```

Let's define Blood. When we instantiate Blood, we'll send it a location, trajectory, color, size, and icon. We'll be using the same images as we used for smoke, but tinted red so they look fine and bloody. We'll be drawing wide and thin, and at the angle of its trajectory, so we get good bits of splatter.

```
class Blood : Particle
{
    public Blood(Vector2 loc,
        Vector2 traj,
        float r,
        float g,
        float b,
        float a,
        float size,
        int icon)
    {
        Location = loc;
        Trajectory = traj;
        this.r = r;
        this.g = g;
        this.b = b;
        this.a = a;
        this.size = size;
        flag = icon;
        owner = -1;
        Exists = true;
        rotation = GlobalFunctions.GetAngle(Vector2.Zero, traj);
        frame = Rand.getRandomFloat(0.3f, 0.7f);
    }
```

When we update the blood, we want it to be slightly affected by gravity, but not so much that it doesn't seem a bit misty.

```
public override void Update(float gameTime, Map map,
                            ParticleManager pMan, Character[] c)
{
    Trajectory.Y += gameTime * 100f;

    if (Trajectory.X < -10f) Trajectory.X += gameTime * 200f;
    if (Trajectory.X > 10f) Trajectory.X -= gameTime * 200f;

    rotation = GlobalFunctions.GetAngle(Vector2.Zero, Trajectory);
```

```
        base.Update(gameTime, map, pMan, c);
}
```

When we draw the blood, notice how the scale we're giving it is new Vector2(size * 2f, size * 0.5f). This will give us wide, thin blood streaks.

```
    public override void Draw(SpriteBatch sprite, Texture2D spritesTex)
    {
        Rectangle sRect = new Rectangle(flag * 64, 0, 64, 64);

        float frameAlpha;

        if (frame > 0.9f)
            frameAlpha = (1.0f - frame) * 10f;
        else
            frameAlpha = (frame / 0.9f);

        sprite.Draw(
            spritesTex,
            GameLocation,
            sRect,
            new Color(new Vector4(r, g, b, a * frameAlpha)),
            rotation,
            new Vector2(32f, 32f),
            new Vector2(size * 2f, size * 0.5f),
            SpriteEffects.None,
            1.0f
            );
    }
}
```

Our last order of business is changing our Bullet.Update() function to allow the bullets to strike zombies.

```
public override void Update(float gameTime,
    ZombieSmashersXNA.map.Map map,
    ParticleManager pMan,
    Character[] c)
{
    if (HitManager.CheckHit(this, c, pMan))
        frame = 0f;

    if (map.CheckParticleCol(loc))
```

Now we're checking for hits from Bullet.Update() and killing off the bullets if they strike anything. Figure 7-15 shows some zombie-shooting action.

Figure 7-15. *Zombie shooting!*

There we have it! We can shoot zombies, and it looks good.

More Zombie Smashing

Let's put the wrench to use. We have a couple of combos mapped out in our guy's character definition file, but they won't do anything until we create some hit triggers and implement them in the game. Starting at the class level of CharacterEditor, define the triggers as follows:

```
const int TRIG_WRENCH_UP = 3;
const int TRIG_WRENCH_DOWN = 4;
const int TRIG_WRENCH_DIAG_UP = 5;
const int TRIG_WRENCH_DIAG_DOWN = 6;
const int TRIG_WRENCH_UPPERCUT = 7;
const int TRIG_WRENCH_SMACKDOWN = 8;
const int TRIG_KICK = 9;
```

Each trigger has a slightly different direction; some of them won't even be used yet. When our guy swings his wrench down and across, that's TRIG_WRENCH_DIAG_DOWN. When he swings it in a wide arc up, that's TRIG_WRENCH_UP. It's easy to figure out the rest.

Normally, this would be considered very poor code design for a few reasons. The biggest issue with declaring constants such as these, or even putting them in an enumeration, is that they are completely dependent on you implementing them in the code. In the grand scheme of game development, implementation of what kind of attacks are allowed and how they are carried out should be split between the game designers and the artists. In this way, artists can draw the attacks and weapons, and the designers can let the game engine know they exist. This way, no major pieces of code need to be written whenever a new attack is developed. However, you are an independent developer trying to get your game out quickly, so this is excusable for now.

Let's move on and make sure to add the string names in `GetTrigName()` of CharacterEditor's Game1:

```
case TRIG_PISTOL_UP:
    return "pistol up";
case TRIG_WRENCH_DOWN:
    return "wrench down";
case TRIG_WRENCH_SMACKDOWN:
    return "wrench smackdown";
case TRIG_WRENCH_DIAG_UP:
    return "wrench diag up";
case TRIG_WRENCH_DIAG_DOWN:
    return "wrench diag down";
case TRIG_WRENCH_UP:
    return "wrench up";
case TRIG_WRENCH_UPPERCUT:
    return "wrench uppercut";
case TRIG_KICK:
    return "kick";
```

We can add our new triggers to just the appropriate frames of animation. For instance, for our ground wrench combo, we'll use this:

- `TRIG_WRENCH_DIAG_DOWN`
- `TRIG_WRENCH_UP`
- `TRIG_WRENCH_DOWN`
- `TRIG_KICK`

Our air combo is about the same, but only three attacks long, culminating in the ever-so-aptly-named `TRIG_WRENCH_SMACKDOWN`. Also, we'll add `TRIG_WRENCH_UPPERCUT` to our uppercut animation. Wrench triggers in the character editor are shown in Figure 7-16.

With all of our spanner-whacking triggers set up, let's implement the action in ZombieSmashers. The first order of business is to bring the new trigger constants (the same ones declared at the class level of CharacterEditor—TRIG_PISTOL_UP, TRIG_PISTOL_DOWN, and so on) to the Character class-level declarations.

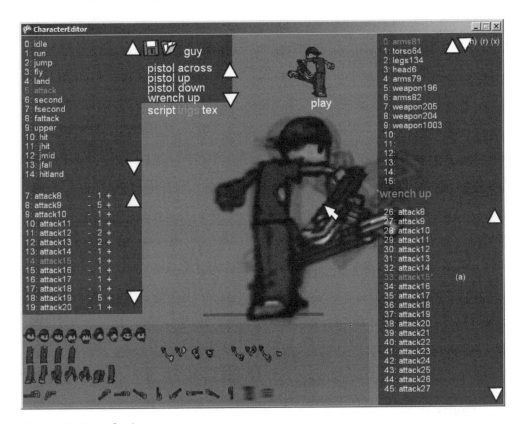

Figure 7-16. *Wrench triggers*

Next, let's create a new `Particle` called `Hit`. We'll use `Hit` for any trigger that's a one-shot attack. By *one-shot*, we mean that the particle is spawned, checks for impact at `Update()`, and dies. Here's what `Hit` looks like:

```
class Hit : Particle
{
    public Hit(Vector2 loc, Vector2 traj, int owner, int flag)
    {

        Location = loc;
        Trajectory = traj;
        Owner = owner;
        flag = flag;

        Exists = true;
        frame = 0.5f;

    }
```

```
public override void Update(float gameTime,
    ZombieSmashersXNA.map.Map map,
    ParticleManager pMan,
    Character[] c)
{
    HitManager.CheckHit(this, c, pMan);

    KillMe();
}

public override void Draw(SpriteBatch sprite, Texture2D spritesTex)
{
    //
}
}
```

We'll be using flag to hold the trigger index. In Update(), we check to see if we've hit anything, and then self-destruct, regardless of whether or not we've hit anything. Notice how we're not doing anything in Draw(), but are still overriding the parent method so nothing gets drawn.

After we handle Bullet impact in HitManager, let's handle particles of type Hit, as follows:

```
if (p is Bullet)
{
    ...
}
else if (p is Hit)
{
    c[i].Face = (tFace==CharDir.Left) ? CharDir.Right : CharDir.Left;
    float tX = 1f;
    if (tFace == CharDir.Left)
        tX = -1f;

    c[i].SetAnim("idle");
    c[i].SetAnim("hit");
```

We'll want the hit character to slide back more if he is grounded. If the character is airborne, we want to keep him closer for air combos.

```
    if (c[i].State == CharState.Grounded)
        c[i].Slide(-200f);
    else
        c[i].Slide(-50f);
```

Next, we do a case-by-case lookup on what to do. For most cases, we just make some blood and set a variable called Game1.slowTime, which we'll explain after we look at the code. The method we're going to create to make blood splashes will accept a location and a trajectory. For some of the heavier moves, we set the victim's animation and toss him around a bit.

```
switch (p.Flag)
{
    case Character.TRIG_WRENCH_DIAG_DOWN:
        pMan.MakeBloodSplash(p.Location,
            new Vector2(50f * tX, 100f));
        Game1.SlowTime = 0.1f;

        break;
    case Character.TRIG_WRENCH_DIAG_UP:
        pMan.MakeBloodSplash(p.Location,
            new Vector2(-50f * tX, -100f));
        Game1.SlowTime = 0.1f;
        break;
      case Character.TRIG_WRENCH_UP:
        pMan.MakeBloodSplash(p.Location,
            new Vector2(30f * tX, -100f));
            Game1.SlowTime = 0.1f;

        break;
    case Character.TRIG_WRENCH_DOWN:
        pMan.MakeBloodSplash(p.Location,
            new Vector2(-50f * tX, 100f));

        Game1.SlowTime = 0.1f;
        break;
    case Character.TRIG_WRENCH_UPPERCUT:
        pMan.MakeBloodSplash(p.Location,
            new Vector2(-50f * tX, -150f));
        c[i].Trajectory.X = 100f * tX;

        c[i].SetAnim("jhit");
        c[i].SetJump(700f);
        Game1.SlowTime = 0.125f;
        break;
    case Character.TRIG_WRENCH_SMACKDOWN:
        pMan.MakeBloodSplash(p.Location,
            new Vector2(-50f * tX, 150f));
        c[i].SetAnim("jfall");
        c[i].SetJump(-900f);
        Game1.SlowTime = 0.125f;

        break;
    case Character.TRIG_KICK:
        pMan.MakeBloodSplash(p.Location,
            new Vector2(300f * tX, 0f));
```

```
            c[i].Trajectory.X = 1000f * tX;

            c[i].SetAnim("jhit");
            c[i].SetJump(300f);

            Game1.SlowTime = 0.25f;
            break;
        }
    }
}
```

Here's a bit of air juggling: if the victim is airborne and we set his animation to hit, we'll make sure he gets tossed up in the air slightly and set to a proper getting-hit-in-air animation.

```
if (c[i].State == Character.STATE_AIR)
{
    if (c[i].AnimName == "hit")
    {
        c[i].SetAnim("jmid");
        c[i].SetJump(300f);
        if (p is Hit)
        {
```

For airborne enemies, we want to make sure our air combos work out just right. What seems to work well is to set the victim's y location to that of the hero if both the hero and victim are airborne and the attack is a melee attack.

```
            if (c[p.Owner].team == Character.TEAM_GOOD_GUYS)
                c[i].Location.Y = c[p.Owner].Location.Y;
        }
    }
}
```

Lastly, let's define MakeBloodSplash() in ParticleManager. It's pretty similar to the bullet blood function, creating spurts of blood mixed with dust:

```
public void MakeBloodSplash(Vector2 loc, Vector2 traj)
{
    traj += Rand.G etRandomVector2(-100f, 100f, -100f, 100f);

    for (int i = 0; i < 64; i++)
    {
        AddParticle(new Blood(loc, traj *
            Rand.GetRandomFloat(0.1f, 3.5f) +
            Rand.GetRandomVector2(-70f, 70f, -70f, 70f),
            1f, 0f, 0f, 1f,
            Rand.GetRandomFloat(0.01f, 0.25f),
            Rand.GetRandomInt(0, 4)));
```

```
        AddParticle(new Blood(loc, traj *
            Rand.GetRandomFloat(-0.2f, 0f) +
            Rand.GetRandomVector2(-120f, 120f, -120f, 120f),
            1f, 0f, 0f, 1f,
            Rand.GetRandomFloat(0.01f, 0.25f),
            Rand.GetRandomInt(0, 4)));
    }
    MakeBulletDust(loc, traj * -20f);
    MakeBulletDust(loc, traj * 10f);
}
```

Here, we create 128 particles of blood—what a mess! Of those, 64 will be "exit wound" type splatters—they will fire off in a tighter cone in the direction of the strike. The other 64 particles will be "entry splatter"—they will come in the opposite direction of the strike and will be in looser form.

We still have a few odds and ends to work out. Let's start with Game1.slowTime. We use that for *Matrix*-esque pauses in action—to accent strikes and to build anticipation for devastating moves. We declare Game1.SlowTime in the Game1 class-level declarations as follows:

```
private static float slowTime = 0f;

public static float SlowTime
{
    get { return slowTime; }
    set { slowTime = value; }
}
```

Then, in Game1.Update(), we reduce frameTime by a factor of 10 if slowTime is greater than zero. This way, if we want a half second of pause, we set slowTime to 0.5.

```
frameTime = (float)gameTime.ElapsedGameTime.TotalSeconds;
if (slowTime > 0f)
{
    slowTime -= frameTime;
    frameTime /= 10f;
}
```

Now that we are using our own timing system that allows us to slow down time, we need to make sure our Character class uses it. Ensure that frameTime in Game1 is a private static field, and then expose it via a static property. Then, in the Character.Update() method, change the local variable et to use the Game1.FrameTime property.

```
float et = Game1.FrameTime;
//float et = (float)gameTime.ElapsedGameTime.TotalSeconds;
```

The next step in the Character class is to make sure we are firing the hits correctly. In the FireTrig() method, update the switch case statement to add a default case.

```
default:
    pMan.AddParticle(new Hit(loc, new Vector2(
        200f * (float)Face - 100f, 0f),
        Id, trig));
    break;
```

Before we test our zombie smashing, we have one last thing to do. Remember how when our characters land, we set them to the land animation? Well, a character who has been knocked into (or out of) the air should land in a hitland animation. Let's change our Character.Land() method to this:

```
private void Land()
{
    state = STATE_GROUNDED;
    switch (animName)
    {
        case "jhit":
        case "jmid":
        case "jfall":
            SetAnim("hitland");
            break;
        default:
            SetAnim("land");
            break;
    }

}
```

Now you should be able to run the game. What you'll discover is that the attacks feel tremendously wrong. Why? We haven't yet implemented character-to-character collision. When you go to do a combo, you just slide right on through whoever you're attacking. So what are we waiting for? Let's remedy this ugliness!

Character-to-Character Collision

We obviously can't have characters just walking through each other, but how should we handle this? Collision detection, as always, is simple enough, but how do we respond? We could implement character-to-character collision response in a few ways:

- Manually move colliding players so that they are not colliding. This is most commonly used, and will give a solid-looking collision response.

- Change the colliding characters' trajectories so that they eventually will not be colliding. This is what was originally used in The Dishwasher game. It gives sort of sloppy collisions, in that it's possible for fast-moving characters to pass through each other.

- Add a new collision trajectory to the colliding characters' trajectories. This is what was eventually used for The Dishwasher. When tweaked properly, it provides a slightly bouncy collision response that isn't too weak.

We chose to go with the third technique. We use essentially the first technique for map collision detection, so you get a good lesson on that as well.

In the `Character` class at the class level, let's declare our collision trajectory value:

```
public float ColMove = 0f;
```

Then in `Update()`, we'll detect and respond to character-to-character collisions:

```
#region Collison w/ other characters
for (int i = 0; i < c.Length; i++)
{
    if (i != Id)
    {
        if (c[i] != null)
        {
```

The next section basically compares our location with that of the other character. We might want to change these values, depending on the feel of the collision response.

```
            if (Location.X > c[i].Location.X - 90f * c[i].Scale &&
                Location.X < c[i].Location.X + 90f * c[i].Scale &&
                Location.Y > c[i].Location.Y - 120f * c[i].Scale &&
                Location.Y < c[i].Location.Y + 10f * c[i].Scale)
            {
```

We've detected a collision; now let's respond. We calculate `dif` as a value that scales up as the two characters get closer to each other. Then we set our `colMove` value and the other character's `colMove` value to opposite values of `dif`, to move them apart.

```
                float dif = (float)Math.Abs
                            (Location.X - c[i].Location.X);
                dif = 180f * c[i].Scale - dif;
                dif *= 2f;
                if (loc.X < c[i].loc.X)
                {
                    ColMove = -dif;
                    c[i].ColMove = dif;
                }
                else
                {
                    ColMove = dif;
                    c[i].ColMove = -dif;
                }
            }
        }
    }
}
```

We'll reduce the value of ColMove to zero, giving our colliding characters a sort of springy response.

```
if (ColMove > 0f)
{
    ColMove -= 400f * et;
    if (ColMove < 0f) ColMove = 0f;
}
else if (ColMove < 0f)
{
    ColMove += 400f * et;
    if (ColMove > 0f) ColMove = 0f;
}
#endregion
```

Later in Update(), when we update our location by trajectory, we add the following:

```
Location.X += Trajectory.X * et;
Location.X += ColMove * et;
```

We're going to include ColMove when we call CheckXCol(). The new function looks like this:

```
public void CheckXCol(Vector2 pLoc)
{
    if (Trajectory.X + ColMove > 0f)
        if (Map.CheckCol(
            new Vector2(Location.X + 25f, Location.Y - 15f)))
            Location.X = pLoc.X;

    if (Trajectory.X + ColMove < 0f)
        if (Map.CheckCol(
            new Vector2(Location.X - 25f, Location.Y - 15f)))
            Location.X = pLoc.X;
}
```

Your project should look and feel good. Our zombie smashing in progress is shown in Figure 7-17.

■**Note** We arrived at a lot of the values we used in the project by tweaking. If you're using this book as a guide and not following along exactly, you may need to make your own adjustments until everything looks right.

Figure 7-17. *Fun air combos!*

Conclusion

Finally, we got to do all the fun stuff in this chapter! Let's go over the improvements we put into Zombie Smashers XNA:

- Implemented a particle system with a particle manager, particle bass class, and a bunch of assorted particles

- Implemented map updating, which we used to make our torch segments generate fire and smoke

- Added triggers to the map editor and game, which we use to make bullets, muzzle flashes, and hits

- Added a hit manager to manage . . . hits, obviously

- Implemented collision detection, giving the movement and combat a good feel

Finally, our project resembles a real game that can actually be played! After all, what would a game called Zombie Smashers be without any actual zombie smashing? However, this isn't the end, because neither our hero or the zombies can die. What this game needs is a goal and ways to impede the player's progress toward that goal. What does this mean in reality? More blood, death, and zombie destruction.

CHAPTER 8

■■■

XACT Audio, Rumble, and More

Sensory Overload

At this point, we have a robust game-playing system—a world we can run and jump around in, zombies to shoot and bash, some fun revolver and wrench moves to shoot and bash zombies with, and oodles of cool combat effects. But something is definitely missing, and, as the chapter title suggests, that something is audio.

To understand the impact audio will have on our game (or any game), consider a game that has sold millions of copies. Think of your favorite game, and now imagine it without sound. Remember how when you fire a gun in a shooter game, you can hear the bullets fire, ricochet, and hit your target. Now try to imagine firing the gun without sound. Audio not only provides entertainment value, but it also gives the player feedback as to what is going on in the game. And as a rule of thumb, the more feedback you can give players without crowding them, the better the game will be.

Audio is another area where a scripting system really shines. Before we had the idea of the character-scripting system, we hard-coded all of the sound. Needless to say, our older games didn't have any really complex audio expression! Of course, there are still instances when we can hard-code sound. For example, remember our `Character.Land()` function? We set the character animation to `hitland` where appropriate, and with that, we could play a thumping sound. If we had to hard-code every character to make the thumping sound in `hitland`, it would be a hassle. Then again, if we want different characters to make different thumping sounds, we might just want to forego the hard-coding. Food for thought!

Because this is the sensory overload chapter, we're also going to implement some rumble. Rumble is often not implemented in games that target the casual game-playing audience, and it is more than frequently left out of games developed by hobbyists. We think that rumble is necessary in most game types, because it gives the player feedback through another area: touch. Players have sound, as you will see in this chapter, and players already have visual feedback. Tactile feedback can help players know immediately what is going on with their character and his surroundings.

Obtaining and Editing Audio

So, we're setting out to add audio to our game. We can't do much if we don't have any good sound files in the first place, can we?

And after we get those audio files, we'll need to edit them to suit our game. Much like the particle systems we created previously, generating good audio is more an art than it is a science. It takes a lot of practice, some creativity, and a lot of testing.

Getting Sound Files

Getting sound files can be a tricky process. Unlike graphics, clean audio is not really something an amateur developer without any expensive equipment can produce. This leaves us with a few options:

Find free sounds: This leads to licensing issues and has varying results. A few good sites to go to are FlashKit (`www.flashkit.com`) and the Freesound Project (`http://freesound.iua.upf.edu/`).

Buy sounds: This may also lead to licensing issues, but typically provides better results than the free route. A number of web sites sell sounds; we like Sounddogs (`www.sounddogs.com`).

Record your own sounds: This typically provides the worst results of all, unless you are a professional audio person—in which case, congratulations, you have a fallback career!

We're going to go with the first option because it provides the best balance between quality and cost. But remember that the term *free* usually means a few things. One major disadvantage of using free resources is that their license is often restrictive. If you're looking to make money off your game, we suggest you get good licenses with your audio. The second large problem with free resources is that you will often find them used in many places. Be sure to look over as much audio as you can stand before deciding.

Tip You can often record some interesting sounds using items found around the house. Trash cans (metal) and pots make excellent clangs, and if you are lucky enough to have a younger brother, he may let you hit him over the head a few times! You may not have professional equipment, but having *some* sound is what is important. For instance, just for fun, a few friends created a Tower Defense clone (a game that involves a lot of sounds) using XNA. During the development process, it was important to get sounds working as soon as possible to know where and how they would fit in. While the team scoured the Internet for decent sounds, they used placeholder sounds, including those that literally consisted of the developers saying words like "click" for a button click. It may not have been pretty, but it worked well enough while the rest of the game was developed.

For Zombie Smashers, we used some sounds from FlashKit. If you go to the Sound FX section of the site and search within the Mayhem category, you should be in pretty good shape! Alternatively, you can use the sound files included with the downloadable materials for this book (available from the Source Code/Download section of `www.apress.com`). We've provided all the audio files used in this chapter.

We'll use an assortment of smacking and crunching sounds:

- Slapstick punch
- Cracking bones

- Skull cracking

- Shot in the face

- 50-caliber (cal) shot

These give use a good enough start. We'll be able to give the game some audio depth without bringing our development pace to a grinding halt.

We can't just put our free audio files into an XACT project. Well, we could, but wouldn't it be nice to clean them up first? Cleaning up audio and changing how it sounds, even to the slightest degree, can remove much of that freebie sound stigma. Also, some audio will have issues like leading or trailing silences, or sounds that are not applicable to the game. For example, our 50-cal shot ends with a shell casing landing (not applicable for a revolver), and our shot in the face starts with a guy yelling. So, let's do some audio editing!

We use Audacity for audio editing. It's free and open source. You can find it at http://audacity.sourceforge.net.

Simple Audio Editing with Audacity

Here, we'll describe what we did with our sound files to end up with some usable sounds. If you are using different sound files, you can apply the same techniques to get rid of unwanted parts and do some other tweaking.

We'll start with the shot-in-the-face sound by dragging the wave file into Audacity. It looks like Figure 8-1. The sound starts with an impact noise, and then has a guy grunting with some splatter. We don't want the guy grunting. There isn't enough sound before the grunt to use, so we can either chop off the entire beginning—impact to grunt—or just try to get rid of the grunt in the middle.

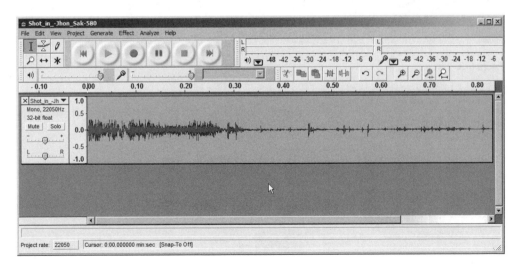

Figure 8-1. *The shot-in-the-face wave file in Audacity*

You can get a feel for when certain parts of an audio track begin and end by a combination of intuition and trial and error. We like to select segments of interest, play them, and make adjustments until we find exactly what we're seeking. You can do this in Audacity simply by clicking the audio trail and dragging. Using this technique, we find that the trailing splatter starts at around 0.20 seconds, as shown in Figure 8-2.

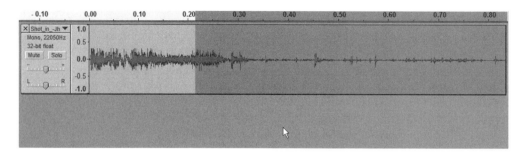

Figure 8-2. *The trailing splatter*

By testing different sections and turning up our speakers a bit, we discover that the grunt starts at around 0.05 seconds, as shown in Figure 8-3. Having found the grunt, we now chop it out. We end up with a nice chunky impact sound, as shown in Figure 8-4.

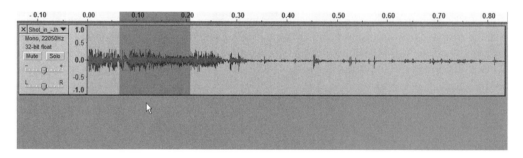

Figure 8-3. *The grunt*

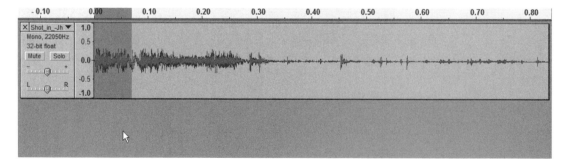

Figure 8-4. *The shot-in-the-face sound without the grunt*

Next, we tackle the 50-cal sound. We like the shot sound, but not the shell-casing sound. Not only do revolvers not eject shells after every shot, but if we did use shell-casing audio, we would want that to have its own sounds. Having a different sound for the shell casing would allow us to change its volume, its timing, and many other properties without affecting the gunshot sound. So the shell casing has to go! We bring it into Audacity, as shown in Figure 8-5.

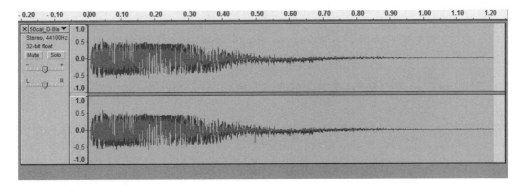

Figure 8-5. *The 50-cal wave file in Audacity*

After a bit of trial and error, we determine that the shell-casing sound begins at about 0.45 seconds, as shown in Figure 8-6. We chop off the shell casing and are left with what you see in Figure 8-7.

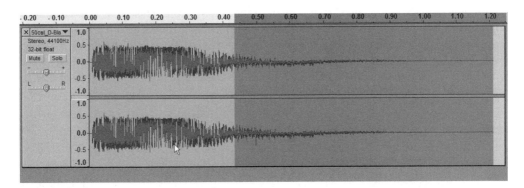

Figure 8-6. *The shell casing*

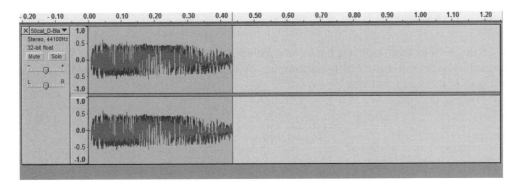

Figure 8-7. *The 50-cal audio without the shell casing*

The problem is that without the shell-casing sound, the shot sound ends very abruptly. We need to remedy this somehow.

First, we apply a Cross Fade Out effect to the second half of the audio. We select from nearly the middle of the audio to the end, and then choose Effect ➤ Cross Fade Out. We get what you see in Figure 8-7.

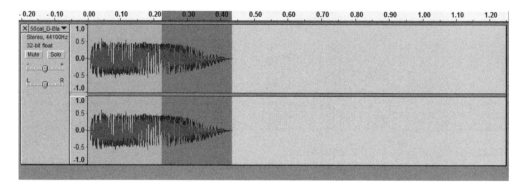

Figure 8-8. *Adding a Cross Fade Out effect to the edited 50-cal sound*

Now it doesn't sound so abrupt, but it would be nice to have a bit of that echo back. Echo will provide us with the subsound that is made at the end of any larger sound. To do this, we apply reverb to the audio. But in order to get a good level of control, we do the reverb in a separate track. We select the first track and choose Edit ➤ Duplicate. Now, in the duplicate track, we want to add some trailing silence (Audacity will not automatically extend the audio when reverb is applied). We choose Generate ➤ Silence and enter a value of 10 to tack 10 seconds of silence to the end of the duplicate track, as shown in Figure 8-9.

■Note When a sound is made, sound waves are emitted from the source in every direction. This provides that initial core sound that your ears pick up. However, as the sound waves travel and bounce off objects and back toward you, you here different versions of the sound at varying levels. Imagine standing in a huge concert hall and yelling at the top of your lungs. It is pretty clear that you will be able to hear an echo of yourself. This is an effect similar to what we want to create for the 50-cal sound here.

Next, we select the duplicate track and choose Effects ➤ GVerb. Because we don't really understand what's going on with the parameters (not all that unusual!), we just click OK, which brings us to the result shown in Figure 8-10.

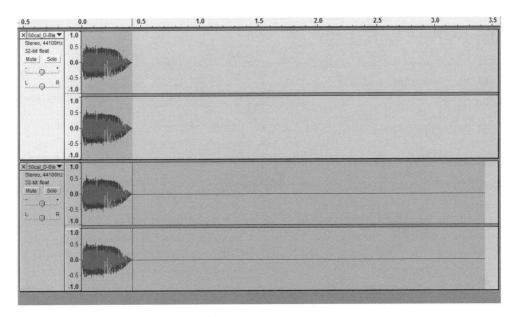

Figure 8-9. *Adding silence to the end of duplicate tracks*

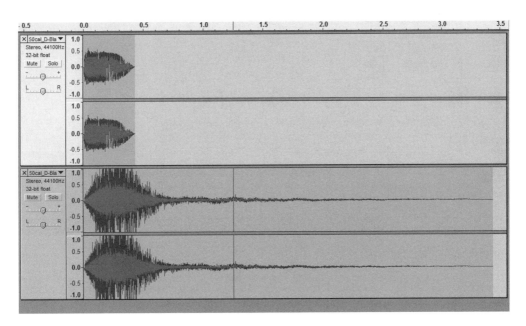

Figure 8-10. *Excessive reverb!*

The result of this is a much distorted sounding reverb effect, so we need to clean it up. First, we only want the echo-sounding part, so we just chop out the early part where it peaks like crazy. We end up with what you see in Figure 8-11.

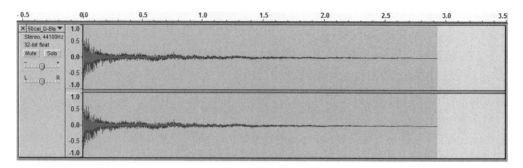

Figure 8-11. *The reverb after removing the peaking part*

For some final cleanup, we quiet the duplicate track a little by selecting Effect ➤ Amplify and entering a negative value of –5, clip off the remaining 5 seconds of silence, and apply a Cross Fade Out to the trailing bit. Figure 8-12 shows the final 50-cal sound for our game.

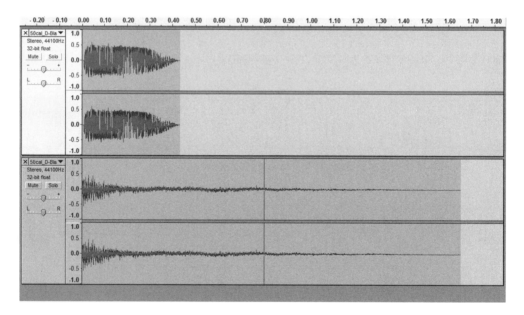

Figure 8-12. *50-cal: the final product*

This should give you an idea of the basic functions that you can accomplish with Audacity and a good idea of how to collect and process audio. It will become more important to understand the workflow of creating a piece of audio as you develop your own games.

In summary, the important audio we ended up with is as follows:

- Gunshot

- Hit

- An assortment of crunching and splatter sounds

We'll use the crunches and splatters to add some flavor to our combat audio. Save all of the audio files as .wav files in ZombieSmashers\Content\sfx. Now let's get all of this set up in XACT!

Adding Audio to the Game

With our audio files ready, we can now add sounds to the game. As you saw in Chapter 2, we use XACT for this task.

XACT organizes sound in a hierarchical manner. You don't need to be intimately familiar with the layout, but it helps to have a vague idea of what's going on:

- *Waves* are raw audio. A *wave bank* is a collection of wave (.wav) files that *could* be used in a game.

- *Sounds* are composed of *tracks* that play simultaneously. Tracks contain *events*. Events can, among other things, play waves. A *sound bank* is the use of files in the wave bank and can apply certain properties to sound files.

- *Cues* play sounds. Cues are what you tell your audio engine to play from within your game. Cues have their own properties that can be applied to sounds.

To look at it from the application end of things, we'll be telling our audio engine to play a *cue*, which will play a *sound*, which will play its *tracks*, which will fire their *events*, which will play *waves*.

There's going to be a bit of *déjà vu* at work here (XNAPong, anyone?), but we'll still hit all of the steps, and in less of a rush this time. Let's get started by setting up our XACT project.

Setting Up the Game Audio in XACT

Fire up XACT. From the Start Menu, you can find XACT in Microsoft XNA Game Studio 2.0 ➤ Tools. Once XACT is up and running, select File ➤ New Project, navigate to your ZombieSmashers\Content\sfx folder, and save the new project as sfxproj, as shown in Figure 8-13.

Next, right-click the Wave Banks item in the navigation pane on the left and select New Wave Bank. Name the new wave bank sfxwavs. Then right-click the Sound Banks item, select New Sound Bank, and name it sfxsnds. XACT automatically gives us the following file paths:

- sfxproj.xgs is the XACT project file.

- sfxwavs.xwb is the XACT wave bank file.

- sfxsnds.xwb is the XACT sound bank file.

Down the road, we'll be loading these three files from ZombieSmashers, so it's a good idea to be vaguely familiar with what they're called and what each represents.

Start off by dragging all of the audio files into the wave bank. They'll show up in red italics, meaning that they are not used in any cues, which we can now start to create.

Figure 8-13. *Creating a new XACT project*

XACT has a shortcut in which you drag a wave from the Wave Bank window into the Cue panel of the Sound Bank window, and let XACT take care of the rest. XACT will create a sound for the wave that has a track that contains the event play wave, as well as a cue that will play the sound we just created. In other words, we can insert a wave file, drag it into the Cue panel of our Sound Bank window, and not worry about all the stuff happening in between. This is what we did when we made XNAPong back in Chapter 2.

We're going to play around with this XACT hierarchy a bit more by making some variable zombie-smacking sounds. We'll create three hit variation sounds that are all called by one cue, which we'll call zomhit.

Drag hit from the Wave Bank window to the Cue panel in the Sound Bank window. Now we have a sound named hit and a cue named hit. Rename the cue to zomhit. Since we want three hit sounds, drag the hit wave into the Sound panel in the Sound Bank window twice (not creating a cue), and rename the three sounds in the Sound panel zomhit1, zomhit2, and zomhit3. Drag zomhit2 and zomhit3, one after another, from the Sound panel into the zomhit cue in the Cue panel. Now we have one cue, zomhit, which will randomly play zomhit1, zomhit2, or zomhit3 when it is run.

Right now, zomhit1, zomhit2, and zomhit3 play only the hit waves, so let's add additional tracks to each sound. In our project, we have three gooey mayhem sounds called crunch, crush, and `splatter`. Adding tracks to sounds is as an easy drag-and-drop operation. Drag `crunch` to `zomhit1`, `crush` to `zomhit2`, and `splatter` to `zomhit3`.

We now have a single cue, `zomhit`, which will play three different sound variations. Each sound plays the hit sound and a different flavor of splatter. Your XACT project should look like the one shown in Figure 8-14.

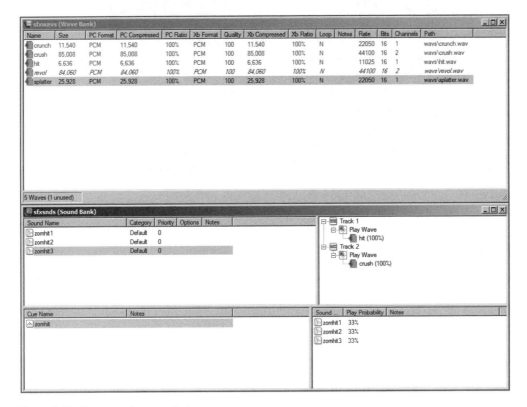

Figure 8-14. *One cue, three variations*

This looks nice enough, but how it sounds could be a very different story. Fortunately, we can listen to the sounds to hear how they will be in our game without actually putting them in the game. Let's start testing and tweaking!

Auditioning Audio

Because XACT is set up to be cross-platform, audio auditioning is handled through a separate program: the XACT Auditioning Utility. You'll find the XACT Auditioning Utility on the Start menu, under Microsoft XNA Game Studio 2.0 ➤ Tools ➤ XACT Auditioning Utility. Windows may give you some trouble about firewalls at some point; allow the program through and let it do its business.

From XACT, select your `zomhit` cue and click the Play button. The XACT Auditioning Utility should subtly let you know it received a connection from XACT, as shown in Figure 8-15, and the sound should play. Try playing it a few times. It will behave just as it will in the game, giving you a different variation each time.

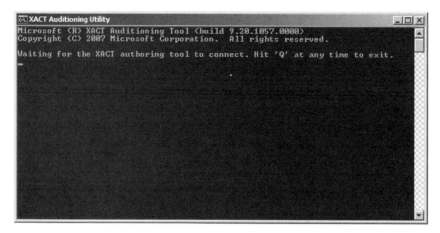

Figure 8-15. *XACT Auditioning Utility*

When we did this, we discovered that the flavoring sounds we put in (crunches, crushes, and splatters) were sometimes overpowering the hit sounds. We want the flavor sounds to be very subtle. Fortunately, we can modify the volume on individual tracks.

For each sound, select the track that plays the flavor sound (it will be Track 2), and in the Properties panel, adjust the volume, as shown in Figure 8-16. You can click the sound in the Sound panel and play it to get a feel for how it's working. Remember that sounds like this will be played quite a bit, so we don't want them to be abrasive or annoying.

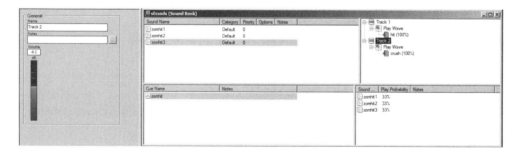

Figure 8-16. *Modifying track volume*

After tweaking, we ended up with only three cues for this iteration of sound project editing: zomhit, revol (for the revolver), and bullethit. We created bullethit by combining hit and crunch, making it quieter than the zomhit variations. The final Sound Bank window looks like Figure 8-17.

Three cues is a good place to start. Our next task is to integrate the sounds into the ZombieSmashersXna project. We can always enrich our audio environment later.

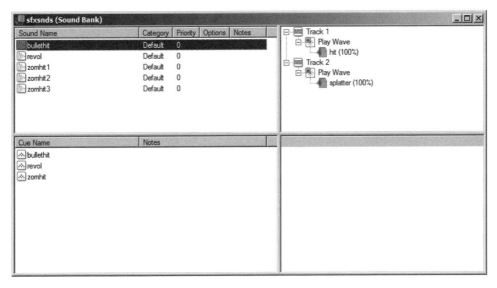

Figure 8-17. *Our three cues*

Bringing Sound into the Game

To bring audio functionality into Zombie Smashers XNA, we need to do three things:

- Add the XACT project to our Content project.

- Create a class to load our XACT project and play cues.

- Hard-code some cues to play at specific spots in our game.

Let's start by adding the XACT project. In the Content project, with Show All Files enabled, refresh Solution Explorer. Then right-click `sfx` and choose Include in Project. Do the same for `sfxproj.xap`, which will automatically be given the proper Content Pipeline properties.

Next, let's create a class to play audio. We'll make all the members public and static so that we can play sounds from anywhere. We are going to be using a special feature of static portions of a class: the static constructor. The static constructor is never declared with a scope (such as public or private) because it is automatically fired before any other static member or method is used. This bit of functionality in the language removes the dependency on creating a basic `initialize` method and making sure it is called only once.

```
using System;
using Microsoft.Xna.Framework.Audio;

namespace ZombieSmashers.Audio
{
    static class Sound
    {
    private static AudioEngine engine;
    private static SoundBank sound;
    private static WaveBank wave;
```

```
    static Sound()
    {
        engine = new AudioEngine(@"Content/sfx/sfxproj.xgs");
        wave = new WaveBank(engine, @"Content/sfx/sfxwavs.xwb");
        sound = new SoundBank(engine,
                            @"Content/sfx/sfxsnds.xsb");
    }

    public static void PlayCue(String cue)
    {
        sound.PlayCue(cue);
    }

    public static Cue GetCue(String cue)
    {
        return sound.GetCue(cue);
    }

    public static void Update()
    {
        engine.Update();
    }
    }
}
```

Now in Game1, we need to make sure that we don't forget to keep the engine updated. Failure to do so will result in terrible things happening (choppy playback, reduced game performance, loss of sleep while trying to determine why performance is going down the drain, and so on). Add Sound.Update() anywhere in Game1.Update().

Next, we'll add some PlayCue() calls. Our first stop will be in HitManager. In CheckHit(), we basically have two big if blocks to choose from when we've hit something: a bullet hit if code block and a default hit if code block. In the bullet hit if statement, add the following:

```
c[i].SetAnim("idle");
c[i].SetAnim("hit");
c[i].Slide(-100f);
Sound.PlayCue("bullethit");
```

Further down, in the default hit if block, add this:

```
c[i].SetAnim("idle");
c[i].SetAnim("hit");
Sound.PlayCue("zomhit");
```

We have one more sound to implement. In Character.FireTrig(), we need a switch where we create particles on a case-by-case basis. Let's set it up to play the revol sound for all three pistol-firing triggers:

```
case TRIG_PISTOL_ACROSS:
    pMan.MakeBullet(loc, new Vector2(2000f, 0f), face, ID);
    Sound.PlayCue("revol");
    break;
case TRIG_PISTOL_DOWN:
    pMan.MakeBullet(loc, new Vector2(1400f, 1400f), face, ID);
    Sound.PlayCue("revol");
    break;
case TRIG_PISTOL_UP:
    pMan.MakeBullet(loc, new Vector2(1400f, -1400f), face, ID);
    Sound.PlayCue("revol");
    break;
```

Great! Now Zombie Smashers has been brought, kicking and screaming, from the silent-movie era into XACT-enriched modern times.

Playing audio at hard-coded points is working well enough so far, but what happens when we want to have a wrench-swishing sound? We couldn't really hard-code that, because there are too many possibilities in a current combo system. So what do we do? The solution is to integrate audio controls into our character-scripting system.

Scripting Audio

We'll start with the sound file. Find a "swing" sound—think swinging a baseball bat or, hey, a wrench! Drag your new swing.wav file into your XACT wave bank, and then drag it from there to the Cue panel in your Sound Bank window. Save the project.

Let's add a new script command to our character-scripting language. In the Commands enumeration, go ahead and add a new one at the end:

```
enum Commands{
    // ...
    PlaySound
}
```

Then, in our big switch case block in DoScript(), we need to add a case to act on our new command, as follows:

```
case Commands.PlaySound:
    Sound.PlayCue(line.SParam);
    break;
```

Finally, we need to add a case to the big switch case block in the constructor for ScriptLine to parse the command string into our script line command format. In the switch block in the constructor for ScriptLine, add this:

```
case "play":
    command = Commands.PlaySound;
    sParam = split[1];
    break;
```

Now add the command play [*sound*] anywhere in the character script.

Run the `CharacterEditor` application and load Guy. Let's add `play swing` commands to our Guy character. For the swing-swing-swing-kick combo, add a `play swing` command near the start of every attack, as shown in Figure 8-18.

Figure 8-18. *Play swing!*

You can see how easy it would be to add sounds for landing, yelling, footsteps, and much, much more. We'll leave that up to you!

Adding Music

We've covered a bit of what XACT has to offer, but there's still a lot more ground in the audio department. A few simple things we can implement are streaming audio, looping audio, categories, and compression—all things we'll need for music implementation.

Music audio can get large. It may not seem like a big deal now, but if we end up with 100MB of music audio in our game, it will make much more sense to load a couple kilobytes of it at a time, swapping blocks in and out of memory, so we've loaded only what we're playing or about to play. This is the essence of streaming audio. This also used to be a big hassle to implement, but it's a snap with XACT.

Now we'll add some music to our game. Of course, you'll need a music track for this. We'll leave this up to you—you can really use anything. We recommend that it be at least three minutes, and it doesn't have to seamlessly loop. Again, FlashKit has some nice tracks available. Also, you can use the music provided with this book's downloadable files, called `music1.wav` (we made this sample track using ACID software).

In XACT, add the wave bank `musicwavs` and the sound bank `musicsnds`. Select `musicwavs` and, in the Properties panel, click the Streaming button. Figure 8-19 shows what's going on. Notice how the wave bank icon now has "DVD" above it. This evidently indicates that these waves would stream from a DVD if our game were based on a DVD. Because it's an XNA title, this won't exactly be the case, but we can forgive Microsoft for this, can't we?

When we load this wave bank, we'll need to set some special parameters to tell our audio engine how to stream, but we'll get to that once we finish in XACT.

Drag `music1.wav` into the `musicwavs` wave bank, and then drag the `music1` wave into the Cue panel of the `musicsnds` Sound Bank window. To set `music1` to loop, click `music1` in the Sound panel of the Sound Bank window and check Infinite under Looping in the Properties panel, as shown in Figure 8-20. Also, set the category to Music.

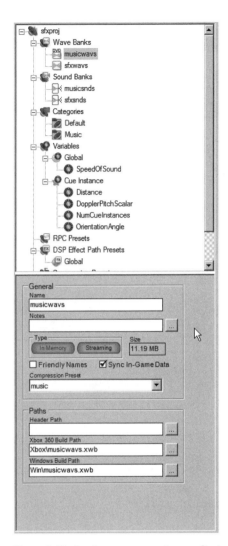

Figure 8-19. *Setting up streaming audio in the wave bank properties*

■**Note** Setting the sound category to Music will cause XNA to not play the audio if the Xbox 360 gamer is playing music through the dashboard—a handy feature!

Finally, we can set the compression of the audio. Right-click Compression Presets and select New Compression Preset. Name the new preset music, and set the parameters. For Xbox 360, we set Quality to 38. For Windows, we set Samples Per Block to 64, as shown in Figure 8-21. You'll need to play with the parameters a bit to see how heavily you can compress your audio before you start to hear artifacts.

Figure 8-20. *Setting up infinite looping*

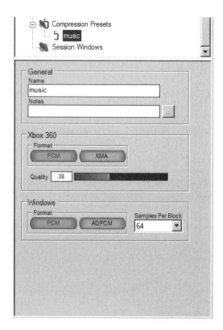

Figure 8-21. *Setting compression presets*

Select the music wave bank again, and in the Properties panel, set the Compression Preset to music.

Now we'll create a Music class in ZombieSmashers. It will use the AudioEngine we have in Sound to load its wave bank and sound bank. When we load our wave bank, we'll do it to work with streaming. We set the parameters to start at offset 0 and keep 16 block chunks of audio in memory. Using smaller block sizes will cause our game music to stutter if things get hectic, but 16 seemed to work fine.

```csharp
using System;
using System.Globalization;
using Microsoft.Xna.Framework.Audio;

namespace ZombieSmashers.Audio
{
    static class Music
    {
        private static WaveBank wave;
        private static SoundBank sound;
        private static Cue musicCue;
        private static string musicStr;

        static Music()
        {
            wave = new WaveBank(Sound.Engine,
                    @"Content/sfx/musicwavs.xwb", 0, 16);

            sound = new SoundBank(Sound.Engine,
                    @"Content/sfx/musicsnds.xsb");
        }

        public static void Play(string musicCueName)
        {
            if (string.Compare(musicStr,
                                musicCueName,
                                true,
                                CultureInfo.InvariantCulture) != 0)
            {
                musicStr = musicCueName;

                if (musicCue != null)
                    musicCue.Dispose();

                musicCue = sound.GetCue(musicStr);

                musicCue.Play();
            }
        }
    }
}
```

In Game1.Update(), call Music.Play("music1"), which will play music1 if nothing else is playing. We now have streaming, looping, compressed, and properly behaving music!

Of course, as this is the "sensory overload" chapter, we have more to do.

Rumble, Quake, and Blast!

We've already worked with force feedback in previous chapters, but we're going to give it a more general implementation this time around. We'll create a global "quake" value that will indicate how much the screen is shaking and how much rumble is to be applied, as well as a cool stylized "blast" effect. We can allow the quake value to be set from character scripts, as well as hard-coded events (certain hits, for example).

Setting Up Quaking, Rumbling, and Blasting

Let's create a few classes to encapsulate and manage all things quakey. We're putting it all in a folder named Shakes.

We'll start with a Rumble class. Remember how the Xbox 360 gamepad works? We have two rumble motors, thoughtfully named leftMotor (the low-frequency motor) and rightMotor (the high-frequency motor). We'll use one Rumble object per gamepad, and let the class know which gamepad it is in the constructor. Our Rumble.Update() method will reduce our vibration values and set our gamepad vibration.

```
using System;
using Microsoft.Xna.Framework;
using Microsoft.Xna.Framework.Input;

namespace ZombieSmashers.Shakes
{
    class Rumble
    {
        private Vector2 rumbleValue = Vector2.Zero;
        private PlayerIndex playerIndex;

        public Rumble(int idx)
        {
            playerIndex = (PlayerIndex)idx;
        }

        public void Update()
        {
            if (rumbleValue.X > 0f)
            {
                rumbleValue.X -= Game1.FrameTime;
                if (rumbleValue.X < 0f) rumbleValue.X = 0f;
            }

            if (rumbleValue.Y > 0f)
            {
                rumbleValue.Y -= Game1.FrameTime;
                if (rumbleValue.Y < 0f) rumbleValue.Y = 0f;
            }
```

```
                GamePad.SetVibration(playerIndex,
                                     rumbleValue.X, rumbleValue.Y);
        }

        public float Left
        {
            get { return rumbleValue.X; }
            set { rumbleValue.X = value; }
        }

        public float Right
        {
            get { return rumbleValue.Y; }
            set { rumbleValue.Y = value; }
        }
    }
}
```

We'll create a Quake class to encapsulate screen shaking. This is pretty easy to implement. Remember how we calculate the scroll value in Game1? Well, we'll just add a random Vector2 calculated by the current quake value to scroll to end up with a shaky camera effect that we can use to accentuate a particular bit of brutality in our Zombie Smashing epic. Otherwise, we're just doing the same linear rundown of our quake value as we did with the Rumble class.

```
class Quake
{
    private float val;

    public void Update()
    {
        if (val > 0f)
            val -= Game1.FrameTime;
        else if (val < 0f)
            val = 0f;
    }

    public float Value
    {
        get { return val; }
        set { val = value; }
    }

    public Vector2 Vector
    {
        get
        {
            if (val <= 0f)
                return Vector2.Zero;
```

```
                return Rand.GetRandomVector2(-val, val, -val, val) * 10f;
            }
        }
    }
```

Our Blast class is very similar:

```
class Blast
{
    private float val;
    private float mag;

    public Vector2 Center;

    public void Update()
    {
        if (val >= 0f)
            val -= Game1.FrameTime * 5f;
        else if (val < 0f)
            val = 0f;
    }

    public float Value
    {
        get { return val; }
        set { val = value; }
    }

    public float Magnitude
    {
        get { return mag; }
        set { mag = value; }
    }
}
```

We'll manage all of this through a class we'll call QuakeManager. This will keep all of our quake-related objects as statics, so that they'll be accessible from anywhere (we'll want to use them from HitManager, Character, and Game1 off the bat).

```
static class QuakeManager
{
    public static Rumble[] Rumbles = new Rumble[4];
    public static Quake Quake;
    public static Blast Blast;

    static QuakeManager()
    {
        Quake = new Quake();
        Blast = new Blast();
```

```
        for (int i = 0; i < Rumbles.Length; i++)
            Rumbles[i] = new Rumble(i);
    }

    public static void Update()
    {
        Quake.Update();
        Blast.Update();

        for (int i = 0; i < Rumbles.Length; i++)
            Rumbles[i].Update();
}
```

The SetBlast() method will accept a magnitude (mag) and a blast center. We'll fire off blasts from our HitManager, to really lay the cool onto finisher moves.

```
    public static void SetBlast(float mag, Vector2 center)
    {
        Blast.Value = mag;
        Blast.Magnitude = mag;
        Blast.Center = center;
    }
```

We use one method, SetQuake(), to set our Quake and Rumble values at once. It's lazy, but it works—99% of the time, when you want some quake, you want some rumble as well. If you want rumble without quake, why, there's a method for that, too!

```
    public static void SetQuake(float val)
    {
        if (Quake.Value < val) Quake.Value = val;

        for (int i = 0; i < Rumbles.Length; i++)
        {
            Rumbles[i].Left = val;
            Rumbles[i].Right = val;
        }
    }

    public static void SetRumble(int i, int motor, float val)
    {
        if (motor == 0) Rumbles[i].Left = val;
        else Rumbles[i].Right = val;
    }
}
```

Let's implement QuakeManager from Game1. We'll start by adding the following in Game1.Update():

```
QuakeManager.Update();

frameTime = (float)gameTime.ElapsedGameTime.TotalSeconds;
...
    Scroll += ((character[0].Location -
        new Vector2(400f, 400f)) - Scroll) * frameTime * 20f;
    Scroll += QuakeManager.Quake.Vector;
```

We'll add a few calls to QuakeManager.SetQuake() and SetBlast() from HitManager. CheckHit(), where we'll do a bit of quaking when certain types of hits, like kicks and uppercuts, connect:

```
case Character.TRIG_WRENCH_UPPERCUT:
    pMan.MakeBloodSplash(p.Location,
        new Vector2(-50f * tX, -150f));
    c[i].Trajectory.X = 100f * tX;

    c[i].SetAnim("jhit");
    c[i].SetJump(700f);
    Game1.SlowTime = 0.125f;
    QuakeManager.SetQuake(.5f);
    QuakeManager.SetBlast(.5f, p.Location);
    break;
```

We can do likewise in Character.FireTrig(). When we fire off revolver bullets, we can check to make sure we're player characters (not AI-controlled bad guys) and set the rumble accordingly.

```
switch (trig)
{
    case TRIG_PISTOL_ACROSS:
    case TRIG_PISTOL_UP:
    case TRIG_PISTOL_DOWN:
        if (team == TEAM_GOOD_GUYS && ID < 4)
        {
            QuakeManager.SetRumble(ID, 1, .5f);
            QuakeManager.SetRumble(ID, 0, .3f);
        }
        break;
}
```

Changing the Render Loop

The last part is a bit of a foray into a much bigger pond. We're going to change our render loop a bit to give us access to a texture with our scene drawn on it. Remember our short discussion about the backbuffer in the previous chapter? One of the major advances in rendering is the idea of drawing to a *faux* backbuffer so we can apply more effects to the image as we render it again. This will allow us to draw the scene multiple times per frame quickly and cheaply, and will also give us a pretty good platform from which to launch into shaders (in Chapter 11).

We set up our render loop to draw everything to the backbuffer. The backbuffer is a piece of texture memory that XNA uses for just this purpose. We clear the backbuffer, draw to the backbuffer, and then present the backbuffer to the screen with the method base.Draw(gameTime).

We'll change our render loop to use a new render target—another piece of texture memory that we can draw to the backbuffer. We'll make it look like this:

- Clear the backbuffer.
- Switch to the render target.
- Clear the render target.
- Draw to the render target.
- Switch to the backbuffer.
- Draw the contents of the render target to the backbuffer.
- If we want blast, draw the render target to the backbuffer a few more times with some alpha and scaling changes.
- Finish up with base.Draw(gameTime).

It's really easy when you get down to it. At the Game1 class level, add this:

```
RenderTarget2D mainTarget;
```

Then in the LoadContent() method, create our new render target with the following code:

```
mainTarget = new RenderTarget2D(GraphicsDevice,
    graphics.PreferredBackBufferWidth,
    graphics.PreferredBackBufferHeight,
    1, SurfaceFormat.Color);
```

Finally, let's modify Draw() to match our new routine:

```
protected override void Draw(GameTime gameTime)
{
    graphics.GraphicsDevice.Clear(Color.Black);

    graphics.GraphicsDevice.SetRenderTarget(0, mainTarget);
    graphics.GraphicsDevice.Clear(Color.Black);

    map.Draw(spriteBatch, mapsTex, mapBackTex, 0, 2);
```

This starts us off by clearing our backbuffer to black, switching to the render target, and clearing *that* to black.

After drawing the map foreground, finish up with this:

```
    map.Draw(spriteBatch, mapsTex, mapBackTex, 2, 3);

    graphics.GraphicsDevice.SetRenderTarget(0, null);
```

```
spriteBatch.Begin(SpriteBlendMode.None);

spriteBatch.Draw(mainTarget.GetTexture(),
    new Vector2(), Color.White);

spriteBatch.End();

if (QuakeManager.Blast.Value > 0f)
{
    spriteBatch.Begin(SpriteBlendMode.AlphaBlend);
    for (int i = 0; i < 5; i++)
    {
        spriteBatch.Draw(
            mainTarget.GetTexture(),
            QuakeManager.Blast.Center - Scroll,
            new Rectangle(0, 0,
                (int)ScreenSize.X, (int)ScreenSize.Y),
            new Color(new Vector4(1f, 1f, 1f,
                .35f * (QuakeManager.Blast.Value /
                QuakeManager.Blast.Magnitude))),
            0f,
            QuakeManager.Blast.Center - Scroll,
            (1.0f + (QuakeManager.Blast.Magnitude -
                QuakeManager.Blast.Value)
                * .1f
                + ((float)(i + 1) / 40f)),
            SpriteEffects.None,
            1f);
    }
    spriteBatch.End();
}

base.Draw(gameTime);
```

If you ignore the if block, we haven't added much. We're just setting the render target back to null (backbuffer), starting a spriteBatch, and drawing our scene contents from the render target to the backbuffer as a sprite. Then we end the spriteBatch and present the scene.

Within the if block, it gets a bit trickier. If we need some blast effect, we draw five copies at the location at Blast.Center, in a translucent white, expanding outward from the center. It's a terrifically ugly line of code, but it gives a nice effect, as shown in Figure 8-22.

Figure 8-22. *Blast effect*

The effect looks better in motion (notice a trend?), but you can see what we're going for. Also, if we were to add more iterations or reverse the order, we might end up with a smoother effect, but we think this works just fine.

Conclusion

Up until this chapter, we've been working on very essential functionality: editors, character movement, collision detection, and particle systems. Now we're starting to add some flavor to the game. In this chapter, we accomplished quite a bit:

- Stitched together some audio in Audacity

- Imported our audio into an XACT project

- Implemented audio in the game, including character script commands

- Added music

- Added vibration and quaking

- Revamped our render loop to use render targets

- Implemented the blast effect

We had a pretty good framework for a game before this chapter, but now that we have audio, we've arrived at a completely new level of legitimacy—you can only get so far without audio, right?

Audio is a tricky beast, but face it: your game must have it. Whether you elect to buy sounds, look for free ones online, or make "pew-pew" noises into a microphone, audio is very important. Really nailing the audio in a game can add a lot to it, while letting your audio get really annoying can make your game nearly unplayable (nails on a chalkboard, anyone?).

Also, a nice bonus of all this Zombie Smashers dressing is that we have our render loop set up to start throwing effects into the mix. We can easily add effects like bloom, blur, water, and the like.

In the next chapter, we'll add a great deal of depth and interactivity to our game with map scripting and enemy AI. We'll add some new enemy triggers to allow our zombies to properly explode, map scripting functionality to give us control over enemy spawning and map features, and more.

CHAPTER 9

■■■

Scripting, AI, and Depth (and Death)
Let's Add Danger!

To be honest, what we have now is basically a glorified punching bag simulator. We walk left, we walk right, we smash, and we shoot. Obviously, when our enemies just stand there, soak up damage, and bleed infinite buckets of blood, we're not offering much in the replayability department. First and foremost, we need to make our enemies die. Then we'll run out of enemies, so we'll need a way to set up a stage to respawn enemies. At some point, we should make our enemies fight back, which means that we'll need to make our hero take damage as well. Much of indie game development heads off into odd job territory, and this chapter, much like the rest of this book, is a shining example. But these odd jobs are what make our punching bag into an actual game. Let's face it: if we don't give the players a reason to play, they might as well be twiddling their thumbs.

Officially, here's the rundown of what we need to do:

- Make enemies killable.

- Make our enemies fight back (including a zombie attack and hero hit animation).

- Add map scripting for enemy respawning and other fun things.

Let's dive in!

Making Enemies Killable

We want to be able to kill our zombies. This sounds easy enough on paper (separate the head or destroy the brain, right?), but we have a few tasks ahead of us to implement all of the facets of zombie death in our game:

- Create zombie death animations.

    - Standing death.

    - Hit the ground death.

- Create blood spray triggers.

    - Implement triggers in the game.

    - Create some new blood particles.

- Add death-related script commands.

    - Implement script commands in the game.

- Add an `init` command to set monster health.

    - Implement the `init` command in the game.

That got out of control in a hurry, didn't it? Let's start with some animations.

Adding Animations

We'll make it so that if you pummel a zombie's hit points (HPs) below 0 while it's standing, the zombie's head will explode. If you knock a zombie into the air and its HP is below 0, it will explode at landing. We'll start in `CharacterEditor`.

In the class level of `Game1`, we'll add some constants for new triggers. We may as well add a "zombie hit" trigger to use for zombies attacking us. The big thing we're adding is a bunch of blood-related triggers for crafting superb zombie bloodsplosions.

```
public const int TRIG_KICK = 9;
public const int TRIG_ZOMBIE_HIT = 10;

public const int TRIG_BLOOD_SQUIRT_UP = 11;
public const int TRIG_BLOOD_SQUIRT_UP_FORWARD = 12;
public const int TRIG_BLOOD_SQUIRT_FORWARD = 13;
public const int TRIG_BLOOD_SQUIRT_DOWN_FORNWARD = 14;
public const int TRIG_BLOOD_SQUIRT_DOWN = 15;
public const int TRIG_BLOOD_SQUIRT_DOWN_BACK = 16;
public const int TRIG_BLOOD_SQUIRT_BACK = 17;
public const int TRIG_BLOOD_SQUIRT_UP_BACK = 18;

public const int TRIG_BLOOD_CLOUD = 19;
public const int TRIG_BLOOD_SPLAT = 20;
```

Then, in `GetTrigName()`, we'll add the strings associated with the constants:

```
case TRIG_ZOMBIE_HIT:
    return "zombie hit";

case TRIG_BLOOD_SQUIRT_UP:
    return "squirt up";
...
case TRIG_BLOOD_SPLAT:
    return "blood splat";
```

Now we can make some animations. We made one called `diehit`, as shown in Figure 9-1.

Figure 9-1. *Decapitation*

We made another animation called `dieland`, as shown in Figure 9-2. It starts out with copious squirts in all directions.

Figure 9-2. *Zombie bloodsplosion*

While we're at it, let's add `attack`. It uses the new zombie hit trigger. Figure 9-3 shows this animation.

Figure 9-3. *Zombie attack!*

Later, we'll add some functionality to our game that will set an animation to `diehit` or `dieland` where appropriate.

As for the animations, we've stuck a lot of blood squirt, cloud, and splat triggers all over. The decapitation animation has blood squirting up, then up and back as the zombie rocks back, then up, up and forward, and finally forward as the creature goes face down (of course, it doesn't have a face). The bloodsplosion animation starts with a lot of squirts in all upward directions, progressing to smatterings of blood splats and clouds.

Defining New Script Commands

We're going to define some new commands:

- `ethereal`: Turns a character "ethereal." Ethereal characters can be walked through and cannot be hit. Not only is this useful for dying animations, but for uninterruptible attacks as well.

- `solid`: Turns an ethereal character solid. Solid means "not ethereal." We'll be turning characters solid at animation changes by default anyway, so we won't need to worry about accidentally leaving our zombies ethereal and breaking the game.

- `speed` *speed*: Sets the character's moving speed to *speed*.

- `hp` *hp*: Sets the character's HP and maximum HP to *hp*.

- `ifdyinggoto` *frame*: If the character's HP is less than 0, goes to *frame*.

- `deathcheck`: If the character's HP is less than 0, flags the character as dead (calls `Killme()`).

- `killme`: Flags the character as dead (calls `Killme()`).

- `ai` *ai*: Sets monster AI to *ai*.

In the next-to-last keyframe of every animation, we'll put the script command `killme`. At the start of dying animations, we put the `ethereal` command, so that enemies in the dying animation cannot be hit again, recycling the dying animation (that would look a bit silly!). Also, we can use `ethereal` for evasive moves—like dodges and uninterruptible superhits.

We're also introducing some initialization script commands— `hp`, `speed`, and `ai`. We'll use these to create a monster initialization script in a new `init` animation we'll create. Our `init` animation is shown in Figure 9-4. We're giving our zombie the following script:

```
speed 80
hp 65
ai zombie
```

We create an `init` animation, add a keyframe (any keyframe will do), and give it some commands. When we implement this in the game, we'll set it up so when a character is initialized, the init script is run. The script for zombie, thus far, is as follows:

- `speed 80`: Zombies shamble.

- `hp 65`: A few spanner-whack combos will do it.

- `ai zombie`: Use the zombie AI, which we'll get to in the "Adding AI" section.

There's quite a bit of implementation to get to in `ZombieSmashersXna`. We'll start with our blood triggers.

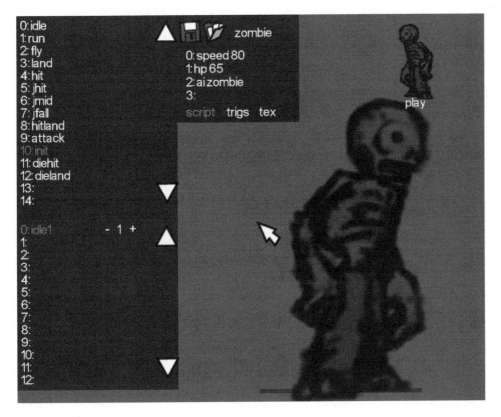

Figure 9-4. *The init animation*

Spraying Blood

Let's implement the triggers in the game. First off, we'll need to add the constants to the class-level declarations in Character.

In FireTrig(), we add some cases for blood squirts, clouds, and splats. The squirts send out streaks of blood in whatever direction (with a bit of randomization) we tell them to go. We're also using a new particle we'll define later called BloodDust, which will be used for various sizes of blood clouds. We can use it for drops, clouds, or whatever.

```
case TRIG_BLOOD_SQUIRT_BACK:
case TRIG_BLOOD_SQUIRT_DOWN:
case TRIG_BLOOD_SQUIRT_DOWN_BACK:
case TRIG_BLOOD_SQUIRT_DOWN_FORNWARD:
case TRIG_BLOOD_SQUIRT_FORWARD:
case TRIG_BLOOD_SQUIRT_UP:
case TRIG_BLOOD_SQUIRT_UP_BACK:
case TRIG_BLOOD_SQUIRT_UP_FORWARD:
    double r = 0.0;
    switch (trig)
```

```
    {
        case TRIG_BLOOD_SQUIRT_FORWARD:
            r = 0.0;
            break;
        case TRIG_BLOOD_SQUIRT_DOWN_FORWARD:
            r = Math.PI * .25;
            break;
        case TRIG_BLOOD_SQUIRT_DOWN:
            r = Math.PI * .5;
            break;
        case TRIG_BLOOD_SQUIRT_DOWN_BACK:
            r = Math.PI * .75;
            break;
        case TRIG_BLOOD_SQUIRT_BACK:
            r = Math.PI;
            break;
        case TRIG_BLOOD_SQUIRT_UP_BACK:
            r = Math.PI * 1.25;
            break;
        case TRIG_BLOOD_SQUIRT_UP:
            r = Math.PI * 1.5;
            break;
        case TRIG_BLOOD_SQUIRT_UP_FORWARD:
            r = Math.PI * 1.75;
            break;
    }
    for (int i = 0; i < 7; i++)
    {
        pMan.AddParticle(new Blood(loc, new Vector2(
            (float)Math.Cos(r) * (Face == CharDir.Right ? 1f : -1f),
            (float)Math.Sin(r)
            ) * Rand.GetRandomFloat(10f, 500f) +
            Rand.GetRandomVector2(-90f, 90f, -90f, 90f),
            1f, 0f, 0f, 1f, Rand.GetRandomFloat(0.1f, 0.5f),
            Rand.GetRandomInt(0, 4)));
    }
    pMan.AddParticle(new BloodDust(loc,
        Rand.getRandomVector2(-30f, 30f, -30f, 30f),
        1f, 0f, 0f, .2f,
        Rand.getRandomFloat(.25f, .5f),
        Rand.getRandomInt(0, 4)));
    break;
case TRIG_BLOOD_CLOUD:
    pMan.AddParticle(new BloodDust(loc,
        Rand.getRandomVector2(-30f, 30f, -30f, 30f),
        1f, 0f, 0f, .4f,
```

```
            Rand.getRandomFloat(.25f, .75f),
            Rand.getRandomInt(0, 4)));
        break;
    case TRIG_BLOOD_SPLAT:
        for (int i = 0; i < 6; i++)
        {
            pMan.AddParticle(new BloodDust(loc,
            Rand.getRandomVector2(-30f, 30f, -30f, 30f),
            1f, 0f, 0f, .4f,
            Rand.getRandomFloat(.025f, .125f),
            Rand.getRandomInt(0, 4)));
        }
        break;
```

We'll create our BloodDust class in our ZombieSmashersXNA.Particles namespace. It's almost the same as our Smoke class, but we've taken out the Update() and simplified Draw() a bit. The idea behind all of these odd particle classes is to reduce functionality and specialize particles. This introduces consistency into our game design as well.

```
class BloodDust : Particle
{
    public BloodDust(Vector2 loc,
        Vector2 traj,
        float r,
        float g,
        float b,
        float a,
        float size,
        int icon)
    {
        Location = loc;
        Trajectory = traj;
        this.r = r;
        this.g = g;
        this.b = b;
        this.a = a;
        this.size = size;
        flag = icon;
        Owner = -1;
        Exists = true;
        frame = 1.0f;
    }
```

```
public override void Draw(SpriteBatch sprite, Texture2D spritesTex)
{
    sprite.Draw(spritesTex, GameLocation,
        new Rectangle(flag * 64, 0, 64, 64), new Color(
        new Vector4(r, g, b, a * frame)),
        rotation, new Vector2(32.0f, 32.0f), size,
        SpriteEffects.None, 1.0f);
}
```

Initializing and Killing the Character

We'll add some fields to the Character class to get it ready for the new functionality we're going to throw at it: an AI object (which we'll get to later), an ethereal field, and a dying frame.

```
public AI Ai;
public bool Ethereal;
public float DyingFrame = -1f;
```

Moving along through Character, we'll create a method to run the init script. It will iterate through all populated keyframes of the init animation, running keyframe scripts.

```
private void InitScript()
{
    SetAnim("init");
    if (AnimName == "init")
    {
        for (int i = 0;
            i < charDef.Animations[Anim].KeyFrames.Length;
            i++)
        {
            if (charDef.Animations[Anim].KeyFrames[i].FrameRef
                    > -1)
                script.DoScript(Anim, i);
        }
    }
}
```

Then, from our Character constructor, call InitScript().

```
InitScript();
Ai = null;
Ethereal = false;
AnimName = "";
SetAnim("fly");
```

In Character.Draw(), we'll add a line to change our draw color for dying characters. When we want to kill a character, we'll set dyingFrame (initialized to –1) to 0. Characters fade to black while fading out as we increase dyingFrame in Update().

```
Color color = new Color(new
    Vector4(1.0f, 1.0f, 1.0f, 1f));
if (DyingFrame > 0f)
    color = new Color(new Vector4(
        1f - DyingFrame,
        1f - DyingFrame,
        1f - DyingFrame,
        1f - DyingFrame));
```

In `Character.Update()`, we'll update our `dyingFrame`. Also, we'll make sure that if a character has been flagged as dying (`dyingFrame >= 0`), we don't update the frame.

```
if (DyingFrame > -1f)
{
    DyingFrame += Game1.frameTime;
}

if (DyingFrame < 0f)
{
    Animation animation = charDef.GetAnimation(anim);
    KeyFrame keyframe = animation.GetKeyFrame(animFrame);

    frame += Game1.FrameTime * 30.0f;

    ...
}
```

Further down in `Update()`, we'll modify our character-collision routine to allow for ethereal characters, who we will not be colliding with:

```
if (c[i] != null)
{
    if (!Ethereal && !c[i].Ethereal)
    {
        if (Location.X > c[i].Location.X - 90f * c[i].Scale &&
```

Also, we need to update our `AI` object (which we'll define soon), sending it the character array, our ID, and the map. For our player character (and by default), we'll leave `ai` set to `null`.

```
if (Ai != null)
    Ai.Update(c, Id, map);
```

Lastly, in `SetAnim()`, when we've successfully set the character animation, we'll add a line to set `ethereal` to `false`.

Implementing the Character Script

Next, let's add our new script commands to the `Script` class. If you forgot how this remarkably simple scripting system worked, you might want to flip back to Chapter 6 to refresh your memory.

If you don't want to flip back but need a really quick refresher, it goes like this: commands are declared and run in Script and parsed in ScriptLine.

First, let's declare our new commands in our enumeration:

```
PlaySound,
Ethereal,
Solid,
Speed,
HP,
DeathCheck,
IfDyingGoto,
KillMe,
AI
```

We need to parse the new script commands in ScriptLine:

```
case "ethereal":
    command = Commands.Ethereal;
    break;
case "solid":
    command = Commands.Solid;
    break;
case "speed":
    command = Commands.Speed;
    iParam = Convert.ToInt32(split[1]);
    break;
case "hp":
    command = Commands.HP;
    iParam = Convert.ToInt32(split[1]);
    break;
case "deathcheck":
    command = Commands.DeathCheck;
    break;
case "ifdyinggoto":
    command = Commands.IfDyingGoto;
    iParam = Convert.ToInt32(split[1]);
    break;
case "killme":
    command = Commands.KillMe;
    break;
case "ai":
    command = Commands.AI;
    sParam = split[1];
    break;
```

Back in Script, we can run the new character script commands. We'll implement AI next.

```
case Commands.Ethereal:
    character.Ethereal = true;
    break;
case Commands.Solid:
    character.Ethereal = false;
    break;
case Commands.Speed:
    character.Speed = (float)line.IParam;
    break;
case Commands.HP:
    character.HP = character.MHP = line.IParam;
    break;
case Commands.DeathCheck:
    if (character.HP < 0)
    {
        character.KillMe();
    }
    break;
case Commands.IfDyingGoto:
    if (character.HP < 0)
    {
        character.SetFrame(line.IParam);
        done = true;
    }
    break;
case Commands.KillMe:
    character.KillMe();
    break;
case Commands.AI:
    switch (line.SParam)
    {
        case "zombie":
            character.Ai = new Zombie();
            break;
        default:
            character.Ai = new Zombie();
            break;
    }
    break;
```

Adding AI

We're calling it AI for artificial intelligence, but make no mistake—there will be absolutely nothing intelligent about our AI class. We're basically going to define a list of simple behaviors (chase and attack, evade, stand still, and so on) in a base AI class, and then create monster-specific classes that will decide which behaviors to use and when.

Making artificial intelligence that looks and feels real is what is important. It doesn't matter how we do it, as long as the player believes that the zombies act like real zombies. As an independent game developer, you should start to realize that the quick and hackish way is often enough, and that you do not need a strong core set of AI algorithms just to make a small game.

We'll call the current behavior a "job," holding the value in the `job` field for a duration of `jobFrame`. We'll keep track of who we're chasing or fleeing with the `targ` field—this will allow us to have friendly nonplayable characters (NPCs) in an all-out side-scrolling zombie war, should it come down to it.

```
public class AI
{
    public const int JOB_IDLE = 0;
    public const int JOB_MELEE_CHASE = 1;
    public const int JOB_SHOOT_CHASE = 2;
    public const int JOB_AVOID = 3;

    protected int job = JOB_IDLE;
    protected int targ = -1;
    protected float jobFrame = 0f;

    protected Character me;
```

In our `Update()` function, we'll take the array of characters, ID of the character we're controlling, and map (it will be nice to know our surroundings, but we won't be implementing that just yet). We start off by setting all of our character's keys to `false`, and then decrement our `jobFrame` and call `DoJob()` to . . . well . . . do our job.

```
    public virtual void Update(Character[] c, int Id, Map map)
    {
        me = c[Id];

        me.KeyLeft = false;
        me.KeyRight = false;
        me.KeyUp = false;
        me.KeyDown = false;
        me.KeyAttack = false;
        me.KeySecondary = false;
        me.KeyJump = false;

        jobFrame -= Game1.FrameTime;

        DoJob(c, Id);
    }
```

In `DoJob()`, we do some case-by-case behavior.

```
    protected void DoJob(Character[] c, int Id)
```

```
{
    switch (job)
    {
        case JOB_IDLE:
            //do nothing!
            break;
```

For all sorts of chasing and avoiding, we make sure we have a valid (greater than –1) target. If we don't, we call FindTarg() and get a new one. We also use ChaseTarg() and FaceTarg(), which return false if they're still working at getting our character within range and facing the correct direction.

```
        case JOB_MELEE_CHASE:
            if (targ > -1)
            {
                if (!ChaseTarg(c, 50f))
                {
                    if (!FaceTarg(c))
                    {
                        me. KeyAttack = true;
                    }
                }
            }
            else
                targ = FindTarg(c);
            break;

        case JOB_AVOID:
            if (targ > -1)
            {
                AvoidTarg(c, 500f);

            }
            else
                targ = FindTarg(c);
            break;

        case JOB_SHOOT_CHASE:
            if (targ > -1)
            {
                if (!ChaseTarg(c, 150f))
                {
                    if (!FaceTarg(c))
                    {
                        me.KeySecondary = true;
                    }
                }
            }
        }
```

```
            else
                targ = FindTarg(c);
            break;
    }
```

In this neat little clause at the end, we determine if the character is just running left or right (not attacking). If this is the case, we check to see if there are any friends in the way. If there are, we stop moving. This way, a chasing zombie next to an idle zombie will not keep walking into the guy, which would look kind of silly.

```
if (!me.KeyAttack && !me.KeySecondary)
{
    if (me.KeyLeft)
    {
        if (FriendInWay(c, Id, CharDir.Left))
            me.KeyLeft = false;
    }
    if (me.KeyRight)
    {
        if (FriendInWay(c, Id, CharDir.Right))
            me.KeyRight = false;
    }
}
}
```

All of our helper functions are up next. Basically, they do a lot of spatial comparisons; the code should really speak for itself.

```
protected int FindTarg(Character[] c)
{
    int closest = -1;
    float d = 0f;

    for (int i = 0; i < c.Length; i++)
    {
        if (i != me.Id)
        {
            if (c[i] != null)
            {
                if (c[i].Team != me.Team)
                {
                    float newD = (me.Location -
                                  c[i].Location).Length();
                    if (closest == -1 || newD < d)
```

```
                {
                    d = newD;
                    closest = i;
                }
            }
        }
    }
}

return closest;
}


private bool FriendInWay(Character[] c, int Id, CharDir face)
{
    for (int i = 0; i < c.Length; i++)
    {
        if (i != Id && c[i] != null)
        {
            if (me.Team == c[i].Team)
            {
                if (me.Location.Y > c[i].Location.Y - 100f &&
                    me.Location.Y < c[i].Location.Y + 10f)
                {
                    if (face == CharDir.Right)
                    {
                        if (c[i].Location.X > me.Location.X &&
                            c[i].Location.X < me.Location.X + 70f)
                            return true;
                    }
                    else
                    {
                        if (c[i].Location.X < me.Location.X &&
                            c[i].Location.X > me.Location.X - 70f)
                            return true;
                    }
                }
            }
        }
    }
    return false;
}
```

ChaseTarg(), AvoidTarg(), and FaceTarg() all return true if the character is in the *wrong* position, meaning the character is still attempting to chase, avoid, or face its target. When we call these methods, we end up doing what we need to be doing when in the correct position (typically attacking) if everything returns false. We thought this way was intuitive, but if you would prefer to word it differently, go for it!

```
protected bool ChaseTarg(Character[] c, float distance)
{
    if (me.Location.X > c[targ].Location.X + distance)
    {
        me.KeyLeft = true;
        return true;
    }
    else if (me.Location.X < c[targ].Location.X - distance)
    {
        me.KeyRight = true;
        return true;
    }
    return false;
}

protected bool AvoidTarg(Character[] c, float distance)
{
    if (me.Location.X < c[targ].Location.X + distance)
    {
        me.KeyRight = true;
        return true;
    }
    else if (me.Location.X > c[targ].Location.X - distance)
    {
        me.KeyLeft = true;
        return true;
    }
    return false;
}

protected bool FaceTarg(Character[] c)
{
    if (me.Location.X > c[targ].Location.X && me.face ==
        CharDir.Right)
    {
        me.KeyLeft = true;
        return true;
    }
    else if (me.Location.X < c[targ].Location.X && me.face ==
        CharDir.Left)
    {
        me.KeyRight = true;
        return true;
    }
    return false;
}
}
```

That does it for our AI class for now. We can easily add new behaviors as we create new and more complex monsters—for instance, a boss character that throws axes when its prey is at a certain distance.

Our Zombie class, which will extend the AI base class, is much simpler:

```
class Zombie : AI
{
    public override void Update(Character[] c, int Id, Map map)
    {
        me = c[Id];

        if (jobFrame < 0f)
        {
            float r = Rand.GetRandomFloat(0f, 1f);
            if (r < 0.6f)
            {
                job = JOB_MELEE_CHASE;
                jobFrame = Rand.GetRandomFloat(2f, 4f);
                targ = FindTarg(c);
            }
            else if (r < 0.8f)
            {
                job = JOB_AVOID;
                jobFrame = Rand.GetRandomFloat(1f, 2f);
                targ = FindTarg(c);
            }
            else
            {
                job = JOB_IDLE;
                jobFrame = Rand.GetRandomFloat(.5f, 1f);
            }
        }

        base.Update(c, ID, map);
    }
}
```

The zombie will chase our character, avoid our character, or stand still. This is not exactly groundbreaking behavior, but then again, it's just a zombie.

Dealing Damage

We need to add some functionality to HitManager.CheckHit(). We now have ethereal characters that we can't hit, as well as dying characters that we can't hit either. In our big series of conditions for checking hit collisions, let's add another if clause to test for both:

```
for (int i = 0; i < c.Length; i++)
{
    if (i != p.Owner)
```

```
    {
        if (c[i] != null)
        {
            if (c[i].DyingFrame < 0f &&
                !c[i].Ethereal)
            {
                if (c[i].InHitBounds(p.Location))
```

Thus far, our `HitManager.CheckHit()` method doesn't actually cause any damage—it just checks for successful hits, creates blood splashes, and sets animations. Let's create a field called `hVal` that will determine our hit damage. We'll give `hVal` a value based on what type of hit it is and then deduct the final damage at the end. If we want to add difficulty levels later, we can scale `hVal` based on those, too. Also, we're adding a case for `TRIG_ZOMBIE_HIT`, our newest hit type.

```
float hVal = 1f;

if (typeof(Bullet).Equals(p.GetType()))
{
    if (!r)
    {
        hVal *= 4f;


        ...

    }
}
if (typeof(Hit).Equals(p.GetType()))
{
    ...

    switch (p.GetFlag())
    {
        case Character.TRIG_ZOMBIE_HIT:
            hVal *= 5f;
            pMan.MakeBloodSplash(p.Location,
                new Vector2(50f * tX, 100f));
            break;

        case Character.TRIG_WRENCH_DIAG_DOWN:
            hVal *= 5f;
            ...
        case Character.TRIG_WRENCH_UPPERCUT:
            hVal *= 15f;
            ...
    }
}

c[i].HP -= (int)hVal;
```

```
if (c[i].HP < 0)
{
    if (c[i].AnimName == "hit")
        c[i].SetAnim("diehit");
}
```

At the end, if our animation had been set to hit, we set it to diehit if the character should
be dead. If our character doesn't have a diehit animation, we'll just end up using the regular
hit animation.

On that note, we also need to employ our dieland animation. We set our enemy animation
to hitland in the Character.Land() method. Let's have it set to dieland if the character should
be dead:

```
case "jhit":
case "jmid":
case "jfall":
    SetAnim("hitland");
    if (HP < 0)
        SetAnim("dieland");
    break;
```

In our dieland and diehit animations, we use the killme command, which calls the
KillMe() method:

```
public void KillMe()
{
    if (DyingFrame < 0f)
    {
        DyingFrame = 0f;
    }
}
```

When we want to add some character building and depth, we could add a few lines in
KillMe() to create coins, health, and so on, as necessary. For now, we can just leave it at setting
DyingFrame to 0, which signals that our character is dead.

Lastly, let's kill off our characters from Game1.Update(). After updating our cháracters,
we'll check their dying status—if dyingFrame is greater than 1, we kill them.

```
character[i].Update(map, pManager, character);
if (character[i].dyingFrame > 1f)
{
    character[i] = null;
}
```

That should do it. We've created some blood-related triggers; created zombie death
animations; created and implemented new script commands; and added health, death, and AI
to characters. Let's run it. We can kill our zombies now! Our zombie head splatter is shown in
Figure 9-5.

Figure 9-5. *Zombie head splatter*

Map Scripting

At this point, you should be gaining an appreciation for the power of scripting. If we were to hard-code the type of stuff we can do with scripting, we would have a very, very messy bunch of classes on our hands. One of James's older games, Zombie Smashers X2, used a modular character system, but hard-coded all animation, sounds, and triggers. It was a terrible mess and had only one character format, with good reason.

Map scripting presents a similar situation, but the question lies in balance between the map format and editor and the script functionality. For instance, say we wanted to let some maps have fog. We could handle that in two ways:

- Add a Fog check box to our editor. In saving the map, we would write the fog value: true or false.

- Create a fog command for our map scripting language. We would add a line in our map script initialization routine to turn on fog.

Both methods have pros and cons. We like putting as much into the scripting language as possible, but the drawback of this is it's easy to forget commands and make syntactical errors. On the other hand, the drawback of incorporating new map functionality into the map format is that it requires interface changes (possibly major). So, if the file format isn't planned for it (as ours isn't), we would need to load and save every last map using the new format if we make a big change mid development.

Because this section is titled "Map Scripting," we're going to choose the script functionality road. Let's get coding! We'll start by making a script editor in MapEditor.

Adding a Script Editor in the Map Editor

Let's declare some new fields at the class level of MapEditor. First, we'll declare a new draw type in our DrawingMode enumeration. Right now, we can draw in select mode, collision map mode, or ledge mode. Let's add script draw mode. We'll also add a text editing mode for script editing and some fields to specify the scroll value of our script and whether any script lines are selected, as well as some highlighting colors for some simple syntax highlighting.

```
int scriptScroll;
int selScript = -1;

const int COLOR_NONE = 0;
const int COLOR_YELLOW = 1;
const int COLOR_GREEN = 2;
```

In Draw(), we add some functionality to draw our script when we're in script draw mode.

```
switch (drawType)
{
    ...
    case DrawingMode.Script:
        layerName = "script";
        break;
}
if (text.DrawClickText(5, 25, "draw: " + layerName,
    mosX, mosY, mouseClick))
    drawType = (DrawingMode)(((int)drawType + 1) % 4);


if (drawType == DrawingMode.Script)
{
```

Draw a translucent black background behind our script.

```
    spriteBatch.Begin(SpriteBlendMode.AlphaBlend);
    spriteBatch.Draw(nullTex, new Rectangle(400, 20, 400, 565),
                new Color(new Vector4(0f, 0f, 0f, .62f)));
    spriteBatch.End();
```

Next, we'll iterate through all visible script lines, drawing and handling selection.

```
    for (int i = scriptScroll; i < scriptScroll + 28; i++)
    {
        if (selScript == i)
        {
            text.Color = Color.White;
            text.DrawText(405, 25 + (i - scriptScroll) * 20,
                i.ToString() + ": " + map.Scripts[i] + "*");
        }
```

```
        else
        {
            if (text.DrawClickText(405, 25 + (i - scriptScroll) * 20,
                i.ToString() + ": " + map.Scripts[i],
                mosX, mosY, mouseClick))
            {
                selScript = i;
                editMode = EditingMode.Script;
            }
        }
    }
```

Now we take care of syntax highlighting. Normally, that would mean we would need to edit our text drawing class to allow some sort of color-designating markup, but here we can cheat a bit. Because we're drawing left-aligned text, we can draw the entire string in white, then draw the string up to the highlighted command in the highlighted color, and then draw the number over that in white. Like so many other techniques we use in these editors, it's ugly but gets the job done.

```
    if (map.Scripts[i].Length > 0)
    {
        String[] split = map.Scripts[i].Split(' ');
```

The GetCommandColor() method will compare our commands against some strings we'll give it.

```
        int c = GetCommandColor(split[0]);
        if (c > COLOR_NONE)
        {
            switch(c)
            {
                case COLOR_GREEN:
                    text.Color = Color.Lime;
                    break;
                case COLOR_YELLOW:
                    text.Color = Color.Yellow;
                    break;
            }
            text.DrawText(405, 25 + (i - scriptScroll) * 20,
                i.ToString() + ": " + split[0]);
        }
    }
    text.Color = Color.White;
    text.DrawText(405, 25 + (i - scriptScroll) * 20,
        i.ToString() + ": ");
}
```

Lastly, we'll draw some scroll buttons.

```
    bool mouseDown = (Mouse.GetState().LeftButton == ButtonState.Pressed);
    if (DrawButton(770, 20, 1, mosX, mosY, mouseDown) &&
        scriptScroll > 0)
        scriptScroll--;

    if (DrawButton(770, 550, 2, mosX, mosY, mouseDown) &&
        scriptScroll < map.Scripts.Length - 28)
        scriptScroll++;
}
```

Implementing Map Script Commands

Let's use the GetCommandColor() method to talk about some of the script commands we'll be
implementing:

```
private int GetCommandColor(String s)
{
    switch (s)
    {
        case "fog":
        case "monster":
        case "makebucket":
        case "addbucket":
        case "ifnotbucketgoto":

        case "wait":

        case "setflag":
        case "iftruegoto":
        case "iffalsegoto":

        case "setglobalflag":
        case "ifglobaltruegoto":
        case "ifglobalfalsegoto":

        case "stop":
            return COLOR_GREEN;
        case "tag":
            return COLOR_YELLOW;
    }
    return COLOR_NONE;
}
```

Map script commands are about the same as character script commands. The only functional difference will be that we'll allow ourselves more than one parameter per command—a
few things would be impossible otherwise. Here's a brief explanation of what we've got so far:

`fog`: Turns map fog on.

`monster` *type x y name*: Creates a monster of *type* type at location *x, y* with the *name* name. A character name is a string identifier that will set a map flag when the character dies. A *flag* is a list of strings that the map system uses to keep track of things. For instance, we can spawn two zombies named `z1` and `z2`, and then end up in a loop that checks whether flags `z1` and `z2` have been set. Flags exist on different scopes. Local flags are reset every time a map is loaded. Global flags are reset every time the user starts a new level, but are persistent otherwise (a player can move from one map screen to another and global flags will not be reset).

`makebucket` *size*: Creates a bucket of size *size*. A *bucket* is basically a list of monsters that will "empty" itself into the game as long as the screen monster population is less than *size*. We can test to see if a bucket is empty.

`addbucket` *type x y*: Adds a monster of type *type* to the bucket. The monster will spawn at location *x, y*.

`ifnotbucketgoto` *tag*: If the bucket is not empty, goes to *tag*. *Tags* are like goto labels. We always start with `tag init`.

`wait` *ticks*: Pauses the script for *ticks* ticks.

`setflag` *flag*: Sets the local map flag *flag*.

`iftruegoto` *flag tag*: If local flag *flag* is set, goes to tag *tag*.

`iffalsegoto` *flag tag*: If local flag *flag* is not set, goes to tag *tag*.

`setglobalflag` *flag*: Sets the global map flag *flag*. As noted, unlike local flags, global flags are persistent throughout the whole level. A good application of this would be to use plain-old (local) map flags to keep track of who you've killed within a room, setting a global `roomcleared` flag once all baddies are cleared. Then when the player reenters the room, we'll see the `roomcleared` global flag and won't try to make them clear the room again.

`ifglobaltruegoto` *flag tag*: If global flag *flag* is set, goes to tag *tag*.

`ifglobalfalsegoto` *flag tag*: If global flag *flag* is not set, goes to tag *tag*.

`stop`: Stops reading the script.

`tag` *tag*: Sets a goto destination.

A simple script could look like this:

```
tag init
fog

ifglobaltruegoto roomclear cleartag

monster zombie 200 100 z1
monster zombie 300 100 z2

tag waitz1
wait 5
```

```
iffalsegoto z1 waitz1
iffalsegoto z2 waitz1

makebucket 3
addbucket zombie 300 100
addbucket zombie 400 100
addbucket zombie 500 100
addbucket zombie 600 100
addbucket zombie 700 100

tag waitb
wait 5
ifnotbucketgoto waitb

setglobalflag roomclear

tag cleartag
stop
```

It should be easy enough to decipher what's going on in this script based on the command definitions and the basic intention of this game. The script starts at the init tag, turns on fog, goes to the last line, and stops if the roomclear global flag has been set. Otherwise, it creates two monsters, loops until they are dead, creates a monster bucket full of zombies, loops until *they* are dead, then sets the roomclear global flag and stops. If the player kills everything in the room, leaves, and comes back, there won't be any zombies spawning.

Notice the wait statements. When we set up the script-running method in ZombieSmashers, we'll have it keep running the script in a while loop until it hits a wait or a stop. We can put in a failsafe (to cry foul, for instance, if we've read more than 1000 lines of script in one go), but we may as well get into the practice of putting wait statements within loops now.

Updating the MapEditor Code

To better punch in map coordinates, let's add some functionality to Update() that lets us just click in the map to add an x, y coordinate to the selected script line:

```
if (drawType == DrawingMode.Ledges)
{
    ...
}
else if (drawType == DrawingMode.Script)
{
    if (selScript > -1)
    {
        if (mosX < 400)
            map.Scripts[selScript] += (" " +
                ((int)((float)mosX + scroll.X / 2f)).ToString() + " " +
                ((int)((float)mosY + scroll.Y / 2f)).ToString());
    }
}
```

The next section we'll update is PressKey(). Our text-editing capacity is fairly rudimentary, but we're going to make it slightly less rudimentary with the introduction of multiline editing. When the user hits Enter, we need to increment the selected script line and push all lines below that down one. When the user tries to press Backspace on an empty line, we decrement the selected line and pull all lines below that up.

```
private void PressKey(Keys key)
{
    String t = "";
    switch (editMode)
    {
        case EditingMode.Path:
            t = map.path;
            break;
        case EditingMode.Script:
            if (selScript < 0)
                return;
            t = map.Scripts[selScript];
            break;
        default:
            return;
    }
```

We'll keep track of whether we've successfully deleted a line with the delLine field. This way, we won't end up overwriting the previous line with a blank string when we delete a line.

We're using the ScriptDelLine() and ScriptEnter() methods to delete lines or carriage returns. These methods return true if successful; false otherwise (for instance, if we try hitting Enter while we're at the last line).

```
    bool delLine = false;

    if (key == Keys.Back)
    {
        if (t.Length > 0)
            t = t.Substring(0, t.Length - 1);
        else if (editMode == EditingMode.Script)
        {
            delLine = ScriptDelLine();
        }
    }
    else if (key == Keys.Enter)
    {
        if (editingText == EditingMode.Script)
        {
            if (ScriptEnter())
            {
                t = "";
            }
        }
    }
```

```
        else
            editingText = EditingMode.None;
    }
    else
    {
        t = (t + (char)key).ToLower();
    }
```

If delLine is true, we'll decrement the selected script line. Otherwise, we'll rewrite the temp string back to our editing string.

```
    if (!delLine)
    {
        switch (editMode)
        {
            case EditingMode.Path:
                map.path = t;
                break;
            case EditingMode.Script:
                map.Scripts[selScript] = t;
                break;
        }
    }
    else
        selScript--;
}
```

Our ScriptEnter() and ScriptDelLine() methods are as follows:

```
private bool ScriptEnter()
{
    if (selScript >= map.Scripts.Length - 1)
        return false;
    for (int i = map.Scripts.Length - 1; i > selScript; i--)
        map.Scripts[i] = map.Scripts[i - 1];
    selScript++;
    return true;
}

private bool ScriptDelLine()
{
    if (selScript <= 0)
        return false;
    for (int i = selScript; i < map.Scripts.Length - 1; i++)
        map.Scripts[i] = map.Scripts[i + 1];
    return true;
}
```

We need to modify the Map class to include the script array, as well as to load and save the new format. At the class level, we'll declare the script as follows:

```
public String[] Scripts = new String[128];
```

At the end of our Write() method, add this:

```
for (int i = 0; i < Scripts.Length; i++)
    file.Write(Scripts[i]);
```

At the end of Read(), add this:

```
for (int i = 0; i < Scripts.Length; i++)
    Scripts[i] = file.ReadString();
```

The tricky bit is dealing with already saved maps. At this point in development, we have only one map, map.zdx. To convert the map to the new format, we change only the Write() method, load the map, save it with the new format, and then change the Read() method. If we had changed both methods, we would get an error while loading the map.

Figure 9-6 shows our script editor in action.

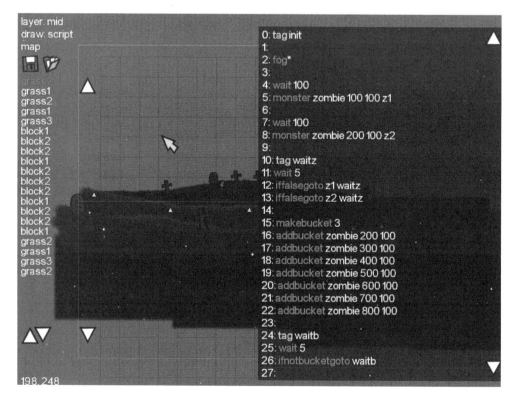

Figure 9-6. *Script editor*

In Figure 9-6, we're using the following script:

```
tag init

fog

wait 100
monster zombie 100 100 z1

wait 100
monster zombie 200 100 z2

tag waitz
wait 5
iffalsegoto z1 waitz
iffalsegoto z2 waitz
makebucket 3

addbucket zombie 200 100
addbucket zombie 300 100
addbucket zombie 400 100
addbucket zombie 500 100
addbucket zombie 600 100
addbucket zombie 700 100
addbucket zombie 800 100

tag waitb
wait 5
ifnotbucketgoto waitb

stop
```

Now we can set up our script processor and reader in the game.

Implementing Map Scripting in the Game

Now we can add some classes to our game to process and run the script. We'll use a similar system to what we used with the character scripting: a `MapScriptLine` class to process and contain the script lines, and a `MapScript` class to manage and run the script. We will also use a new enumeration for our commands.

```
enum MapCommands
{
    Fog = 0,
    Monster,
    MakeBucket,
    AddBucket,
    IfNotBucketGoto,
    Wait,
```

```
        SetFlag,
        IfTrueGoto,
        IfFalseGoto,
        SetGlobalFlag,
        IfGlobalTrueGoto,
        IfGlobalFalseGoto,
        Stop,
        Tag
}
public class MapScript
{
    Map map;

    public MapScriptLine[] Lines;
```

All of our map script command constants follow. We'll be using these when we process our map script line strings in MapScriptLine. We'll keep track of which line of script we're currently reading with curLine.

```
    int curLine;
    float waiting;
    public bool IsReading;

    public MapFlags Flags;
```

Our constructor will take a reference from the map that is using it, create a new MapFlags object of size 32, and create an array of 128 script lines. The MapFlags constructor we'll create will just take the size of the string array to create.

```
    public MapScript(Map _map)
    {
        map = _map;
        Flags = new MapFlags(32);
        Lines = new MapScriptLine[128];
    }
```

DoScript() is the big method we use to run any and all script commands. If the script is waiting, it will count down the waiting value a bit; otherwise, it will continuously run line after line of script until it's told to stop.

```
    public void DoScript(Character[] c)
    {
        if (waiting > 0f)
        {
            waiting -= Game1.FrameTime;
        }
        else
        {
            bool done = false;
            while (!done)
```

```
        {
            curLine++;
            if (Lines[curLine] != null)
            {
```

Our case-by-case script-running functionality follows.

```
                switch (scriptLine[curLine].Command)
                {
                    case MapCommands.Fog:
                        map.fog = true;
                        break;
```

When a MapScriptLine parses a command, it will split the command into a string array called sParam. Also, for certain types of commands, it will convert what we intend to be vectors (that is, x y coordinates) into a Vector2 called vParam, and integers into iParam.

For our monster command, we use vParam for the spawn location, sParam[1] for the monster type, and sParam[4] for the monster name.

```
                    case MapCommands.Monster:
                        for (int i = 0; i < c.Length; i++)
                        {
                            if (c[i] == null)
                            {
                                c[i] = new Character(
                                    Lines[curLine].VParam,
                                    Game1.CharDefs
                                    [GetMonsterFromString
                                    (Lines[curLine]
                                        .SParam[1])],
                                    i,
                                    Character.TEAM_BAD_GUYS);
                                if (Lines[curLine]
                                        .SParam.Length > 4)
                                    c[i].Name = Lines[curLine]
                                        .SParam[4];
                                break;
                            }
                        }
                        break;
                    case MapCommands.MakeBucket:
                        map.Bucket = new
                            Bucket(Lines[curLine].IParam);
                        break;
```

```
case MapCommands.AddBucket:
    map.bucket.AddItem
        (Lines[curLine].VParam,
        GetMonsterFromString
        (Lines[curLine].SParam[1]));
    break;
case MapCommands.IfNotBucketGoto:
    if (map.bucket.IsEmpty)
        GotoTag(Lines[curLine].SParam[1]);
    break;
```

When we run a wait command, we'll set done to true. This means there won't be any more script processing until the waiting value isn't greater than zero.

```
case MapCommands.Wait:
    waiting =
        (float)Lines[curLine].IParam / 100f;
    done = true;
    break;
```

Our MapFlags setting and evaluating is fairly straightforward. Remember that these are local scope map flags, which will be reset whenever a player enters a new map segment.

```
case MapCommands.SetFlag:
    Flags.SetFlag(Lines[curLine].SParam[1]);
    break;
case MapCommands.IfTrueGoto:
    if(Flags.GetFlag
            (Lines[curLine].SParam[1]))
        GotoTag(Lines[curLine].SParam[2]);
    break;
case MapCommands.IfFalseGoto:
    if (!Flags.GetFlag
            (Lines[curLine].SParam[1]))
        GotoTag(Lines[curLine].SParam[2]);
    break;
```

We'll declare a MapFlags object called globalFlags in map and use that for our global flag setting and evaluation. When the player leaves one map segment and enters another (we'll implement this later), the global map flags will remain on, but the local map flags will all be reset.

```
case MapCommands.SetGlobalFlag:
    map.GlobalFlags.SetFlag
        (Lines[curLine].SParam[1]);
    break;
```

```
                case MapCommands.IfGlobalTrueGoto:
                    if (map.GlobalFlags.GetFlag
                            (Lines[curLine].SParam[1]))
                        GotoTag(Lines[curLine].SParam[2]);
                    break;
                case MapCommands.IfGlobalFalseGoto:
                    if (!map.GlobalFlags.GetFlag
                            (Lines[curLine].SParam[1]))
                        GotoTag(Lines[curLine].SParam[2]);
                    break;
                case MapCommands.Stop:
                    IsReading = false;
                    done = true;
                    break;
                case MapCommands.Tag:
                    //
                    break;
            }
        }
    }
}
```

Our GotoTag() method tries to go to the tag we give it. It returns false if it can't find the tag.

```
public bool GotoTag(String tag)
{
    for (int i = 0; i < Lines.Length; i++)
    {
        if (Lines[i] != null)
        {
            if (Lines[i].Command == MapCommands.Tag)
            {
                if (Lines[i].SParam[1] == tag)
                {
                    curLine = i;
                    return true;
                }
            }
        }
    }
    return false;
}
```

We'll just do a case-by-case check for monster type strings in GetMonsterFromString(). We have only one monster so far. We'll use this method for any addbucket and monster commands, which refer to monsters by string names.

```
    public static int GetMonsterFromString(String m)
    {
        switch (m)
        {
            case "zombie":
                return CharacterDefinitions.Zombie;

        }
        return CharacterDefinitions.Zombie;
    }
}
```

Our MapScriptLine class does all of the parsing. The script line that is parsed is split into a string array called sParam, and integers and vectors are converted into iParam and vParam, where necessary.

```
class MapScriptLine
{
    public MapCommands Command;
    public int IParam;
    public Vector2 VParam;
    public string[] SParam;

    public MapScriptLine(string line)
    {
        if (line.Length < 1)
            return;

        SParam = line.Split(' ');
        switch (SParam[0])
        {
            case "fog":
                Command = MapCommands.Fog;
                break;
            case "monster":
                Command = MapCommands.Monster;
                VParam = new Vector2(
                    Convert.ToSingle(SParam[2]),
                    Convert.ToSingle(SParam[3])
                    );
                break;
            case "makebucket":
                Command = MapCommands.MakeBucket;
                IParam = Convert.ToInt32(SParam[1]);
                break;
```

```
                case "addbucket":
                    Command = MapCommands.AddBucket;
                    VParam = new Vector2(
                        Convert.ToSingle(SParam[2]),
                        Convert.ToSingle(SParam[3])
                        );
                    break;
                case "ifnotbucketgoto":
                    Command = MapCommands.IfNotBucketGoto;
                    break;
                case "wait":
                    Command = MapCommands.Wait;
                    IParam = Convert.ToInt32(SParam[1]);
                    break;
                case "setflag":
                    Command = MapCommands.SetFlag;
                    break;
                case "iftruegoto":
                    Command = MapCommands.IfTrueGoto;
                    break;
                case "iffalsegoto":
                    Command = MapCommands.IfFalseGoto;
                    break;
                case "setglobalflag":
                    Command = MapCommands.SetGlobalFlag;
                    break;
                case "ifglobaltruegoto":
                    Command = MapCommands.IfGlobalTrueGoto;
                    break;
                case "ifglobalfalsegoto":
                    Command = MapCommands.IfGlobalFalseGoto;
                    break;
                case "stop":
                    Command = MapCommands.Stop;
                    break;
                case "tag":
                    Command = MapCommands.Tag;
                    break;
            }
        }
    }
```

Next, let's create a Bucket class!

Implementing Monster Buckets

Our Bucket class contains an array of bucket items, which are monster spawn locations and
types. We can add items to the bucket as our script reads them. The main function of the
bucket is to make sure that the number of enemies on screen is not less than the size we give it.
We supply a stream of monsters until the bucket is empty.

```
public class Bucket
{
    BucketItem[] bucketItem = new BucketItem[64];
    public int Size;
    float updateFrame = 0f;
    public bool IsEmpty = false;

    public Bucket(int size)
    {
        for (int i = 0; i < bucketItem.Length; i++)
            bucketItem[i] = null;

        Size = size;
    }

    public void AddItem(Vector2 loc, int charDef)
    {
        for (int i = 0; i < bucketItem.Length; i++)
        {
            if (bucketItem[i] == null)
            {
                bucketItem[i] = new BucketItem(loc, charDef);
                return;
            }
        }
    }

    public void Update(Character[] c)
    {
        updateFrame -= Game1.frameTime;

        if (updateFrame > 0f)
            return;
        updateFrame = 1f;

        int monsters = 0;

        for (int i = 0; i < c.Length; i++)
            if (c[i] != null)
                if (c[i].team == Character.TEAM_BAD_GUYS)
                    monsters++;
```

```
    if (monsters < Size)
    {
        for (int i = 0; i < bucketItem.Length; i++)
        {
            if (bucketItem[i] != null)
            {
                for (int n = 0; n < c.Length; n++)
                {
                    if (c[n] == null)
                    {
                        c[n] = new
                            Character(bucketItem[i].Location,
                            Game1.CharDefs[bucketItem[i].CharDef],
                            n, Character.TEAM_BAD_GUYS);
                        bucketItem[i] = null;
                        return;
                    }
                }
            }
        }
        if (monsters == 0)
            IsEmpty = true;
    }

    }
}
```

BucketItem contains only a spawn location and character type integer:

```
class BucketItem
{
    public Vector2 Location;
    public int CharDef;

    public BucketItem(Vector2 _loc, int _charDef)
    {
        Location = _loc;
        CharDef = _charDef;
    }
}
```

Bringing It All Together

We've set up our map script lines, our map script processing and reading, and our monster buckets. Now we'll update our Map class so that our Read() method handles the new file format, namely by loading, processing, and running our new scripts. We also need to get around to implementing that fog, and for that, we'll use a frame field as a sort of map timer.

At the class level, we'll add some fields:

```
public MapScript mapScript;
public MapFlags GlobalFlags;

public bool Fog;

public Bucket Bucket;
protected float pFrame;
protected float frame;
```

In the `Map` constructor, create the `globalFlags` to store our global scope map flags. These flags will be reset only when the player starts a new level.

```
GlobalFlags = new MapFlags(64);
```

We'll add some lines at the beginning of our `Map.Update()` method to update the script, update the monster bucket, increment the map frame, and create a fog particle every one-tenth second if fog is on.

```
if (mapScript.IsReading)
    mapScript.DoScript(c);

if (Bucket != null)
{
    if (!Bucket.IsEmpty)
        Bucket.Update(c);
}

frame += Game1.FrameTime;

if (Fog)
{
    if ((int)(pFrame * 10f) != (int)(frame * 10f))
    {
        pMan.AddParticle(new Fog(
            Rand.GetRandomVector2(0f, 1280f, 600f, 1000f)));
    }
}
```

We also need to update our `Read()` method by adding a few lines toward the end of the file-reading routine, immediately after reading the collision map data. We'll create a new `MapScript` object, thus wiping the map scope flags. Then we'll read and process the map script line by line. Finally, we'll turn off fog and run the script from the `init` tag (which, in the case of the script we're using, will turn fog back on!).

```
for (int x = 0; x < 20; x++)
    for (int y = 0; y < 20; y++)
        col[x, y] = file.ReadInt32();
```

```
mapScript = new MapScript(this);

for (int i = 0; i < mapScript.Lines.Length; i++)
{
    String s = file.ReadString();
    if (s.Length > 0)
        mapScript.Lines[i] = new MapScriptLine(s);
    else
        mapScript.Lines[i] = null;
}

file.Close();

Fog = false;
if (mapScript.GotoTag("init"))
    mapScript.IsReading = true;
```

We create fog particles in Map.Update(). Fog particles spawn within a thick, horizontal band near the map's lower boundaries and slowly drift up and to the right. Because we don't really need much variation in fog, we can create it with only a location in the constructor and then manually populate all of the fields. Our Fog class looks like this:

```
class Fog : Particle
{
    public Fog(Vector2 loc)
    {
        this.Location = loc;
        this.Trajectory = new Vector2(80f, -30f);
        this.size = Rand.GetRandomFloat(6f, 8f);
        this.flag = Rand.GetRandomInt(0, 4);
        this.owner = -1;
        this.Exists = true;
        this.frame = (float)Math.PI * 2f;
        this.Additive = true;
        this.rotation = Rand.GetRandomFloat(0f, 6.28f);
    }
```

The alpha value we're using uses a bit of trig, which is why we created the fog particle with a frame value of PI * 2. The sine of frame will give us an alpha value that follows a sinusoidal curve—brighten quickly, stay bright for a while, and then darken quickly.

```
    public override void Draw(SpriteBatch sprite, Texture2D spritesTex)
    {
        sprite.Draw(spritesTex, GameLocation,
            new Rectangle(flag * 64, 0, 64, 64),
            new Color(
            new Vector4(1f, 1f, 1f, (float)Math.Sin(frame / 2f) * .2f)
```

```
            ),
            rotation + frame / 4f, new Vector2(32.0f, 32.0f), size,
            SpriteEffects.None, 1.0f);
    }
}
```

Our map scripting system is now in place. We just need to add our MapFlags class.

```
public class MapFlags
{
    String[] flags;

    public MapFlags(int size)
    {
        flags = new String[size];
        for (int i = 0; i < flags.Length; i++)
            flags[i] = "";
    }

    public bool GetFlag(String flag)
    {
        for (int i = 0; i < flags.Length; i++)
        {
            if (flags[i] == flag)
                return true;
        }
        return false;
    }

    public void SetFlag(String flag)
    {
        if (GetFlag(flag))
            return;

        for (int i = 0; i < flags.Length; i++)
        {
            if (flags[i] == "")
            {
                flags[i] = flag;
                return;
            }
        }
    }
}
```

There's one last bit of cleanup to do: remove the for loop in our Game1 initialize routine that spawns our ten zombies. We'll be spawning all of our zombies from map scripts from here on out.

With our map in place using its brand-new script, run ZombieSmashers. You'll see something like Figure 9-7.

Figure 9-7. *Final product of this chapter*

Conclusion

We've covered some fairly varied ground in this chapter. The main goal was to introduce map scripting, but we ended up adding quite a bit of functionality to our characters: blood sprays, initialization and death, and rudimentary AI. We know that we say this every chapter, but we're a lot closer to having a fleshed-out game.

To recap, we accomplished the following:

- Added all sorts of blood sprays and spurts to the character editor

- Created zombie attack, decap, and bloodsplode animations

- Added initialization scripts

- Implemented the new blood effects in our game

- Implemented character initialization and death

- Added AI

- Defined a map scripting language

- Added script-editing functionality to the map editor

- Introduced map level and global level flags

- Added fog

In the next chapter, we'll introduce player death, map transitions, a HUD, and game menus.

As we near the completion of our game, it is important to keep our head in the game and not get distracted by the want or need to change things that are done. One of the biggest problems that plagues independent developers is their constant desire to fix old code, no matter how well it works.

The best thing to do at this point is finish the game first, and then go back.

■■■

CHAPTER 10

Menus, a HUD, and Deployment
At Last, the Coveted Xbox 360 Deployment

We'll warn you right off the bat: this is going to be another odds-and-ends chapter. The initial design was to produce all of the interface-related items we would need: a health bar, score, map transitions, and a main menu. However, since these tie in with the constraints we'll be dealing with on the Xbox 360, and because thus far we haven't touched the thing, it seemed like a perfect time to introduce the concept of deployment.

If you don't have an Xbox 360 and/or an XNA Creators Club membership, you can blissfully skip the deployment section of this chapter. But, honestly, if you've gotten this far in the book and still don't have any intention of playing around with an Xbox 360, you've got some issues. Granted, they might be good issues (thriftiness?), but they are issues nonetheless.

Here's the rundown of what we'll be doing in this chapter:

- Add a player HUD to display the health and score. We'll need to implement scoring and map transitions, and add scripting functionality to support map transitions.

- Add a menu system.

- Implement player death. We'll need to have a menu system in place to deal with this.

- Dive into Xbox 360 deployment.

There will be a bit of "we need to do *A*, but to get there we need to have *B* and *C* in place," so bear with us.

Adding a HUD

Our HUD will consist of a row of five hearts for our health and a score, as shown in Figure 10-1. The hearts will just be a visual representation of our integer health value, not some sort of atomic unit of health. For instance, if you have 82/100 HP, you'll have 4.1 hearts. We just thought hearts would look cute.

Figure 10-1. *Health and score display*

Creating the HUD Class

The HUD class will deal with all things related to the interface: updating the health display and fading transitions, and drawing the health, score, and transitions. Just like everything else so far, we'll be calling the Update() and Draw() functions from Game1.

```
class HUD
{
    SpriteBatch sprite;
    Texture2D spritesTex;
    Texture2D nullTex;

    Character[] character;

    Map map;
```

We'll be using a new object, scoredraw, to draw numbers. "But wait," you may be saying, "why not just use a text class and ToString() to draw text?" The long and the short of it is that ToString() generates a ton of garbage when used every frame; this kills performance on the Xbox 360. We'll use a more efficient algorithm that you may have seen in a Computer Science 101 class:

```
    ScoreDraw scoreDraw;
```

We will talk more about ScoreDraw in the next section.

We'll use the field heartFrame to let our hearts sort of waver in a classic comic, cutesy fashion. We're using the fHP field (think floating health points) for a sort of catch-up health bar. When we take damage or get health, we want our health bar to smoothly transition from the previous value to the current value. When we call HUD.Update(), we'll have the floating bar try to get to where the real bar is. Then when we Draw(), we'll draw more prominently at the floating position than the real position. This technique is infinitely more professional-looking than just drawing the current health value.

```
float heartFrame;
float fHP;
```

For the constructor, we'll just send it all of the objects it will need: the ever-present SpriteBatch, some textures, and the Character array and Map.

```
public HUD(SpriteBatch _sprite, Texture2D _spritesTex,
    Texture2D _nullTex,
    Character[] _character,
    Map _map)
{
    sprite = _sprite;
    spritesTex = _spritesTex;
    character = _character;
    map = _map;
    nullTex = _nullTex;
    scoreDraw = new ScoreDraw(sprite, spritesTex);
}
```

As promised, the Update() function increments our heartFrame and tries to get fHP to match with our goal HP.

```
public void Update()
{
    heartFrame += Game1.FrameTime;
    if (heartFrame > 6.28f)
        heartFrame -= 6.28f;

    if (character[0].HP > fHP)
    {
        fHP += Game1.FrameTime * 15f;
        if (fHP > character[0].HP)
            fHP = character[0].HP;
    }
    if (character[0].HP < fHP)
    {
        fHP -= Game1.FrameTime * 15f;
        if (fHP < character[0].HP)
            fHP = character[0].HP;
    }
}
```

Our Draw() method will first draw the score, then some black background hearts (our floating health hearts), and finally our real health hearts.

We're using the same sprites texture we previously used it for smoke, flame, and muzzle flashes, but we'll add some hearts and numbers to it. The new image is shown in Figure 10-2.

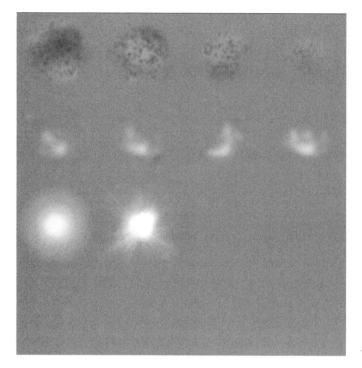

Figure 10-2. *Updated sprites texture*

The hearts all start at 0, 192 and are 32 × 32.

```
public void Draw()
{
    sprite.Begin(SpriteBlendMode.AlphaBlend);

    scoreDraw.Draw(Game1.Score, new Vector2(50f, 78f),
Color.White, Justification.Left);
```

Likening our health meter to a progress bar, we'll call our floating health value `fProg` and our health value `prog`. Each value will be between 0 and 5, since we're using 5 hearts. When we iterate through our five hearts, we can figure out if we're using a full heart, no heart, or a portion of a heart by the difference between the currently drawn heart and our progress value.

```
        float fProg = fHP / character[0].MHP;
        float prog = character[0].HP / character[0].MHP;
        fProg *= 5f;
        prog *= 5f;
        for (int i = 0; i < 5; i++)
        {
```

We'll be using the `r` float to determine how much to rotate our hearts. The value is a function of our `heartFrame` value and the current heart index. This way, the hearts don't all rotate in sync. Since it's a cosine function, the hearts bob one way or another.

```
float r = (float)Math.Cos((double)heartFrame * 2.0 +
    (double)i) * 0.1f;
```

First, we draw the dark background hearts:

```
    sprite.Draw(spritesTex, new Vector2(
66f + (float)i * 32f, 66f),
            new Rectangle(i * 32, 192, 32, 32),
            new Color(new Vector4(0.5f, 0f, 0f, .25f)),
            r, new Vector2(16f, 16f), 1.25f,
            SpriteEffects.None, 1f);
```

Next, we compute how much of a heart is shown, by getting the difference between the progress value and the current heart index, and draw the floating health heart:

```
    float ta = fProg - (float)i;
    if (ta > 1f) ta = 1f;
    if (ta > 0f)
    {
        sprite.Draw(spritesTex, new Vector2(
66f + (float)i * 32f, 66f),
            new Rectangle(i * 32, 192, (int)(32f * ta), 32),
            new Color(new Vector4(1f, 0f, 0f, .75f)),
            r, new Vector2(16f, 16f), 1.25f,
            SpriteEffects.None, 1f);
    }
```

Finally, compute another heart sliver width and draw the real health heart:

```
    ta = prog - (float)i;
    if (ta > 1f) ta = 1f;
    if (ta > 0f)
    {
        sprite.Draw(spritesTex, new Vector2(
66f + (float)i * 32f, 66f),
            new Rectangle(i * 32, 192, (int)(32f * ta), 32),
            new Color(new Vector4(.9f, 0f, 0f, 1f)),
            r, new Vector2(16f, 16f), 1.25f,
            SpriteEffects.None, 1f);
    }
}
```

Lastly, we're implementing some fade-to-black functionality. We'll have transition values in the map soon, for entering and exiting segments, as well as for when we first start a game. Based on where the map is transition-wise, we'll draw our nullTex over the entire screen with an appropriate alpha value.

```
        float a = map.GetTransVal();
        if (a > 0f)
        {
            sprite.Draw(nullTex, new Rectangle(0, 0,
                (int)Game1.ScreenSize.X,
                (int)Game1.ScreenSize.Y), new Color(
                new Vector4(0f, 0f, 0f, a)));
        }
        sprite.End();
    }
}
```

Drawing the Score

We referred to a ScoreDraw class earlier. Let's define it here:

```
public enum Justification
{
    Left = 0,
    Right
}
class ScoreDraw
{
    SpriteBatch spriteBatch;
    Texture2D spritesTex;

    public ScoreDraw(SpriteBatch _spriteBatch, Texture2D _spritesTex)
    {
        spriteBatch = _spriteBatch;
        spritesTex = _spritesTex;
    }
```

For our drawing, we're just applying a simple loop to our original score. We calculate modulus 10, draw the modulus 10 value, divide by 10, shift our position left, and repeat until nothing remains. For instance, if we give it the number 123, we'll do this:

- Compute 123 mod 10 = 3

- Draw 3, shift left a bit

- Divide 123 by 10 = 12

- Compute 12 mod 10 = 2

- Draw 2, shift left a bit

- Divide 12 by 10 = 1

- Compute 1 mod 10 = 1

- Draw 1, shift left a bit

- Divide 1 by 10 = 0

- *Fini!*

Computer science professors love to use this problem as an introduction to modulus arithmetic.

```
public void Draw(long score, Vector2 loc,
  Color color, Justification justify)
    {
        int place = 0;
```

The obnoxiously ugly part is in left-justified text. Drawing and shifting left as necessary is fine, but if we can't draw and shift right, we would get a reverse score. Instead, we apply our divide-by-10 loop to the score to determine the entire string width, shift our draw position *right* by that much, and proceed as normal.

```
        if (justify == Justification.Left)
        {
            loc.X -= 17f;
            long s = score;
            if (s == 0)
                loc.X += 17f;
            else
                while (s > 0)
                {
                    s /= 10;
                    loc.X += 17f;
                }
        }
```

The numbers use the same sprites texture. They start at 0, 224, and their dimensions are 16 × 32.

```
        while (true)
        {
            long digit = score % 10;
            score = score / 10;

            spriteBatch.Draw(spritesTex, loc +
        new Vector2((float)place * -17f, 0f),
                new Rectangle((int)digit * 16, 224, 16, 32),
                color);
            place++;
            if (score <= 0)
                return;
        }
    }
}
```

And that does it for our HUD. We have updating and drawing functionality for health, score, and map transitions. That leaves quite a bit of implementation to do. Let's start with map transitions!

Creating Map Transitions

As we described in Chapter 4, our game world will be made up of map *segments*. When the player walks all the way to the left or right on a map, the previous or subsequent segment will load. An example of a segmented map is shown in Figure 10-3. For the hero in segment 1 to get to the house in segment 4, three map transitions are necessary.

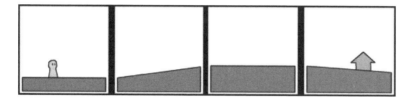

Figure 10-3. *Four map segments*

Designating Segment Transitions

To designate segment transitions, we'll add some scripting to our functionality to define exits and entrances. We'll use the terminology as follows:

Exit: This is the destination map we'll transition to upon hitting a boundary. For instance, if leftexit is map1, we'll transition to map map1 if our player hits the map segment's left boundary. If rightexit is "", there is no right exit.

Entrance: This is the vector for our player when we transition to a new map. For example, if we've just transitioned to map1 by exiting map2 to the left, we'll place our player at the vector defined as rightentrance.

At this point, we'll be using only leftexit, rightexit, leftentrance, rightentrance, and initentrance. We'll use initentrance to define an entrance vector for starting a new game.

New Script Commands

We need to add the new script commands to our MapScript and MapScriptLine classes. First, let's define them in our MapCommands enumeration:

```
enum MapCommands
{
    Fog = 0,
    ...,
    SetLeftExit,
    SetLeftEntrance,
```

```
    SetRightExit,
    SetRightEntrance,
    SetIntroEntrance
}
```

We'll parse them in the `MapScriptLine` constructor. The expected syntax is as follows:

```
setleftexit path
setrightexit path
setleftentrance x y
setrightentrance x y
setleftexit x y
```

It's the usual string-to-constant model, with added attention to the vectors we're using for entrance locations.

```
case "setleftexit":
    Command = MapCommands.SetLeftExit;
    break;
case "setleftentrance":
    Command = MapCommands.SetLeftEntrance;
    VParam = new Vector2(Convert.ToSingle(SParam[1]),
        Convert.ToSingle(SParam[2]));
    break;
case "setrightexit":
    Command = MapCommands.SetRightExit;
    break;
case "setrightentrance":
    Command = MapCommands.SetRightEntrance;
    VParam = new Vector2(Convert.ToSingle(SParam[1]),
        Convert.ToSingle(SParam[2]));
    break;
case "setintroentrance":
    Command = MapCommands.SetIntroEntrance;
    VParam = new Vector2(Convert.ToSingle(SParam[1]),
        Convert.ToSingle(SParam[2]));
    break;
```

Back in `MapScript`, we'll run the new commands. Here are our exits:

```
case MapCommands.SetLeftExit:
    map.TransitionDestination[(int)TransitionDirection.Left] =
        Lines[curLine].SParam[1];
    break;
case MapCommands.SetRightExit:
    map.TransitionDestination[(int)TransitionDirection.Right] =
        Lines[curLine].SParam[1];
    break;
```

In our `Map` class, we'll use an array of enumeration `TransitionDirection` to hold transition destinations. We're also referring to fields that we'll add to `Map`. We'll get to the `Map` updates in the next section.

Let's move on to our entrances:

```
case MapCommands.SetLeftEntrance:
    if (map.TransDir == TransitionDirection.Right)
    {
        c[0].Location = Lines[curLine].VParam;
        c[0].Face = CharDir.Right;
        c[0].SetAnim("fly");
        c[0].State = CharState.Air;
        c[0].Trajectory = new Vector2(200f, 0f);
        map.TransDir = TransitionDirection.None;
    }
    break;
case MapCommands.SetRightEntrance:
    if (map.TransDir == TransitionDirection.Left)
    {
        c[0].Location = Lines[curLine].VParam;
        c[0].Face = CharDir.Left;
        c[0].SetAnim("fly");
        c[0].State = CharState.Air;
        c[0].Trajectory = new Vector2(-200f, 0f);
        map.TransDir = TransitionDirection.None;
    }
    break;
case MapCommands.SetIntroEntrance:
    if (map.TransDir == TransitionDirection.Intro)
    {
        c[0].Location = Lines[curLine].VParam;
        c[0].Face = CharDir.Right;
        c[0].SetAnim("fly");
        c[0].State = CharState.Air;
        c[0].Trajectory = new Vector2(0f, 0f);
        map.TransDir = TransitionDirection.None;
    }
    break;
```

When we set the entrances, we're not actually *setting* anything. We're checking to see what type of transition has just occurred leading up to this latest map initialization. If the transition matches whichever one we're checking for, we'll set the player to the appropriate location, complete with the proper animation, airborne state, and so on.

Map Transition Enum and Fields

Now, a bit out of order, we'll define some of the fields we just talked about at the class level of Map. But first, let's define our enumeration:

```
public enum TransitionDirection : int
{
    None = -1,
    Left = 0,
    Right = 1,
    Intro = 2
}
```

The fields transInFrame and transOutFrame will be used to operate the map transitioning:

```
public float transInFrame = 0f;
public float transOutFrame = 0f;

public string[] transitionDestination = { "", "", "" };

public TransitionDirection TransDir;
```

When we first trigger a transition, transOutFrame will be set to 1, and as transOutFrame decreases to 0, the screen will fade to black. When transOutFrame hits 0, we'll load the new map (which will in turn set the player to the right entrance location), and set transInFrame to 1. As transInFrame decreases to 0, the screen will fade in from black.

Remember the GetTransVal() function we use in HUD to black out the screen? Here it is:

```
public float GetTransVal()
{
    if (transInFrame > 0f)
    {
        return transInFrame;
    }
    if (transOutFrame > 0f)
    {
        return 1 - transOutFrame;
    }
    return 0f;
}
```

We're just returning a value between 0f and 1f, based on transInFrame and transOutFrame.

Checking for Transitions

Now we'll define a function to check if a transition should be triggered. We'll check for transitions based on player index 0's location. If it's at the left boundary, we'll transition left; if it's at the right boundary, we'll transition right. We have also started to correct a mistake that was made in a previous chapter. As we add more and more code that is dependent on the size of the map, we want to move that value into a private variable or two. Here, we define two variables: xSize and ySize, both with a value of 20.

```
public void CheckTransitions(Character[] c)
{
    if (transOutFrame <= 0f && transInFrame <= 0f)
    {
        if (c[0].DyingFrame > 0f)
            return;

        if (c[0].Location.X > xSize * 64f - 32f &&
            c[0].Trajectory.X > 0f)
        {
            if (transitionDestination[(int)TransitionDirection.Right]
                != "")
            {
                transOutFrame = 1f;
                TransDir = TransitionDirection.Right;
            }
        }
        if (c[0].Location.X < 64f + 16f &&
            c[0].Trajectory.X < 0f)
        {
            if (transitionDestination[(int)TransitionDirection.Left]
                  != "")
            {
                transOutFrame = 1f;
                TransDir = TransitionDirection.Left;
            }
        }
    }
}
```

In Map.Update(), we have some extra work to do. We'll need to call CheckTransitions(), of course, and update our transition frames, switching maps if necessary.

```
public void Update(ParticleManager pMan, Character[] c)
{
    CheckTransitions(c);
    if (transOutFrame > 0f)
    {
        transOutFrame -= Game1.FrameTime * 3f;
        if (transOutFrame <= 0f)
        {
            path = TransitionDestination[(int)TransDir];
            Read();
            transInFrame = 1.1f;
            for (int i = 1; i < c.Length; i++)
                c[i] = null;
            pMan.Reset();
```

```
        }
    }
    if (transInFrame > 0f)
    {
        transInFrame -= Game1.FrameTime * 3f;
    }

    if (mapScript.IsReading)
        mapScript.DoScript(c);
```

Uh-oh, looks like we snuck another new method in there. We added `Reset()` to our `ParticleManager` class. It just iterates through all particles, setting each to `null`.

Now we have the map transition functionality in place. However, at this point in development, there's only one map!

Adding a Map

Let's make a new map, and link the two maps together. We created a new one called `start`, as shown in Figure 10-4.

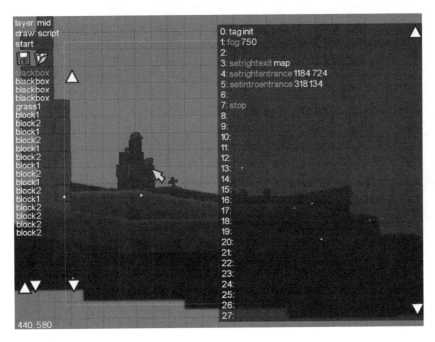

Figure 10-4. *The new start map*

The initialization script for our start map is as follows:

```
tag init
fog 750

setrightexit map
setrightentrance 1184 724
setintroentrance 318 134

stop
```

We're giving the map a right exit, which is map—the first map we created. So, this new start map is basically our starting point. The player can then navigate to the right to get to the map with the zombies.

Now we need to add some transition scripting to map, as shown in Figure 10-5.

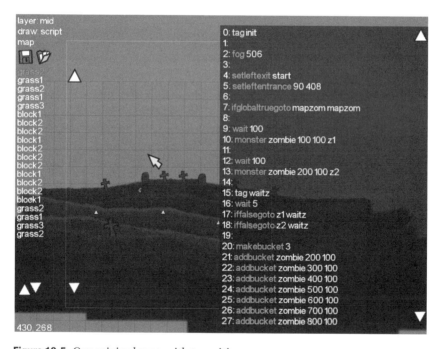

Figure 10-5. *Our original map with transitions*

We'll add a bit to the initialization script for this one:

```
tag init
fog 506

setleftexit start
setleftentrance 90 408
...
```

So, start has map defined as the right exit, and map has start defined as the left exit. Tedious? We got used to it. There are most likely better ways to do it, such as by incorporating adjoining map data into the map definition, rather than the script. However, for a quick solution, this works fairly well. It handled the more than 100 map segments in The Dishwasher: Dead Samurai game easily enough.

Remember that setintroentrance command? We're getting to that main menu!

Adding Menus

We'll create a big fat Menu class to deal with all things menu-related. Our class will have menu functionality in levels—a main level, options level, quit-are-you-sure? level, and so on—where we can be on one level or transitioning from one level to another.

We also want to be able to use our Menu class as a pause menu and a you-are-dead menu. Hitting start while in a game will bring up the menu in pause mode; dying will bring up the menu in dead mode. Each mode will carry certain restrictions. For instance, hitting Start in the main menu is functionally the same as pressing A, but hitting Start in the pause menu will return the player to the game, because Start is meant to work as a pause toggle.

Designing the Menu

We want our menu to look excellent. Figure 10-6 shows a rough sketch of the look we have in mind.

Figure 10-6. *Main renu, rough draft*

Our menu options are at left, slightly staggered. Our hero is at right in a prominent, wrench-wielding pose. In the foreground, we have a zombie hand underfoot.

We'll use a series of layers to do this. Our hero will be one image, as shown in Figure 10-7.

Figure 10-7. *Our hero poses in pose.png*

The black foreground will pan in a slightly more exaggerated way than the hero pose, giving an illusion of depth (it's that crazy parallax again!) Also, we can draw some fog between our hero and the foreground. Figure 10-8 shows the foreground image.

Figure 10-8. *Pose foreground in posefore.png*

On the left side of the menu will be some buttons. While it would be more robust to use a text-drawing class for these buttons, it's a lot easier (and perfectly acceptable) to use images. We put together a sprite sheet, shown in Figure 10-9.

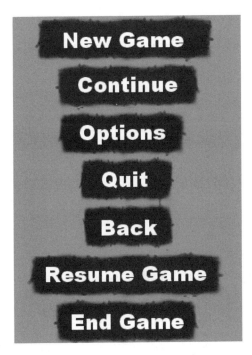

Figure 10-9. *Game options (more to come) in options.png*

We'll set it up to have a layer of smoothly animated fog, a hero, the buttons, another layer of fog, and the foreground, with everything slowly panning left and right in parallax. Figure 10-10 shows what we're going for.

Figure 10-10. *The main menu final product*

Let's get to creating the class.

Creating the Menu Class

We'll start with a rather lengthy list of class-level declarations, dealing with both game logic and render logic.

```
public class Menu
{
```

When transitioning from one level to another, sometimes we want just the buttons to fade out, and sometimes we want everything to fade out. The `Trans` enumeration takes care of that:

```
public enum Trans : int
{
    Buttons = 0,
    All = 1
}
```

Our `Level` enumeration defines all of our menu levels. Some of these aren't literal levels, but indicate a level transition destination. For example, `Main` is a literal level, with options like New Game, Continue, and so on, while `Quit` is just a destination. When we try to transition to the `Quit` level, we simply kill the game.

```
public enum Level : int
{
    Main = 0,
    Options = 1,
    Quit = 2,
    NewGame = 3,
    ResumeGame = 4,
    EndGame = 5,
    Dead = 6
}
```

Our `Option` enumeration defines all possible menu options. Notice an uncanny resemblance between this list and Figure 10-9.

```
public enum Option : int
{
    None = -1,
    NewGame = 0,
    Continue = 1,
    Options = 2,
    Quit = 3,
    Back = 4,
    ResumeGame = 5,
    EndGame = 6
}
```

The `MenuMode` enumeration defines the menu modes we discussed earlier: main, paused, and dead.

```
public enum MenuMode : int
{
    Main = 0,
    Pause = 1,
    Dead = 2
}
```

With our enumerations out of the way, let's use them for something!

We'll use transFrame for level-to-level transitions, transType to define the type of transition going on, and transGoal to specify the destination menu level. Obviously, level is our current menu level. Finally, selItem is the currently selected menu item.

```
public float transFrame = 1f;
public Trans transType = Trans.All;
public Level transGoal;
public Level level = Level.Main;
public int selItem;

Texture2D poseTex;
Texture2D poseForeTex;
Texture2D optionsTex;
Texture2D backTex;
Texture2D spritesTex;
SpriteBatch sprite;
```

While we're using selItem to indicate which item is currently selected, we can keep track of which item had been currently selected on all levels with levelSel[].

```
int[] levelSel = new int[32];
```

We'll use a method called PopulateOptions(), which we'll define later (in the "Option Population" section), to figure out the available options for the particular menu level. For instance, the Main level could have the options New Game, Continue, Options, and Quit; the Dead level will have End Game and Quit. PopulateOptions() will populate option[] and totalOptions. We'll use optionFrame[] to smoothly transition to the selected option.

```
Option[] option = new Option[10];
float[] optionFrame = new float[10];

int totalOptions = 0;
```

For our fog particles, we'll use fog[]. We can calculate each fog particle's location, size, and speed by its index and some snazzy modulus arithmetic.

```
Vector2[] fog = new Vector2[128];
```

We'll use frame for our slow parallax panning.

```
float frame;
```

Because we'll be handling input for the menu as well, we'll need to keep track of previous gamepad states to determine new button presses.

```
GamePadState[] oldState = new GamePadState[4];

public MenuMode menuMode = MenuMode.Main;
```

That should do it for the class-level variables!

Our constructor will set us up with our SpriteBatch and textures, and randomly scatter fog about.

```
public Menu(Texture2D _poseTex,
    Texture2D _poseForeTex,
    Texture2D _optionsTex,
    Texture2D _backTex,
    Texture2D _spritesTex,
    SpriteBatch _sprite)
{
    poseTex = _poseTex;
    poseForeTex = _poseForeTex;
    optionsTex = _optionsTex;
    sprite = _sprite;
    backTex = _backTex;
    spritesTex = _spritesTex;

    for (int i = 0; i < fog.Length; i++)
    {
        fog[i] = Rand.GetRandomVector2(-50f,
            Game1.ScreenSize.X + 50f,
            Game1.ScreenSize.Y - 100f,
            Game1.ScreenSize.Y);
    }
}
```

Updates

Our Update() method comes next. The rundown on what needs to be updated goes as follows:

- Update the frame value.

- Update the menu transition, triggering certain events (such as quitting) as necessary.

- Update fog.

- Update option frames.

- Process input, changing selected items and transitioning as necessary.

We'll call a few methods that we'll define later (par for the course, right?).

```
public void Update(Game1 game)
{
    frame += Game1.FrameTime / 2f;
    if (frame > 6.28f) frame -= 6.28f;
```

When we update transFrame, we're looking at it as 0f. 1f is transitioning out, and 1f - 2f is transitioning in. If the previous frame is less than 1f and the current frame is greater equal than 1f, we set the current level to transGoal. If transGoal is one of those metaphorical levels we discussed (such as Quit), we'll do something.

```
    if (transFrame < 2f)
    {
        float pFrame = transFrame;
        transFrame += Game1.FrameTime;
        if (transType == Trans.Buttons)
            transFrame += Game1.FrameTime;
        if (pFrame < 1f && transFrame >= 1f)
        {
            levelSel[(int)level] = selItem;
            level = transGoal;
            selItem = levelSel[(int)level];
            switch (level)
            {
                case Level.NewGame:
                    game.NewGame();
                    break;
                case Level.ResumeGame:
                    Game1.GameMode = Game1.GameModes.Playing;
                    break;
                case Level.EndGame:
                    menuMode = MenuMode.Main;
                    level = Level.Main;
                    break;
                case Level.Quit:
                    game.Quit();
                    break;
            }
        }
    }
}
```

Next, we'll update the fog. We're updating the vector location by a function of frameTime, and updating the index with a bit of modulus arithmetic applied for a sort of scattered look. When the fog rolls past the left edge of the screen, we give it a new random location beyond the right edge.

```
for (int i = 0; i < fog.Length; i++)
{
    fog[i].X -= Game1.FrameTime * (50f + (float)(i % 20 + 2));
    fog[i].Y += Game1.FrameTime * (float)(i % 14 + 5);
    if (fog[i].X < -150f)
    {
        fog[i].X = Game1.ScreenSize.X +
            Rand.GetRandomFloat(150f, 200f);
        fog[i].Y = Game1.ScreenSize.Y -
            Rand.GetRandomFloat(0f, 300f);
    }
}
```

We'll use optionFrame[] to determine how "selected" each option is. The currently selected option tries to be at 1; the rest try to be at 0.

```
for (int i = 0; i < optionFrame.Length; i++)
{
    if (selItem == i)
    {
        if (optionFrame[i] < 1f)
        {
            optionFrame[i] += Game1.FrameTime * 7f;
            if (optionFrame[i] > 1f) optionFrame[i] = 1f;
        }
    }
    else
    {
        if (optionFrame[i] > 0f)
        {
            optionFrame[i] -= Game1.FrameTime * 4f;
            if (optionFrame[i] < 0f) optionFrame[i] = 0f;
        }
    }
}
```

Now, we'll process input from all gamepads (if applicable). We'll start by calling PopulateOptions(), which will make sure option[] and totalOptions are current with our current menu level.

```
PopulateOptions();

for (int i = 0; i < 4; i++)
{
    GamePadState gs = GamePad.GetState((PlayerIndex)i);
```

If the D-pad or left analog stick is newly pressed Up or Down, we switch selItem to the next or previous item, done here with more modulus arithmetic.

```
        if (totalOptions > 0)
        {
            if ((gs.ThumbSticks.Left.Y > 0.3f &&
                oldState[i].ThumbSticks.Left.Y <= 0.3f) ||
                (gs.DPad.Up == ButtonState.Pressed &&
                oldState[i].DPad.Up == ButtonState.Released))
            {
                selItem = (selItem + (totalOptions - 1))
    % totalOptions;
            }

            if ((gs.ThumbSticks.Left.Y < -0.3f &&
                oldState[i].ThumbSticks.Left.Y >= -0.3f) ||
                (gs.DPad.Down == ButtonState.Pressed &&
                oldState[i].DPad.Down == ButtonState.Released))
            {
                selItem = (selItem + 1) % totalOptions;
            }
        }
```

Finally, we'll process button presses.

For starters, we'll process button presses only if we're nearly fully transitioned in.

We're using the ok value to determine whether a button has been pressed. If the A button is newly pressed, this always is a button press, but if menuMode is Pause, a Start button press will cause the game to resume; otherwise, it will count as a normal button press.

```
        bool ok = false;
        if (transFrame > 1.9f)
        {
            if (gs.Buttons.A == ButtonState.Pressed &&
                oldState[i].Buttons.A == ButtonState.Released)
                ok = true;
            if (gs.Buttons.Start == ButtonState.Pressed &&
                oldState[i].Buttons.Start == ButtonState.Released)
            {
                if (menuMode == MenuMode.Main ||
                    menuMode == MenuMode.Dead)
                    ok = true;
                else
                {
                    Transition(Level.ResumeGame, true);
                }
            }
        }
```

If we have the go-ahead, we'll do a case-by-case analysis and transition accordingly. A lot of this is a bit placeholder, as you'll see.

```
if (ok)
{
    switch (level)
    {
        case Level.Main:
            switch (option[selItem])
            {
                case Option.NewGame:
                    Transition(Level.NewGame, true);
                    break;
                case Option.ResumeGame:
                    Transition(Level.ResumeGame, true);
                    break;
                case Option.EndGame:
                    Transition(Level.EndGame, true);
                    break;
                case Option.Continue:

                    break;
                case Option.Options:
                    Transition(Level.Options);
                    break;
                case Option.Quit:
                    Transition(Level.Quit, true);
                    break;
            }
            break;
        case Level.Dead:
            switch (option[selItem])
            {
                case Option.EndGame:
                    Transition(Level.EndGame, true);
                    break;
                case Option.Quit:
                    Transition(Level.Quit, true);
                    break;
            }
            break;
        case Level.Options:
            switch (option[selItem])
            {
                case Option.Back:
                    Transition(Level.Main);
                    break;
```

```
                    }
                    break;
                }
            }
        }
        oldState[i] = gs;
    }
}
```

Transitions

Here's our `Transition()` function. We're setting our goal, setting `transFrame` to `0f`, and setting our transition type.

```
private void Transition(Level goal)
{
    Transition(goal, false);
}

private void Transition(Level goal, bool all)
{
    transGoal = goal;
    transFrame = 0f;
    if (all)
        transType = Trans.All;
    else
        transType = Trans.Buttons;
}
```

When we get to the drawing, we'll want a function to quickly get the alpha value we'll be using for the options and rest of the scene where the alpha will reflect the current transition values. `GetAlpha()` is the function for the job.

```
private float GetAlpha(bool buttons)
{
    if (!buttons && transType == Trans.Buttons)
        return 1f;
    if (transFrame < 2f)
    {
        if (transFrame < 1f)
            return 1f - transFrame;
        else
            return transFrame - 1f;
    }
    return 1f;
}
```

Drawing

The big Draw() function is up next, starting out like this:

```
public void Draw()
{
    sprite.Begin(SpriteBlendMode.AlphaBlend);
```

It will go as follows:

- Draw the background.

- Draw a layer of fog.

- Draw the hero.

- Draw the options.

- Draw another layer of fog.

- Draw the foreground.

When we draw the background, if we're in main menu mode, we'll draw the background with the moon, looking very much like a background. Otherwise, we'll draw a small rectangle of the background with a low alpha transparency, looking very much like a blue film.

```
if (menuMode == MenuMode.Main)
{
    sprite.Draw(backTex, new Rectangle(0, 0,
        1280, 720), new Color(new Vector4(GetAlpha(false),
        GetAlpha(false), GetAlpha(false), 1f)));
}
else if (menuMode == MenuMode.Pause)
{
    sprite.Draw(backTex, new Rectangle(0, 0,
        1280, 720),
        new Rectangle(600, 400, 200, 200),
        new Color(new Vector4(1f, 1f, 1f, .5f)));
}

sprite.End();
sprite.Begin(SpriteBlendMode.Additive);
```

We're using the pan variable to determine how far to pan everything. It's a cosine function, which means that everything getting panned will sort of slowly sway, a bit like the hearts but without rotating.

We draw the fog as follows:

```
float pan = (float)Math.Cos((double)frame) * 10f + 10f;
for (int i = fog.Length / 2; i < fog.Length; i++)
{
    sprite.Draw(spritesTex, fog[i] + new Vector2(pan, 0f),
        new Rectangle((i % 4) * 64, 0, 64, 64),
        new Color(new Vector4(1f, 1f, 1f,
```

```
.1f * GetAlpha(false))),
        (fog[i].X + fog[i].Y) / 100f,
        new Vector2(32f, 32f),
        (float)(i % 10) * .5f + 2f, SpriteEffects.None, 1f);
}

sprite.End();
sprite.Begin(SpriteBlendMode.AlphaBlend);
```

Next, we'll draw our posing hero. We won't draw him at all in our dead mode (it just wouldn't be appropriate). If we're in the pause mode, we'll draw him as a black silhouette.

```
float poseA = GetAlpha(false);
if (menuMode != MenuMode.Dead)
{
    if (menuMode != MenuMode.Main)
        poseA = 0f;

    sprite.Draw(poseTex,
        new Vector2(Game1.ScreenSize.X -
        (Game1.ScreenSize.Y / 480f) * 380f *
        (.5f * GetAlpha(false) + .5f)
        + (float)Math.Cos((double)frame) * 10f + 10f,
        0f),
        new Rectangle(0, 0, 421, 480),
        new Color(new Vector4(poseA, poseA, poseA, 1f)), 0f,
        new Vector2(), (Game1.ScreenSize.Y / 480f),
        SpriteEffects.None, 1f);
}
```

For the option drawing, we're incorporating optionFrame[] quite a bit. We're using it to nudge options right a bit, rotate them a bit, and tint them red. Unselected options appear with white text and skewed. Selected options appear with red text, straightened, and slightly to the right. Using our optionFrame[] array allows us to smoothly transition between these two modes of appearance.

```
PopulateOptions();

for (int i = 0; i < totalOptions; i++)
{
    sprite.Draw(optionsTex,
        new Vector2(190f + (float)i * 5f + pan +
optionFrame[i] * 10f
        + GetAlpha(true) * 50f,
        300f + (float)i * 64f - (float)totalOptions * 32f),
        new Rectangle(0, (int)option[i] * 64, 320, 64),
new Color(
        new Vector4(1f, 1f - optionFrame[i],
```

```
    1f - optionFrame[i], GetAlpha(true))),
            (1f - optionFrame[i]) * -.1f,
  new Vector2(160f, 32f), 1f, SpriteEffects.None, 1f);
      }



    sprite.End();
```

If we're not in dead mode, draw the second layer of fog and foreground graphic:

```
    if (menuMode != MenuMode.Dead)
    {
        sprite.Begin(SpriteBlendMode.Additive);


        pan *= 2f;
        for (int i = 0; i < fog.Length / 2; i++)
        {
            sprite.Draw(spritesTex, fog[i] + new Vector2(pan, 0f),
                new Rectangle((i % 4) * 64, 0, 64, 64),
                new Color(new Vector4(1f, 1f, 1f,
.1f * GetAlpha(false))),
                (fog[i].X + fog[i].Y) / 100f,
                new Vector2(32f, 32f),
                (float)(i % 10) * .5f + 2f,
SpriteEffects.None, 1f);
        }

        sprite.End();
        sprite.Begin(SpriteBlendMode.AlphaBlend);

        sprite.Draw(poseForeTex,
            new Vector2(Game1.ScreenSize.X - (Game1.ScreenSize.Y
  / 480f) * 616f * GetAlpha(false)
            + (float)Math.Cos((double)frame) * 20f + 20f,
            Game1.ScreenSize.Y - (Game1.ScreenSize.Y / 480f)
  * 286f),
            new Rectangle(0, 0, 616, 286),
            new Color(new Vector4(GetAlpha(false),
            GetAlpha(false), GetAlpha(false), 1f)), 0f,
            new Vector2(), (Game1.ScreenSize.Y / 480f),
SpriteEffects.None, 1f);

        sprite.End();
    }
}
```

Options Population

Now, let's take a look at our `PopulateOptions()` method. It's just a bunch of cases again. The only odd bit is for the main level: if we're in pause mode, our main level will be a bit different than for the other modes.

```
private void PopulateOptions()
{
    for (int i = 0; i < option.Length; i++)
        option[i] = Option.None;

    switch (level)
    {
        case Level.Main:
            if (menuMode == MenuMode.Pause)
            {
                option[0] = Option.ResumeGame;
                option[1] = Option.EndGame;
                option[2] = Option.Options;
                option[3] = Option.Quit;
                totalOptions = 4;
            }
            else
            {
                option[0] = Option.NewGame;
                option[1] = Option.Continue;
                option[2] = Option.Options;
                option[3] = Option.Quit;
                totalOptions = 4;
            }
            break;
        case Level.Options:
            option[0] = Option.Back;
            totalOptions = 1;
            break;
        case Level.Dead:
            option[0] = Option.EndGame;
            option[1] = Option.Quit;
            totalOptions = 2;
            break;
        default:
            totalOptions = 0;
            break;
    }
}
```

Pausing and Dying

We'll be using the `Pause()` and `Die()` methods from elsewhere in our game to set all of the appropriate flags to pause or go into you-are-dead mode.

```
public void Pause()
{
    menuMode = MenuMode.Pause;
    Game1.GameMode = Game1.GameModes.Menu;

    transFrame = 1f;
    level = Level.Main;
    transType = Trans.All;
}

public void Die()
{
    menuMode = MenuMode.Dead;
    Game1.GameMode = Game1.GameModes.Menu;

    transFrame = 1f;
    level = Level.Dead;
    transType = Trans.All;
}

}
```

That concludes our big bad `Menu` class. We've done a lot of coding this chapter, but it has all been fairly simple, using techniques that are definitely not new. We are going to keep going, because we need to clean up and update our current classes before we run the game.

Updating the Game

We need to plug everything in to `Game1`, and we also need to sort out some stuff.

Adding the HUD and Menu to the Game

We'll start at the class level of `Game1` by declaring our `HUD` and `Menu`. We also need a new enumeration called `GameModes`, which we'll use to define the current state: playing or at the menu. Remember that paused and dead count as being in the menu.

```
HUD hud;

public enum GameModes : int
{
    Menu = 0,
    Playing = 1
}
```

```
private static Menu menu;
private static long score = 0;
private static GameModes gameMode;

public static GameModes GameMode
{
    get { return gameMode; }
    set { gameMode = value; }
}

public static Menu Menu
{
    get { return menu; }
    set { menu = value; }
}

public static long Score
{
    get { return score; }
    set { score = value; }
}
```

From Menu.Update(), we called NewGame() and Quit(). Let's define them next.

NewGame() clears all characters and particles, sets the map path to start, resets the map flags, reads the map, sets the map transition direction to Intro, and tells the map that it is transitioning in. When the map is loaded and the game mode switches over to GameMode.Playing, our setintroentrance command will see that we are in a TransitionDirection.Intro transition and plant our new character at the intro location we gave it.

```
public void NewGame()
{
    gameMode = GameModes.Playing;

    character[0]
        = new Character(new Vector2(100f, 100f),
        CharDefs[(int)CharacterDefinitions.Guy],
        0,
        Character.TEAM_GOOD_GUYS);
    character[0].HP = character[0].MHP = 100;
    for (int i = 1; i < character.Length; i++)
        character[i] = null;

    pManager.Reset();
    map.Path = "start";
    map.GlobalFlags = new MapFlags(64);
    map.Read();
    map.TransDir = TransitionDirection.Intro;
    map.transInFrame = 1f;
```

```
}

public void Quit()
{
    this.Exit();
}
```

In LoadContent(), we'll create our new Menu and HUD, sending them all of the right textures. Since we won't need our pose, pose foreground, and options textures elsewhere, we can load them directly in the constructor, rather than loading them in the Game1 scope and passing a reference.

```
nullTex = Content.Load<Texture2D>(@"gfx/1x1");

menu = new Menu(
    Content.Load<Texture2D>(@"gfx/pose"),
    Content.Load<Texture2D>(@"gfx/posefore"),
    Content.Load<Texture2D>(@"gfx/options"),
    mapBackTex[0],
    spritesTex,
    spriteBatch);

hud = new HUD(spriteBatch, spritesTex, nullTex, character, map);
```

Next, we need to do some reorganizing.

Reorganizing the Code

We previously updated all of the game logic in Update() and all of the game-drawing logic in Draw(). However, now that we have two game modes, we need some more complicated cases to determine whether we want to update game logic or draw the game, so let's move the code into UpdateGame() and DrawGame(), respectively.

The UpdateGame() method (well, most of it) looks like this:

```
private void UpdateGame()
{
    scroll += ((character[0].loc -
        new Vector2(400f, 400f)) - scroll) * frameTime * 20f;
    ...

    if (scroll.Y > yLim) scroll.Y = yLim;

    if (map.transOutFrame <= 0f)
    {
        pManager.UpdateParticles(frameTime, map, character);

        if (character[0] != null)
        {
```

```
            ...
        }
        for (int i = 0; i < character.Length; i++)
        {
            if (character[i] != null)
            {
                character[i].Update(map, pManager, character);
                if (character[i].dyingFrame > 1f)
                {
                    ...
                }
            }
        }
    }

    map.Update(pManager, character);
    hud.Update();
}
```

The basic functionality is the same as the code lifted from Update(), but we won't be updating the particles or characters if the map is transitioning out. Otherwise, we would be able to walk to the edge, trigger a transition, and start walking back in the opposite direction, which would look all wrong! Also, we added a hud.Update() at the end.

Similarly, DrawGame() takes a big chunk from Draw(). The only change we're doing for now is to draw the main screen a bit darker if we're paused or dead. When we start playing with shaders in the next chapter, we'll be able to draw the main screen in a grayscale or sepia tone if the pause menu is overlaid.

```
private void DrawGame()
{
    graphics.GraphicsDevice.SetRenderTarget(0, mainTarget);
    graphics.GraphicsDevice.Clear(Color.Black);

    map.Draw(spriteBatch, mapsTex, mapBackTex, 0, 2);

    ...

    graphics.GraphicsDevice.SetRenderTarget(0, null);

    spriteBatch.Begin(SpriteBlendMode.None);
    spriteBatch.Draw(mainTarget.GetTexture(), new Vector2(),
        (gameMode == GameModes.Menu ? Color.Gray : Color.White));
    spriteBatch.End();
```

```
    spriteBatch.Begin(SpriteBlendMode.AlphaBlend);
    if (QuakeManager.blast.val > 0f)
    {
        ...
    }
    spriteBatch.End();
}
```

Now that we've extracted some important functionality from Update() and Draw(), we need to sort things out within these methods. The sound-updating and frameTime-calculating stuff is the same, but if we're in you-are-dead menu mode, we still want to update the game, albeit slightly slower.

```
protected override void Update(GameTime gameTime)
{

    Sound.Update();
    Music.Play("music1");
    QuakeManager.Update();

    frameTime = (float)gameTime.ElapsedGameTime.TotalSeconds;

    if (slowTime > 0f)
    {
        slowTime -= frameTime;
        frameTime /= 10f;
    }

    switch (gameMode)
    {
        case GameModes.Playing:
            UpdateGame();

            break;
        case GameModes.Menu:
            if (menu.menuMode == Menu.MenuMode.Dead)
            {
                float pTime = frameTime;
                frameTime /= 3f;
                UpdateGame();

                frameTime = pTime;
            }
            menu.Update(this);
            break;
    }

    base.Update(gameTime);
}
```

Our Draw() method shrinks a bit, too. If we're playing the game, we'll draw the game and then draw the HUD. If we're in menu mode, we'll draw the menu. If it's a pause or dead menu, we'll make sure the game gets drawn under it. We need to draw the HUD only while we're playing the game. If the HUD is shown while the pause or dead menu is up, the interface gets a bit crowded.

```
protected override void Draw(GameTime gameTime)
{
    graphics.GraphicsDevice.Clear(Color.Black);

    switch (gameMode)
    {
        case GameModes.Playing:
            DrawGame();
            hud.Draw();
            break;
        case GameModes.Menu:
            if (menu.menuMode == Menu.MenuMode.Pause ||
                menu.menuMode == Menu.MenuMode.Dead)
                DrawGame();
            menu.Draw();
            break;
    }

    base.Draw(gameTime);
}
```

This should complete the vicious cycle we've just introduced. We now have a pause screen, as shown in Figure 10-11. We also have a you-are-dead screen, as shown in Figure 10-12.

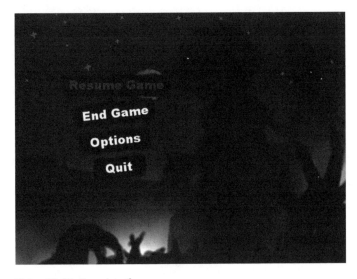

Figure 10-11. *Pausing the game*

Figure 10-12. *After death*

Lastly, and compared to the rest of this, certainly least, we should implement some sort of functionality for scoring.

Scoring

We'll add some fairly basic scoring functionality. Since score is a public static in Game1, it's simple enough to set from anywhere. We'll be setting it from Character.KillMe() and from HitManager.CheckHit().

Also, we need to add a new field to Character at the class level:

```
public int LastHitBy = -1;
```

A Character can use this to determine who hit him last.

In HitManager, after we've determined a successful hit, we'll set lastHitBy to the index of the hit owner.

```
if (c[i].InHitBounds(p.Location))
{
    float hVal = 1f;

    c[i].LastHitBy = p.Owner;
```

Further down, after we've fully calculated hVal, we'll add some points (50 times hVal) to the static score value if the hit owner index is 0.

```
if (c[i].LastHitBy == 0)
    Game1.Score += (int)hVal * 50;
```

In Character, we'll add more to the score if the character was last hit by character index 0.

```
public void KillMe()
{
    if (DyingFrame < 0f)
    {
        DyingFrame = 0f;
        if (LastHitBy == 0)
            Game1.Score += MHP * 50;
    }
}
```

There we have it—scoring is implemented! Our final product is shown in Figure 10-13.

Figure 10-13. *In-game scoring*

■**Note** Scoring in The Dishwasher game used a fairly complicated combo system. Any points scored would feed into a combo score, and combo hits and kills would increase the combo multiplier. Once a combo ended, the combo score would be multiplied by the combo multiplier, and the final score would be added to the main player score (think Tony Hawk with buckets of blood). It added a lot of strategy to the combat for players seeking the best scores. For our Zombie Smashers XNA game, we'll leave it up to you to implement more complex scoring, if that interests you.

Deploying to Xbox 360

Let's tackle the fun part: trying the game on Xbox 360. For this, we'll need to create a new project and connect the Xbox 360 to XNA Game Studio.

If you have not yet purchased a Creators Club Premium Membership (required to deploy to Xbox 360), you can do so at http://creators.xna.com/en-US/membership. You'll be required to have a Gamertag and at least a four-month subscription (currently $49).

Creating the Xbox 360 Project

To begin, right-click the ZombieSmashers project in Solution Explorer and select Create Copy of Project for Xbox 360, as shown in Figure 10-14. You'll see a dialog informing you that you'll have two separate projects to maintain now; click OK. A new Xbox 360 project is created.

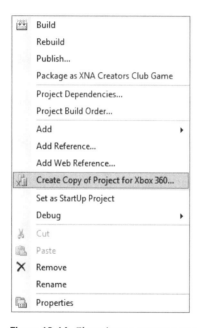

Figure 10-14. *Choosing to create a copy of the project for Xbox 360*

We were a bit put off by the prospect of maintaining two separate projects, but warmed up to it in time. The files referenced by both projects are the same, and both share a Content project, so the inconvenience of keeping both projects current typically comes down to a few rounds of refreshing Solution Explorer with Show All Files enabled, and adding all of the classes and folders that were newly added in the other project.

Visual Studio creates the new project as Xbox 360 Copy of ZombieSmashers. We renamed it to ZombieSmashers360. Right-click the new project and select Set as StartUp Project. The Solution Platforms drop-down list should show x86. Change this to Xbox 360, as shown in Figure 10-15.

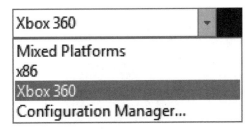

Figure 10-15. *Choosing Xbox 360 as the solution platform*

Connecting to the XBox 360

Now you need to add the Xbox 360 to the Device Center. In the XNA Game Studio Device Management 2.0 toolbar, click Add New Device. You're prompted to enter a device name, as shown in Figure 10-16.

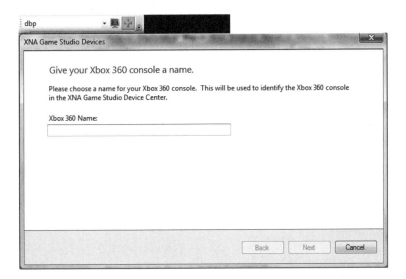

Figure 10-16. *Adding a new device*

At this point, jog (or swivel) over to your Xbox 360. You'll need to download an application called XNA Game Studio Connect.

On your Xbox 360, sign in with your Live-enabled account and navigate to the Marketplace. Select Game Store ➤ All Games ➤ XNA Creators Club. Select and download XNA Game Studio Connect.

After your download is finished, navigate to the Games blade, select Games Library ➤ My Games, and find and launch XNA Game Studio Connect. You'll see a connection key, as shown in Figure 10-17.

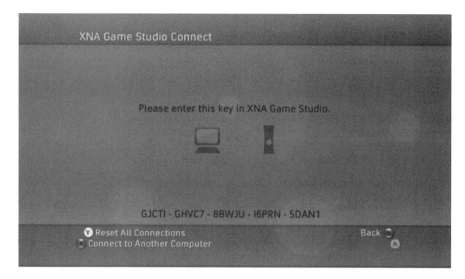

Figure 10-17. *Running XNA Game Studio Connect*

Jog (or swivel) back to your computer. Give your Xbox 360 a name and click Next. You're prompted to enter a connection key, as shown in Figure 10-18. Plug in the numbers from XNA Game Studio Connect and click Next. You should see a dialog saying that you're ready to go.

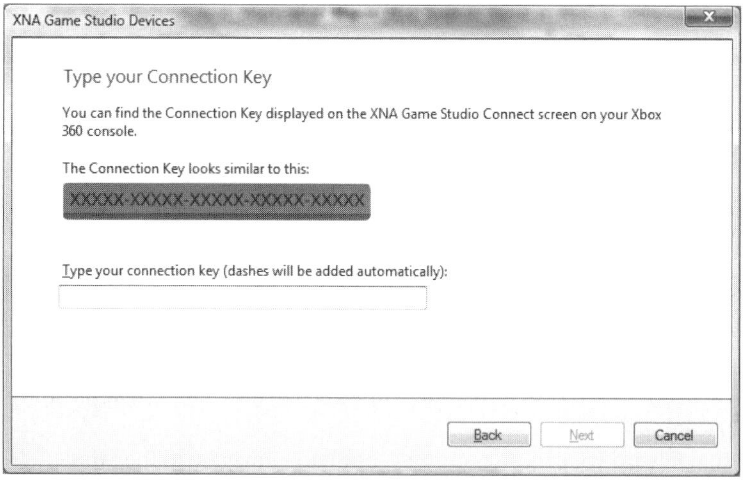

Figure 10-18. *You'll need to enter the connection key from XNA Game Studio Connect.*

This is a 99% painless process. If you're using some old analog TV for your Xbox 360 (we use one of these as a minimum setup test), the numbers on the screen will require a bit of squinting to decipher—watch out for the zeros and *O* characters, and the ones and *I* characters.

Assuming you hit no snags, you should be good to go.

Debugging

Click Debug or press F5, and jog (or swivel) back to your Xbox 360. If all went according to plan, you should have Zombie Smashers running like a dream on your Xbox 360.

While debugging code on Xbox 360, you can still break and step from your computer, but you won't be able to make code changes. We tend to use pause, code, resume programming as a total crutch. Usually (particularly earlier on), we'll do 99% of the development work on Windows, switching over to Xbox 360 every couple of days to make sure we didn't royally screw anything up. What can be royally screwed up? The big ones for us have been the safe zone and garbage collection.

The *safe zone* is easy enough to work with. It's the region of a screen that is viewable on even the cheapest TV: 80% of the entire screen is usually safe; anything beyond 90% is almost assuredly cut out. On the TV we used to test Zombie Smashers, the hearts were entirely in frame, but by a thread. It wouldn't hurt to bump them a little farther into the frame.

Garbage collection (GC), on the other hand, is something we've lost sleep over. While Windows can run GC frequently and with relative ease, Xbox 360 really chokes on GC. It's not uncommon to see GC take more than 1000 ms, during which time the game is basically frozen. It breaks up action a bit!

■**Note** Through our first experience with GC, we discovered that a bitmap-based text renderer class we made was the culprit. The class would call ToCharArray() on whatever string it was to render each time, and then evidently the char array would be flagged as garbage. Rendering at 60 fps and drawing half a dozen strings per frame would lead to those nasty 1000+ ms GC calls every minute or so.

You can use the XNA Framework Remote Performance Monitor for Xbox 360 (available on the Start ➤ XNA Game Studio 2.0 ➤ Tools menu) to track collections for clues on when and how much garbage is being produced. However, what we've found to be really helpful is the CLR Profiler.

The CLR Profiler for the .NET Framework 2.0 is a free application available for download from Microsoft.com. If you use it to launch the x86 binary (it's in ZombieSmashersXna/bin/x86), you'll end up with an enormous (gigabytes, not megabytes) log file, detailing pretty much everything that ever occurred since launch. In the Summary section, you can view a timeline of GC statistics; navigate through all manner of graphs, histograms, and timelines; and, with any luck, root out GC-related problems.

Still, garbage generation is typically inevitable. What you don't want is *a lot* of garbage; a little you can handle. In order to keep the inevitable bit of garbage low, you can force a collection at an opportune time, using GC.Collect(). In The Dishwasher, GC is forced every time a new map is loaded, allowing collection of any garbage that is inadvertently generated without disrupting game play too much. This is actually a preferred technique, because rather than introducing interruptions into the game play, you can force a larger interruption when the player is used to sitting around and waiting. The worst thing you could do is have consistent or large pauses in the middle of game play.

Conclusion

Our primary focus of this chapter was the game interface. We set up the HUD, created a quick yet somewhat robust menuing system, and rearranged things to work with this new setup. And, as is usually the case, we added an assortment of supporting functionality, like scoring and map transitions.

We also jumped into Xbox 360 deployment, both the process (which is quite simple) and some of the more problematic considerations of console deployment. We briefly looked at some strategies and tools to use when tackling deployment issues. And by deployment issues, we're talking about terrible, horrible, no-good, very bad GC. For information about storage on Xbox 360, check out Appendix B.

In the next chapter, we'll be covering some fun graphics effects.

CHAPTER 11

■■■

Postprocessing Effects
Some Graphical Glitz

Let's be honest: right now, our game is pretty dull in the graphics department. Of course, considering that we're creating a 2D game, there's only so much we can do, but there's still a lot of fun to be had. We can add effects like color filters (black and white, sepia tone, and so on), blurring, bloom, and water.

We'll use pixel shaders to generate these effects. Pixel shaders—once scary, inaccessible, complicated bits of programming—are quite easy to work with in XNA Game Studio 2.0.

Here's what we'll be doing:

- Create a color filter effect.

- Modify our main game logic to load and implement the color filter.

- Implement a water effect (must be implemented in the map script as well).

- Add refract effects (must be implemented as a type of particle).

The Absolute Minimum You Need to Know About Pixel Shaders

Very large books have been (and are still being) written about shaders. They're created by a very comprehensive and potentially complicated technology that provides the means to add huge amounts of depth to rich 3D environments. Here, we'll just be scratching the surface of this technology.

We'll be writing a very simple pixel shader, which we'll refer to as an *effect*. Our effect will take as input a texture and an input coordinate, and output a single pixel. This means that our effect program will be run on *every single pixel* that we draw to the screen. For example, here is the pseudocode for producing a photographic negative effect:

```
float4 color = Input Texture at Input coordinate x, y
return 1 - color
```

This simple effect would give us a game that looked like the image shown in Figure 11-1 (what it lacks in appeal it makes up for in educational value).

Figure 11-1. *Photographic negative effect*

And really, that's all the background you should need. So, let's get started on a shader.

Color Filter Effects

Our game is written with the C# programming language. Shaders, on the other hand, are written in the High Level Shading Language (HLSL) programming language. It's a lot like C#. Let's take a look at the code for the negative effect you see in Figure 11-1:

```
//negative.fx
sampler samplerState;

struct PS_INPUT
{
    float2 TexCoord : TEXCOORD0;
};

float4 Neg(PS_INPUT Input) : COLOR0
{
    float4 col = tex2D(samplerState, Input.TexCoord.xy);
    col.rgb = 1 - col.rgb;
    return col;
}
```

```
technique Negative
{
    pass P0
    {
        PixelShader = compile ps_2_0 Neg();
    }
}
```

From the get-go, it looks fairly cryptic. But if you examine it, you'll see that all of the functionality of the pseudocode is within the second pair of curly brackets:

```
float4 Neg(PS_INPUT Input) : COLOR0
{
    ...
}
```

Our Neg() function returns a float4, which is how we refer to colors in our shader program. The function accepts our defined PS_INPUT struct as input, which sets us up with the correct texture coordinates. Our input texture is samplerState. The functionality, just as in the pseudocode, involves grabbing the float4 color from the input texture at the input texture coordinate, calculating one minus the color's RGB value, and returning the result. That's some heavy math!

The technique Negative function sets up our techniques and passes for the shader. When we call it from our program, we can specify which pass of which technique we'll be using. For simplicity's sake, we will use only one technique with one pass per shader file.

Add this file as negative.fx in the ZombieSmashers Content project, under an fx folder.

To load it into ZombieSmashers, we'll start by declaring the Effect object in the Game1 class level:

```
Effect negEffect;
```

In LoadContent(), we'll use the content manager to load our effect:

```
negEffect = Content.Load<Effect>(@"fx/negative");
```

Moving along, we'll modify our DrawGame() function. Currently, there is a block that looks like this:

```
graphics.GraphicsDevice.SetRenderTarget(0, null);

spriteBatch.Begin(SpriteBlendMode.None);
spriteBatch.Draw(mainTarget.GetTexture(), new Vector2(),
    (gameMode == GameMode.Menu ? Color.Gray : Color.White));
spriteBatch.End();
```

A fairly commonly used effect is to draw the game with a different shader—like blurred or low saturation—when the pause menu is drawn over it. No one ever uses the negative, so let's start a trend. We'll modify the block like this:

```
if (gameMode == GameMode.Menu)
{
    negEffect.Begin();
```

```
        spriteBatch.Begin(SpriteBlendMode.None,
                        SpriteSortMode.Immediate,
                        SaveStateMode.SaveState);
        EffectPass pass = negEffect.CurrentTechnique.Passes[0];
        pass.Begin();
        spriteBatch.Draw(mainTarget.GetTexture(),
                        Vector2.Zero, Color.White);
        pass.End();
        spriteBatch.End();
        negEffect.End();
    }
    else
    {
        spriteBatch.Begin(SpriteBlendMode.None);

        spriteBatch.Draw(mainTarget.GetTexture(),
                        Vector2.Zero, Color.White);

        spriteBatch.End();
    }
```

The final product, as shown in Figure 11-2, is interesting, though probably not one we'll keep.

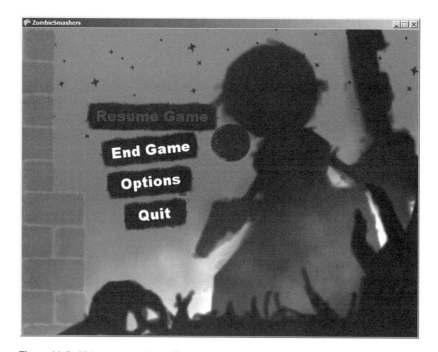

Figure 11-2. *Using a negative effect in our pause menu*

A Blurry Grayscale Pause Effect

Let's create a better-looking pause effect. Our pause effect will blur the image by combining each pixel with its neighbors, and then compute the grayscale by averaging the RGB values. Here's the code:

```
//pause.fx
sampler samplerState;
```

We'll use an array of float2's (basically the same thing as a Vector2) as a lookup table to store the offsets for our neighbors—it will basically save us a lot of trig calculations.

```
const float2 offsets[12] =
{
    -0.326212, -0.405805,
    -0.840144, -0.073580,
    -0.695914,  0.457137,
    -0.203345,  0.620716,
     0.962340, -0.194983,
     0.473434, -0.480026,
     0.519456,  0.767022,
     0.185461, -0.893124,
     0.507431,  0.064425,
     0.896420,  0.412458,
    -0.321940, -0.932615,
    -0.791559, -0.597705,
};


struct PS_INPUT
{
    float2 TexCoord : TEXCOORD0;
};
```

For our main function, we'll sum all of our neighbors' color values, compute the average of the sum's RGB values, turning it into a grayscale sum, and then compute the average of the grayscale sum and return that value as the new color's RGB value.

```
float4 Pause(PS_INPUT Input) : COLOR0
{
    float4 col = 0;
    for (int i = 0; i < 12; i++)
    {
        col += tex2D(samplerState, Input.TexCoord + 0.005 *
            offsets[i]);
    }
    float a = (col.r + col.g + col.b) / 3.0f;
    a /= 12.0f;

    col.rgb = a;
```

```
        return col;
}

technique PauseTechnique
{
    pass P0
    {
        PixelShader = compile ps_2_0 Pause();
    }
}
```

Let's plug it in. Just as with the negative effect, create a new Effect in the Game1 class level as pauseEffect, load it in LoadContent(), and in Game1.DrawGame(), change all instances of negEffect to pauseEffect. Our pause screen should now look like Figure 11-3.

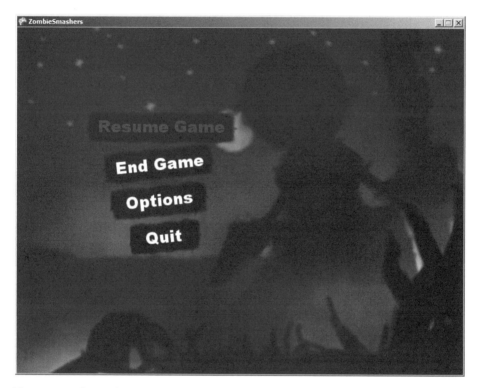

Figure 11-3. *Blur and grayscale in a pause effect*

This is a much more fitting look for our pause screen. It's official: we're next-gen!

Blurry grayscale pause menu? Check. What else do we need? Why, bloom and earth tones, of course!

A Little Bloom Never Hurt Anyone

For our bloom effect file, we'll use a strategy similar to what we used with our pause effect. We'll average a pixel with its neighbors and return the value with a reduced alpha. Also, we're using the parameter v to determine how far we'll reach out when comparing a pixel with its neighbors.

Parameters declared at the class level of an HLSL file can be changed on the fly from the game—from Game1 in our case. We can set v from Game1 to give us a pulsing bloom effect. Here's the file:

```
//bloom.fx

sampler samplerState;

float v = 0.01f;
float a = 0.25f;

const float2 offsets[12] = {
    -0.326212, -0.405805,
    -0.840144, -0.073580,
    -0.695914,  0.457137,
    -0.203345,  0.620716,
     0.962340, -0.194983,
     0.473434, -0.480026,
     0.519456,  0.767022,
     0.185461, -0.893124,
     0.507431,  0.064425,
     0.896420,  0.412458,
    -0.321940, -0.932615,
    -0.791559, -0.597705,
};

struct PS_INPUT
{
    float2 TexCoord : TEXCOORD0;
};

float4 Bloom(PS_INPUT Input) : COLOR0
{
    float4 col = tex2D(samplerState, Input.TexCoord);
    for (int i = 0; i < 12; i++)
        col += tex2D(samplerState, Input.TexCoord + v *
            offsets[i]);

    col /= 13.0f;
    col.a = a;
```

```
        return col;
}

technique BloomTechnique
{
    pass P0
    {
        PixelShader = compile ps_2_0 Bloom();
    }
}
```

From `Game1`, our strategy for using the effect will be a little complex. Our previous loop looked like this:

- Set render target to `mainTarg`

- Draw the game

- Set render target to backbuffer

- Draw `mainTarg`

- Draw HUD

- Present

Our new loop will look like this (new bits are italicized):

- Set render target to `mainTarg`

- Draw the game

- *Set render target to* `bloomTarg[0]`

- *Draw* `mainTarg` *with bloom effect*

- *Set render target to* `bloomTarg[1]`

- *Draw* `mainTarg` *with bloom effect*

- *Set render target to* `gameTarg`

- *Draw* `mainTarg`

- *Draw* `bloomTarg[0]`

- *Draw* `bloomTarg[1]`

- Set render target to backbuffer

- Draw `gameTarg`

- Draw HUD

- Present

When we create `bloomTarg` in `LoadContent()`, we'll create the two surfaces with the following code:

```
bloomTarget = new RenderTarget2D[2];
bloomTarget[0] =
    new RenderTarget2D(GraphicsDevice,
    128, 128, 1, SurfaceFormat.Color);
bloomTarget[1] =
    new RenderTarget2D(GraphicsDevice,
    256, 256, 1, SurfaceFormat.Color);
```

This gives us a 128×128 render target and a 256×256 render target.

We'll be changing `DrawGame()` around a bit. We'll use a `float[]` called `bloomPulse` to determine how far each pixel will reach out when looking for neighbors; as v increases and decreases, glowing objects will have a pulsing effect. We're using two bloom targets to give a smoother effect.

```
private void DrawGame()
{
    graphics.GraphicsDevice.SetRenderTarget(0, mainTarget);
    graphics.GraphicsDevice.Clear(Color.Black);

    ...

    map.Draw(spriteBatch, mapsTex, mapBackTex, 2, 3);

    for (int i = 0; i < 2; i++)
    {
        graphics.GraphicsDevice.SetRenderTarget(0, bloomTarget[i]);

        bloomEffect.Parameters["a"].SetValue(.25f);
        bloomEffect.Parameters["v"].SetValue((float)(i + 1) * 0.01f *
            ((float)Math.Cos((double)bloomPulse[i]) * .25f + 0.7f));
        bloomEffect.Begin();
        spriteBatch.Begin(SpriteBlendMode.None,
            SpriteSortMode.Immediate,
            SaveStateMode.SaveState);
        EffectPass pass = bloomEffect.CurrentTechnique.Passes[0];
        pass.Begin();

        spriteBatch.Draw(mainTarget.GetTexture(),
            new Rectangle(0, 0, 128 * (i + 1), 128 * (i + 1)),
            Color.White);

        pass.End();
        spriteBatch.End();
        bloomEffect.End();
    }
```

```
graphics.GraphicsDevice.SetRenderTarget(0, gameTarget);

if (gameMode == GameMode.Menu)
{
    ...
}
else
{
    spriteBatch.Begin(SpriteBlendMode.None);

    spriteBatch.Draw(mainTarget.GetTexture(), new Vector2(),
        Color.White);

    spriteBatch.End();
```

We'll overlay our bloom targets with additive blending:

```
    spriteBatch.Begin(SpriteBlendMode.Additive);

    for (int i = 0; i < 2; i++)
        spriteBatch.Draw(bloomTarget[i].GetTexture(),
        new Rectangle(0, 0, (int)ScreenSize.X,
        (int)ScreenSize.Y), Color.White);

    spriteBatch.End();
}

graphics.GraphicsDevice.SetRenderTarget(0, null);

spriteBatch.Begin(SpriteBlendMode.None);

spriteBatch.Draw(gameTarget.GetTexture(), Vector2.Zero,
    Color.White);

spriteBatch.End();
spriteBatch.Begin(SpriteBlendMode.AlphaBlend);

if (QuakeManager.blast.val > 0f)
{
    for (int i = 7; i >= 0; i--)
    {
        spriteBatch.Draw(gameTarget.GetTexture(),
            ...
    }
}

spriteBatch.End();
}
```

In UpdateGame(), we'll update our bloomPulse values. If we do them both at different rates, we get a more natural-looking bloom pulse:

```
bloomPulse[0] += frameTime * .5f;
bloomPulse[1] += frameTime * .9f;
for (int i = 0; i < bloomPulse.Length; i++)
    if (bloomPulse[i] > 6.28f) bloomPulse[i] -= 6.28f;
```

Our restructured render loop will produce the image shown in Figure 11-4.

Figure 11-4. *Bloom!*

Earth Tones

For our official earth tones, we'll create a simple yet robust color filter that will allow us to tune RGB, saturation, brightness, and "burn." For those unfamiliar with color terms (particularly the one we made up at the end), here's the rundown:

RGB: The red, green, and blue channels of a color. Our shader will multiply existing RGB values by the input color.

Saturation: The dominance of hue in a color. Think of low saturation as grayscale and high saturation as vibrant color.

Brightness: The overall value added to the image. We can use negative numbers to darken the image. A positive value will turn black into dark gray.

Burn: The amount to which color is degraded toward the edges of an image. This gives the image an old film, moody look.

Here's the code for `filter.fx`:

```
//filter.fx
sampler samplerState;

float burn = 0.01f;
float saturation = 1.0f;
float r = 1.0f;
float g = 1.0f;
float b = 1.0f;
float brite = 0.0f;

struct PS_INPUT
{
    float2 TexCoord : TEXCOORD0;
};

float4 Filter(PS_INPUT Input) : COLOR0
{
    float4 col = tex2D(samplerState, Input.TexCoord.xy);
    float2 tex = Input.TexCoord;
    float d = sqrt(pow((tex.x - 0.5), 2) + pow((tex.y - 0.5), 2));

    col.rgb -= d * burn;
        float a = col.r + col.g + col.b;
    a /= 3.0f;
        a *= 1.0f - saturation;
        col.r = (col.r * saturation + a) * r;
    col.g = (col.g * saturation + a) * g;
    col.b = (col.b * saturation + a) * b;
        col.rgb += brite;
        return col;
}

technique Filter
{
    pass P0
    {
        PixelShader = compile ps_2_0 Filter();
    }
}
```

Then we'll hook it up to DrawGame(), right after we draw our pause screen.

```
else
{
```

We'll set our filter effect parameters first. We'll do a slight amount of burn, very low saturation (nearly black and white), a slightly reddish tint, and a bit of a bump in brightness.

```
filterEffect.Parameters["burn"].SetValue(.15f);
filterEffect.Parameters["saturation"].SetValue(0.05f);
filterEffect.Parameters["r"].SetValue(1.0f);
filterEffect.Parameters["g"].SetValue(0.98f);
filterEffect.Parameters["b"].SetValue(0.85f);
filterEffect.Parameters["brite"].SetValue(0.05f);

filterEffect.Begin();
spriteBatch.Begin(SpriteBlendMode.None, SpriteSortMode.Immediate,
    SaveStateMode.SaveState);
EffectPass pass = filterEffect.CurrentTechnique.Passes[0];
pass.Begin();

spriteBatch.Draw(mainTarget.GetTexture(),
    new Vector2(), Color.White);

pass.End();
spriteBatch.End();
filterEffect.End();

spriteBatch.Begin(SpriteBlendMode.Additive);
```

We'll end up with what you see in Figure 11-5. We call this the *Gears-eriffic* color filter. It won't be very evident in a black-and-white image, so use your imagination. It's a very next-gen look.

The really neat thing about setting up a generic color filter is that you can control the tone of certain areas of your game through map scripting. The Dishwasher: Dead Samurai game used "map themes" for different effects. A cemetery map theme, for instance, had bluer tones; a city theme had redder tones; and a catacombs theme had very burnt yellowish tones. Using a map script command called setmaptheme, the various themes were set; for example, setmaptheme cem in the init script set a cemetery-themed map. We have only one theme in Zombie Smashers, so we don't need such an implementation at this point, but it's definitely something to check out.

Figure 11-5. *Earth tones (not highly evident in black and white)*

A Water Effect

Let's add water to the game. Our water will be strictly cosmetic—that means no swimming! Our plan of attack, shown in Figure 11-6, is as follows:

- Set the map water level (shown in the first panel).

- Draw to a water target from the main target using a water effect (second panel).

- Draw the water target back over the main target (third panel).

This looks and sounds simple enough, but we'll run into a bit of trouble with our map foreground, as you'll see.

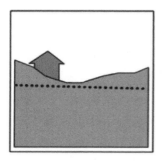 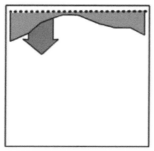 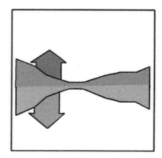

Figure 11-6. *A nice plan for water*

Here's the shader we'll be using:

```
// water.fx
sampler samplerState;

float horizon = 0.5;
float delta;
float theta;

struct PS_INPUT
{
    float2 TexCoord : TEXCOORD0;
};

float4 Water(PS_INPUT Input) : COLOR0
{
    float4 sum = 0;
    float2 tex = Input.TexCoord;
        if (tex.y < 1.0)
    {
        tex.y = horizon - tex.y;
        tex.y += (cos(tex.x * 50.0 + delta) / 500.0f);
        tex.y += (sin(tex.y * 250.0 + theta) / 120.0f);
        tex.x += (tex.y * (sin(tex.y * 750.0 + theta) / 250.0f));
                sum = tex2D(samplerState, tex);
    }
        if (Input.TexCoord.y < 0.2f)
        sum.a = 0.0;
    else if (Input.TexCoord.y < 0.25f)
        sum.a = (Input.TexCoord.y - 0.2) * 20.0;
    else sum.a = 1.0;

    return sum;
}
```

```
technique Water
{
    pass P0
    {
        PixelShader = compile ps_2_0 Water();
    }
}
```

It's a bit of ugly trig, but here's the gist: we tell our shader where the water "horizon" is (denoted by the dotted line in Figure 11-6), and then feed it two values: delta and theta, which are floats that range between 0 and 2π. Since we can't update variables from one to the next in a shader, we'll be updating these values from Game1 and feeding them into our water shader.

For the technique function, we set tex.y as horizon - tex.y, resulting in a flipped image where the line of symmetry is 0 (panel 2 of Figure 11-6). Then, applying some trig functions (which, honestly, were reached by trial and error), we nudge our texture coordinates around a bit, resulting in the rippling effect. Finally, we smoothly fade out the top 20% of the image.

As for implementing this in the game, we have a problem. The way we have our map set up, it would look really nice to have the water drawn between the main draw (map, characters, particles, and so on) and the foreground. However, if we kept everything else intact and introduced water between the main draw and the foreground, we would need to either introduce another render target or draw the foreground twice. Let's see how the solutions would pan out.

Adding a new render target goes like this:

- Set render target to mainTarg

- Draw background and main (characters, particles, and so on)

- *Set render target to waterTarg*

- *Draw with water effect*

- *Set render target to auxTarg*

- *Draw mainTarg and waterTarg to auxTarg*

- Set render target to bloomTarg[0]

- *Draw auxTarg with bloom effect*

- Set render target to bloomTarg[1]

- *Draw auxTarg with bloom effect*

- Set render target to gameTarg

- *Draw auxTarg*

- Draw bloomTarg[0]

- Draw bloomTarg[1]

- Set render target to backbuffer

- Draw gameTarg

- Draw HUD

- Present

And here's what we would need to do to draw the foreground twice:

- Set render target to `mainTarg`

- Draw the game

- *Set render target to* `waterTarg`

- *Draw with water effect*

- Set render target to `bloomTarg[0]`

- Draw `mainTarg` with bloom effect

- Set render target to `bloomTarg[1]`

- Draw `mainTarg` with bloom effect

- Set render target to `gameTarg`

- Draw `mainTarg`

- *Draw* `waterTarg`

- *Draw map foreground*

- Draw `bloomTarg[0]`

- Draw `bloomTarg[1]`

- Set render target to backbuffer

- Draw `gameTarg`

- Draw HUD

- Present

This goes to show how trying to work a simple change into the render loop—where render targets are concerned—can really throw a wrench in things. Both solutions are feasible but a little wasteful. So we came up with a third solution that *doesn't* leave our current setup intact—it adds a bit of feedback to our bloom.

The way our bloom is set up currently, we draw the image, then calculate the bloom, and then apply the bloom to the image. To use feedback, we need to draw the image, apply the bloom, and then calculate the bloom to use on the next frame. We must make sure that we don't draw any bloom on the first frame, of course, but every subsequent frame will be fine. This will give us a sort of dreamy, hazy effect, and is also a bit dangerous. Since we're operating on the *previous* frame, if we set our bloom alpha too high, the image will rapidly grow brighter until it is solid white.

The render loop to use feedback looks like this:

- Set render target to `mainTarg`

- Draw background and main (characters, particles, and so on)

- *Set render target to `waterTarg`*

- *Draw with water effect*

- Set render target to `gameTarg`

- Draw `mainTarg`

- *Draw `waterTarg`*

- *Draw map foreground*

- *Draw `bloomTarg[0]`*

- *Draw `bloomTarg[1]`*

- *Set render target to `bloomTarg[0]`*

- *Draw `mainTarg` with bloom effect*

- *Set render target to `bloomTarg[1]`*

- Draw `mainTarg` with bloom effect

- Set render target to backbuffer

- Draw `gameTarg`

- Draw HUD

- Present

This gives us the best of both worlds, and the feedback bloom effect is really appropriate for our moody cemetery. Here's the actual code:

```
graphics.GraphicsDevice.SetRenderTarget(0, mainTarget);
...

pManager.DrawParticles(spritesTex, false);

EffectPass pass;
```

We add a class-level field to `Map` called `water`. The `water` field specifies the water level; 0 for no water. We also add a new script command, `COMMAND_WATER`, to let us set the water level through the map init script.

```
float waterLevel = map.water - (.2f * screenSize.Y);
if (map.water > 0f)
{
    graphics.GraphicsDevice.SetRenderTarget(0,
        waterTarget);

    float wLev =
        (screenSize.Y / 2f + waterLevel - scroll.Y) / screenSize.Y;

    waterEffect.Parameters["delta"].SetValue(waterDelta);
    waterEffect.Parameters["theta"].SetValue(waterTheta);
    waterEffect.Parameters["horizon"].SetValue(wLev);
    waterEffect.Begin();
    spriteBatch.Begin(SpriteBlendMode.None,
            SpriteSortMode.Immediate,
            SaveStateMode.SaveState);
    pass = waterEffect.CurrentTechnique.Passes[0];
    pass.Begin();

    spriteBatch.Draw(mainTarget.GetTexture(),
        new Rectangle(0, 0, 256, 256), Color.White);

    pass.End();
    spriteBatch.End();
    waterEffect.End();
}

graphics.GraphicsDevice.SetRenderTarget(0, gameTarget);

if (gameMode == GameMode.Menu)
{
    ...
}
else
{
    filterEffect.Parameters["burn"].SetValue(.15f);
    ...
    filterEffect.End();

    if (map.water > 0f)
    {
        spriteBatch.Begin(SpriteBlendMode.AlphaBlend);

        spriteBatch.Draw(waterTarget.GetTexture(), new Rectangle(0,
            (int)(waterLevel - scroll.Y),
            (int)screenSize.X, (int)screenSize.Y), Color.White);
```

```
        spriteBatch.End();
    }

    map.Draw(spriteBatch, mapsTex, mapBackTex, 2, 3);
```

We'll use a class-level float, hasBloom, to let us know that our bloom targets have been drawn on. Once we draw our bloom targets a few lines later, hasBloom will always be true, but if we don't throw this failsafe in, we'll get an error.

```
    if (hasBloom)
    {
        spriteBatch.Begin(SpriteBlendMode.Additive);

        for (int i = 0; i < 2; i++)
            spriteBatch.Draw(bloomTarget[i].GetTexture(),
            new Rectangle(0, 0, (int)screenSize.X,
            (int)screenSize.Y), Color.White);

        spriteBatch.End();
    }
}
```

Now we'll calculate our bloom from our already-bloomed gameTarget (we previously used mainTarget).

```
for (int i = 0; i < 2; i++)
{
    hasBloom = true;
    graphics.GraphicsDevice.SetRenderTarget(0, bloomTarget[i]);

    bloomEffect.Parameters["a"].SetValue(.25f);
    ...
    spriteBatch.Draw(gameTarget.GetTexture(),
        new Rectangle(0, 0, 128 * (i + 1), 128 * (i + 1)),
        Color.White);
    ...
    bloomEffect.End();
}

graphics.GraphicsDevice.SetRenderTarget(0, null);

spriteBatch.Begin(SpriteBlendMode.None);

spriteBatch.Draw(gameTarget.GetTexture(), new Vector2(),
    Color.White);

spriteBatch.End();
spriteBatch.Begin(SpriteBlendMode.AlphaBlend);
```

```
if (QuakeManager.blast.val > 0f)
{
    ...
}

spriteBatch.End();
```

In `UpdateGame()`, we update the theta and delta values:

```
waterDelta += frameTime * 8f;
waterTheta += frameTime * 10f;
```

The end result (provided we implemented the new map script command) is shown in Figure 11-7.

Figure 11-7. *Reflecting water*

Refraction Effects

Moving up the complexity ladder, we arrive at refraction. Refraction involves distorting the produced image specifically. We can use it for effects like shockwaves and heat haze.

Our strategy is shown in Figure 11-8. It will go something like this:

- Draw the main stuff to a render target (first panel)

- Draw the refraction stuff to a second render target (second panel)

- Draw a third image using one shader and the two render target textures on separate
  texture levels (third panel)

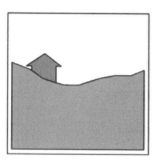  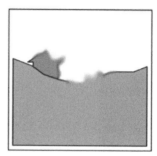

Figure 11-8. *A refraction plan*

This is actually really easy to set up. We can start off by just changing the filter.fx to
accept another sampler and adding the refraction functionality.

All the refraction functionality is handled through a function called GetDif(), which gets
the difference in the red value of horizontally and vertically neighboring pixels and adjusts the
texture coordinates accordingly, returning the adjusted amount as a float2.

```
//filter.fx
sampler samplerState;
sampler refractSampler;

float burn = 0.01f;
float saturation = 1.0f;
float r = 1.0f;
float g = 1.0f;
float b = 1.0f;
float brite = 0.0f;

struct PS_INPUT
{
    float2 TexCoord : TEXCOORD0;
};

float2 GetDif(float2 _tex)
{
    float2 dif;
        float2 tex = _tex;
    float2 btex = _tex;
    tex.x -= 0.003;
    btex.x += 0.003;
```

```
        dif.x = tex2D(refractSampler, tex).r
        - tex2D(refractSampler, btex).r;
            tex = _tex;
        btex = _tex;
        tex.y -= 0.003;
        btex.y += 0.003;
            dif.y = tex2D(refractSampler, tex).r
        - tex2D(refractSampler, btex).r;
            tex = _tex;
        dif *= (1.5 - tex2D(refractSampler, tex).r);
            return dif;
}

float4 Filter(PS_INPUT Input) : COLOR0
{
        float2 tex = Input.TexCoord + GetDif(Input.TexCoord) * 0.1f;
        float4 col = tex2D(samplerState, tex);
        float d = sqrt(pow((tex.x - 0.5), 2) + pow((tex.y - 0.5), 2));
        ...
```

That's all we need for our filter.fx.

Now we'll modify Game1 just enough to show that refraction is working. We'll start by creating a class-level RenderTarget2D called refractTarget, which will instantiate in LoadContent() to be identical to mainTarget.

Then, in DrawGame(), we'll draw our sprites texture to refractTarget as a test, immediately after we finish drawing the main game stuff:

```
pManager.DrawParticles(spritesTex, false);

graphics.GraphicsDevice.SetRenderTarget(0, refractTarget);
graphics.GraphicsDevice.Clear(Color.Black);
spriteBatch.Begin(SpriteBlendMode.AlphaBlend);
spriteBatch.Draw(spritesTex, new Rectangle(0, 0, 800, 600), Color.Red);
spriteBatch.End();
```

Moving along, we draw. mainTarget to gameTarget using the filter effect. Since we've modified filter.fx to include another sampler, we need to set our graphics device to include the additional sampler:

```
graphics.GraphicsDevice.Textures[1] = refractTarget.GetTexture();
filterEffect.Parameters["burn"].SetValue(.15f);

...

filterEffect.End();

graphics.GraphicsDevice.Textures[1] = null;
```

The result of this is shown in Figure 11-9. Notice how the text looks like it puts an inner bevel on the explosion. Also, can you see the hearts in the row above the text?

Figure 11-9. *Refraction test*

It's not much of an extra stretch to plug this effect into our game. We'll just modify our particle setup by adding a Boolean to the Particles base class: refract. Any particles for which refract is true will be drawn to our refractTarget; otherwise, particles will be drawn as normal.

After adding the refract Boolean, we make a refract particle called Heat. We'll use it for heat haze, which we can attach to our muzzle flashes, rocket contrails, torches, and so on. Heat looks like this:

```
class Heat : Particle
{
    public Heat(Vector2 loc,
        Vector2 traj,
        float size)
    {
        this.Location = loc;
        this.Trajectory = traj;
```

```
        this.Size = size;
        this.Flag = Rand.GetRandomInt(0, 4);
        this.Owner = -1;
        this.Exists = true;
        this.rotation = Rand.GetRandomFloat(0f, 6.28f);
        this.Frame = Rand.GetRandomFloat(.5f, .785f);
        this.Refract = true;
    }

    public override void Draw(SpriteBatch sprite, Texture2D spritesTex)
    {

        Rectangle sRect = new Rectangle(flag * 64, 64, 64, 64);

        a = (float)Math.Sin((double)frame * 4.0) * .1f;

        sprite.Draw(spritesTex, GameLocation, sRect, new Color(
            new Vector4(1f, 0f, 0f, a)),
            rotation + frame * 16f, new Vector2(32.0f, 32.0f),
            Size,
            SpriteEffects.None, 1.0f);
    }
}
```

We'll add some special cases to our DrawParticles() method in ParticleManager. Currently, it draws all alpha-blended particles, and then draws all additive-blended particles. We need to add a little condition to make sure it doesn't try to draw any refract particles:

```
public void DrawParticles(Texture2D spritesTex, bool background)
{
    sprite.Begin(SpriteBlendMode.AlphaBlend);
    foreach (Particle p in particle)
    {
        if (p != null)
        {
            if (!p.Additive && p.Background == background
                && !p.Refract)
                p.Draw(sprite, spritesTex);
        }
    }
    sprite.End();

    sprite.Begin(SpriteBlendMode.Additive);
    foreach (Particle p in particle)
    {
        if (p != null)
```

```
        {
            if (p.Additive && p.Background == background &&
                !p.Refract)
                p.Draw(sprite, spritesTex);
        }
    }
    sprite.End();
}
```

Then we create a new method, `DrawRefractParticles()`, to iterate through our particle array again, drawing only refract particles.

```
public void DrawRefractParticles(Texture2D spritesTex)
{
    sprite.Begin(SpriteBlendMode.AlphaBlend);
    foreach (Particle p in particle)
    {
        if (p != null)
        {
            if (p.Refract)
                p.Draw(sprite, spritesTex);
        }
    }
    sprite.End();
}
```

Back in `Game1.DrawGame()`, we can change our refract test, in which we just drew the whole sprites texture, to this:

```
graphics.GraphicsDevice.SetRenderTarget(0, refractTarget);
graphics.GraphicsDevice.Clear(Color.Black);
pManager.DrawRefractParticles(spritesTex);
```

Now we're set up for our refraction effect. All that's left is to add some `AddParticle()` lines here and there to create heat haze where heat haze is necessary. For instance, in `ParticleManager.MakeMuzzleFlash()`, add this:

```
for (int i = 4; i < 12; i++)
    AddParticle(new Heat(
        Location+ (Trajectory* (float)i) * 0.001f
        + Rand.GetRandomVector2(-30f, 30f, -30f, 30f),
        Rand.GetRandomVector2(-30f, 30f, -100f, 0f),
        Rand.GetRandomFloat(.5f, 1.1f)));
```

And in `Map.Update()`, where we create our torch fire, we add the following:

```
for (int i = 0; i < 64; i++)
```

```
{
    if (mapSeg[LAYER_MAP, i] != null)
    {
        if (segDef[mapSeg[LAYER_MAP, i].Index].Flags ==
            SegmentFlags.Torch)
        {
            ...
            pMan.AddParticle(new Heat(mapSeg[LAYER_MAP, i].Location
                * 2f + new Vector2(20f, -50f),
                Rand.GetRandomVector2(-50f, 50f, -400f, -300f),
                Rand.GetRandomFloat(1f, 2f)));
```

The results, as shown in Figure 11-10, look pretty nice. You can see heat haze on the moon, as well as a little in the star over our hero, where he has just fired a shot. As the mantra goes, the effects look better in motion.

Figure 11-10. *In-game refraction*

Refraction effects are a lot of fun to play with and very easy to abuse. With a fresh technology, it's typical to throw as much of it into a game as possible, only to realize a few weeks later that too much of a good thing is a bad thing. The same goes for bloom. In fact, the effects in this chapter are probably a bit too overpowering, but at least in this case, we can hide behind the premise of "educational purposes."

Conclusion

We had a lot of fun making this chapter, not because the implementation was exciting (to be honest, most of the shaders were taken almost line for line from The Dishwasher game), but because we're suckers for graphics. We really like how much we were able to make this game shine in under 30 pages.

We implemented basic color filters; created a generic mood filter for hue, saturation, and a moody burn effect; added bloom; added water and bloom feedback; and implemented refraction in our particle system. Along the way, we switched the render loop around about a half dozen times, it seems, but that's par for the course. Working out the render loop is fairly important, and you should understand the thinking that goes behind developing a good strategy for getting all of your effects in there.

CHAPTER 12

■ ■ ■

Networking
Console on the Interwebs!

Honestly, networking is a terrific hassle. It involves dealing with a lot of fault tolerance and tweaking in a cumbersome testing environment. However, once you've cleared the numerous hurdles, networking can really do a great deal to define your game.

The XNA Framework alleviates a number of classic networking hassles, like ensuring data ordering and delivery, and network game state management. Even better, it allows you to take advantage of Xbox Live matchmaking features. With a good grasp on networking with XNA Game Studio, you could feasibly make your own Soldat-like 31-player deathmatch game, complete with a searchable server list, all with much, much less effort than you would need to exert doing things the old way. For those of you familiar with DirectX of old, you can consider networking in XNA to be everything DirectPlay should have been and more. Not only do you get built-in local-area network (LAN) and Xbox Live capabilities, you also get built-in voice chat.

To set up networking in Zombie Smashers XNA, here's what we'll be doing:

- Add gamer services to the game, enabling networking.

- Add functionality to allow us to create, find, and join matches from the main menu.

- Add functionality to send and receive game messages (locations of characters, particles, and so on) during a game session.

Our final product will be a two-player online co-op arcade game in which two zombie-smashing heroes face off against wave after wave of zombies.

Networking with XNA Game Studio

We have a few requirements for networking with XNA Game Studio. Our first order of business is the physical setup of our development environment.

You can't use two instances of the same game running on the same machine; you can have only one instance per machine. *Machine*, of course, means Windows PC or Xbox 360. You can use the two devices interchangeably for some cross-platform debugging.

Because we'll be implementing just a two-player co-op, your setup can be two Xbox 360s (which can be deployed from the same Windows machine), two Windows PCs, or one Windows PC and one Xbox 360. If you can deploy the game (as discussed in Chapter 10), you have the Windows PC and Xbox 360 setup. You should be able to have two instances of Visual C# Express open: one set to deploy as x86 and one set to deploy as Xbox 360, using the same source. Since this is probably the most common setup and an easy transition from normal Xbox 360 deployment, we'll assume the Windows PC/Xbox 360 setup in this chapter.

You need one Xbox Live Silver membership per machine. Fortunately, Silver Live memberships are free! You won't be able to do any Live matchmaking with a Silver account; it's System Link (LAN) only. Again, fortunately, this is all you need for testing purposes. We'll simulate lag on System Link to get a good feel for how our game will play over Games for Windows LIVE.

For any Xbox 360 deployment, you will need one XNA Creators Club membership per Xbox 360—at least, that's what the XNA documentation says. At the time of writing, we would get an exception while attempting to create a System Link session from a Windows game where no profile was signed in, and would also get an exception when signing in to a profile without a Creators Club membership. It seems like the way to go is one Xbox Silver Live membership and one XNA Creators Club membership *per account*.

Adding the Gamer Service Component

To make our game network-ready, we need to initialize a component called the Gamer Services Component. This just requires adding the following line to the `Game1` constructor:

```
Components.Add(new GamerServicesComponent(this));
```

After adding this line, you'll discover a few things have changed. The most readily apparent change is that the game now takes a few more seconds to load.

Once you get over the shock of a less-than-snappy debug process, you'll notice that in Windows, pressing the big Guide button in the middle of your Xbox 360 controller will bring up the Games for Windows LIVE Guide, allowing you to sign in and out, just like on Xbox 360, as shown in Figure 12-1.

■**Note** You can use the Games for Windows LIVE Guide in Windows to test profile functionality, but here's the deal: if you sign on with a profile that does not have an XNA Creators Club membership, XNA Game Studio will cry foul, throwing a `GamerServicesNotAvailable` exception in `Game1.Update()`. You can opt to either leave profiles alone on the Windows environment or make sure you use only compliant profiles.

Of course, we didn't add the Gamer Services Component to play around with the Guide all day. We added it to enable network functionality.

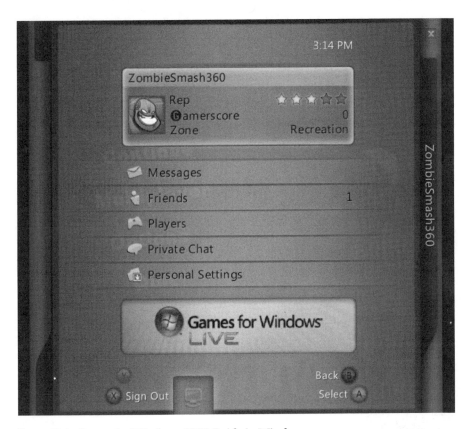

Figure 12-1. *Games for Windows LIVE Guide in Windows*

Adding Multiplayer Options to the Menu

We'll be working with a simple System Link connection, which is basically the Xbox name for a LAN connection. Normally, we would allow our game to reach a server list. To simplify things, we'll just have our client join the first server it finds. Here's how our multiplayer game will pan out (we'll bring Alice and Bob along from Networking 101):

- Alice selects Host Game. Her game begins a network session, sitting in lobby mode, waiting for another player to join. Alice just sees a "waiting" screen.

- Bob selects Join Game. His game searches the LAN for an active multiplayer game in lobby mode. Bob, likewise, sees a "waiting" screen.

- Bob's search returns one or more running multiplayer games. Alice's could be the first. Because we're just testing, we can be pretty sure that this will be the case.

- Bob's game joins Alice's game.

- Alice's game, seeing that Bob has joined, switches over to playing mode. This affects the whole session, so Bob's game sees playing mode now.

- Both Alice's game and Bob's game, upon discovering that they've entered playing mode, launch into the game.

Discussing the workflow for networking using Alice and Bob can be fun, but let's get the ball rolling. We'll start by modifying the main menu. Add some buttons to the options image, as shown in Figure 12-2.

Figure 12-2. *Options.png with new multiplayer options*

Options and Levels

By now, we expect you to be pretty fluent in both C# and ZombieSmashers, and as such, we'll leave out many of the details and focus on the main modifications.

We'll add the new options to the Option enumeration in Menu:

```
Multiplayer = 7,
HostGame = 8,
JoinGame = 9,
RumbleOn = 10,
RumbleOff = 11,
Cancel = 12,
AwaitingConnection = 13
```

■**Note** Between Chapter 10 and here, we snuck in a Rumble button at the options level. You can see the code for this in Appendix B, where we use it as an example of saving settings.

We'll add some new menu levels as well in our Level enumeration:

```
Multiplayer = 7,
HostGame = 8,
JoinGame = 9,
NewArena = 10
```

The NewArena level will work like our NewGame level. When the player transitions to this level, we'll trigger a method to start our game.

We'll change PopulateOptions() around a little. We need to add a new button to the main menu level and define our three new levels: Multiplayer, HostGame, and JoinGame:

```
case Level.Main:
    if (menuMode == MenuMode.Pause)
    {
        ...
    }
    else
    {
        option[0] = Option.NewGame;
        option[1] = Option.Continue;
        option[2] = Option.Multiplayer;
        option[3] = Option.Options;
        option[4] = Option.Quit;
        totalOptions = 5;
    }
    break;
...
case Level.Multiplayer:
```

```
    option[0] = Option.HostGame;
    option[1] = Option.JoinGame;
    option[2] = Option.Back;
    totalOptions = 3;
    break;
case Level.HostGame:
    option[0] = Option.AwaitingConnection;
    option[1] = Option.Cancel;
    totalOptions = 2;
    break;
case Level.JoinGame:
    option[0] = Option.AwaitingConnection;
    option[1] = Option.Cancel;
    totalOptions = 2;
    break;
```

We'll do a bit of hacking here. Notice how we're setting the first option on the HostGame and JoinGame levels to AwaitingConnection? This isn't a selectable option. What we'll do is throw a line in Update() to lock the selected item to index 1 if the item at index 0 is AwaitingConnection. Right after we update selItem in Update(), we add this line:

```
if (option[0] == Option.AwaitingConnection) selItem = 1;
```

This will make Cancel always be highlighted, as shown in Figure 12-3.

Figure 12-3. *The HostGame/JoinGame level*

Navigation

In Update(), we'll add some navigation functionality.

```
case Level.Main:
    switch (option[selItem])
    {
        ...
        case Option.Multiplayer:
            Transition(Level.Multiplayer);
            break;
        ...
case Level.Multiplayer:
    switch (option[selItem])
    {
        case Option.Back:
            Transition(Level.Main);
            break;
        case Option.HostGame:
            Transition(Level.HostGame);
            break;
        case Option.JoinGame:
            Transition(Level.JoinGame);
            break;
    }
    break;
case Level.HostGame:
    switch (option[selItem])
    {
        case Option.Cancel:
            Transition(Level.Main);
            Game1.netPlay.netConnect.Disconnect();
            break;
    }
    break;
case Level.JoinGame:
    switch (option[selItem])
    {
        case Option.Cancel:
            Transition(Level.Main);
            Game1.netPlay.netConnect.Disconnect();
            break;
    }
    break;
```

Note the Disconnect() call. We have two classes to define between here and Disconnect(), but essentially what we'll be doing is disconnecting our network session when the user chooses Cancel.

We use button presses to transition in the menu system for most cases, but for our HostGame and JoinGame levels, we'll be monitoring our netConnect object for updates. We used a field, ok, to check whether A or (as long as we're not paused) Start has been pressed. If no button has been pressed, we can check for network-induced transitions:

```
if (ok)
{
    ... /* A or Start has been pressed */
}
else
{
    switch (level)
    {
        case Level.JoinGame:
            if (Game1.netPlay.joined)
                Transition(Level.NewArena);
            break;
        case Level.HostGame:
            if (Game1.netPlay.netSession != null)
            {
                if (Game1.netPlay.netSession.AllGamers.Count == 2)
                    Transition(Level.NewArena);
            }
            break;
    }
}
```

We'll trigger our new level changes in Update() as well. Earlier in the Update() function, we had a switch block that would trigger special-case levels, like NewGame, Quit, and so on. Let's add HostGame, JoinGame, and NewArena.

```
case Level.HostGame:
    Game1.netPlay.netConnect.Host();
    break;
case Level.JoinGame:
    Game1.netPlay.netConnect.Find();
    break;
case Level.NewArena:
    game.NewGame(true);
    Game1.netPlay.netConnect.NewGame();
    break;
```

We're using some more methods to be defined in the future again here, but the functionality of Host() and Find() should be apparent enough at this point.

Also, we've overloaded Game1.NewGame() to allow for our new Arena game type. We've added some new class-level items to specify game type and players. Here's the code:

```
public enum GameType
{
    Solo = 0,
    Arena = 1
}

public static GameType gameType;
public static int players;
```

Arena Play

Our overloaded NewGame() method allows us to specify a new arena. This will set players to 2, load the correct map (arena), and spawn the right amount of players in the right places.

```
public void NewGame()
{
    NewGame(false);
}

public void NewGame(bool arena)
{
    gameMode = GameMode.Playing;

    pManager.Reset();

    if (arena)
    {
        map.Path = "arena";
        gameType = GameType.Arena;
        players = 2;
    }
    else
    {
        map.Path = "start";
        gameType = GameType.Solo;
        players = 1;
    }

    for (int i = 0; i < players; i++)
    {
        character[i]
            = new Character(new Vector2(300f
            + (float)i * 200f, 100f),
```

```
            charDef[(int)CharacterDefinitions.Guy],
            i,
            Character.TEAM_GOOD_GUYS);
        character[i].HP = character[i].MHP = 100;
    }
    for (int i = players; i < character.Length; i++)
        character[i] = null;

    map.GlobalFlags = new MapFlags(64);
    map.Read();
    map.TransDir = Map.TransitionDirection.Intro;
    map.transInFrame = 1f;
}
```

Our new arena map is shown in Figure 12-4. It's basically a locked-in area that will keep spawning baddies.

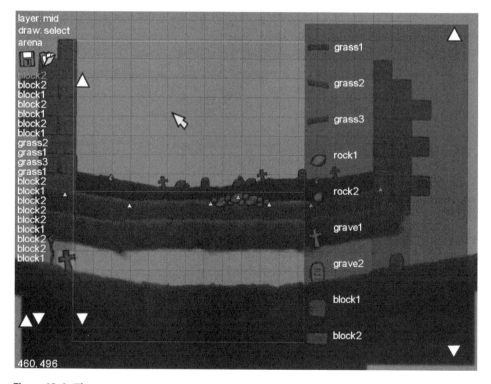

Figure 12-4. *The arena map*

Creating, Finding, and Joining Sessions

We've already referred to a couple of classes that don't exist yet, so let's go over the classes we'll be creating:

`NetPlay`: Overarching network control class, responsible for updating connections and game network objects as necessary.

`NetConnect`: Maintains network connections, including finding, joining, and leaving games, and detecting when others have done so.

`NetGame`: Maintains game data interactions, such as sending and receiving character and particle data.

`NetPacker`: A class full of static helper methods we'll use to pack and unpack data in smaller data types, such as floats to shorts.

We'll cover `NetPlay` and `NetConnect` here, and get to `NetGame` and `NetPacker` in the next section, when we talk about sending and receiving game messages.

Network Control

We'll start with `NetPlay`:

```
public class NetPlay
{
    public NetConnect netConnect;
    public NetGame netGame;
```

`NetworkSession` is the object that the XNA Framework will use for all network session management: player states, data sending and receiving, and so on. `NetworkSession` does a lot of work on its own, provided we `Update()` it every frame.

```
    public NetworkSession netSession;

    public bool hosting = false;
    public bool joined = false;

    public NetPlay()
    {
        netConnect = new NetConnect(this);
        netGame = new NetGame(this);
    }
```

```
    public void Update(Character[] c, ParticleManager pMan)
    {
        if (netSession != null)
            if (!netSession.IsDisposed)
                netSession.Update();

        netConnect.Update();

        if (netSession != null)
        {
```

NetworkSession.SessionState can be in either the Lobby state or the Playing state, and keeping all gamers informed on the current state is one of the automatic functions of NetworkSession. If we're in Playing state, we'll call NetGame.Update().

```
            if (netSession.SessionState == NetworkSessionState.Playing)
            {
                netGame.Update(c, pMan);
            }
        }
    }
}
```

Network Connections

From Menu, we made some calls to NetConnect. NetConnect is a class that we'll use for all network connection maintenance issues: creating matches, finding matches, and so on. Because a lot of network connection activity takes time, we'll be doing a lot of stuff asynchronously. So, for the three actions we'll be taking—hosting, finding, and joining—we can be in one of three states: doing nothing, pending a result, or having a completed result.

For instance, say we want to host a game. The state transitions will go like this:

- pendingHost = false, hosting = false. We are unconnected.

- Begin creating a game. pendingHost = true.

- Idle while our game has not yet been created.

- Complete creating a game. pendingHost = false, hosting = true.

Using this asynchronous routine lets our game go about its network duties somewhat smoothly. If we used synchronous calls to create, find, and join games, everything would have frozen for the duration of the call. Our fog would have stopped rolling, our scene would have stopped scrolling, and our users would be in the middle of saying, "Oh no, this amazing game just crashed!" We clearly do not want that situation on our hands, so we prevent it from being even remotely possible.

Here's our async-friendly `NetConnect` class:

```
public class NetConnect
{
    public bool pendingHost = false;
    public bool pendingJoin = false;
    public bool pendingFind = false;

    IAsyncResult createResult;
    IAsyncResult findResult;
    IAsyncResult joinResult;

    NetPlay netPlay;
```

We'll construct the class with a reference to our `NetPlay` object.

```
    public NetConnect(NetPlay _netPlay)
    {
        netPlay = _netPlay;
    }

    public void Disconnect()
    {
        if (netPlay.hosting || netPlay.joined)
        {
            netPlay.netSession.Dispose();
            netPlay.hosting = false;
            netPlay.joined = false;
        }
    }

    public void Host()
    {
        if (netPlay.netSession != null)
            netPlay.netSession.Dispose();

        NetworkSessionProperties props = new
            NetworkSessionProperties();
```

We're using our asynchronous result interface, `createResult`, to asynchronously create our new game session. While `pendingHost` is true, we'll keep checking on `createResult` to see how our progress is moving along. We're creating a game with one local gamer, two maximum gamers, and zero private gamer slots.

```
        createResult =
            NetworkSession.BeginCreate(NetworkSessionType.SystemLink,
            1, 2, 0, props, new AsyncCallback(GotResult), null);
        pendingHost = true;
    }
```

Our Find() method works in roughly the same way. We're looking for another System Link game and have one local gamer.

```
public void Find()
{
    NetworkSessionProperties props = new
        NetworkSessionProperties();

    findResult =
        NetworkSession.BeginFind(NetworkSessionType.SystemLink,
        1, props, new AsyncCallback(GotResult), null);
    pendingFind = true;
}
```

Our Update() function looks at all of our pending processes and behaves accordingly.

```
public void Update()
{
    if (pendingHost)
    {
        if (createResult.IsCompleted)
        {
            netPlay.netSession =
                NetworkSession.EndCreate(createResult);
            netPlay.hosting = true;
            pendingHost = false;
        }
    }
    if (pendingFind)
    {
        if (findResult.IsCompleted)
        {
```

Here's a neat case:

```
            AvailableNetworkSessionCollection availableSessions =
                NetworkSession.EndFind(findResult);
            if (availableSessions.Count > 0)
            {
                joinResult = NetworkSession.BeginJoin(
                    availableSessions[0], new
                    AsyncCallback(GotResult), null);
                pendingJoin = true;

            }
            pendingFind = false;
        }
    }
```

```
if (pendingJoin)
{
    if (joinResult.IsCompleted)
    {
        netPlay.netSession =
            NetworkSession.EndJoin(joinResult);
        netPlay.joined = true;
        pendingJoin = false;
    }
}

if (netPlay.hosting)
{
    //
}
if (netPlay.joined)
{
    //
}
```

In this case, if our find is complete, we launch into an asynchronous join of the first session that was returned. Of course, the *right* way to do it would be to take the list and put it into the user interface, allowing the user to choose which server to join. However, because we can be fairly sure that we'll be looking at a list of one, we might as well cut to the chase and join that first session.

If we are in an active network game, we should check to see if anything went wrong that would prompt us to quit—namely, the client leaving or the host killing the game. If the gamer count drops below two (meaning the client quit) or the server quits, we fire an EndGame(), kill our session, and set our appropriate fields.

```
if (netPlay.netSession != null)
{
    if (!netPlay.netSession.IsDisposed)
    {
        bool ended = false;
        if (netPlay.netSession.SessionState ==
            NetworkSessionState.Playing)
        {
            if (netPlay.netSession.AllGamers.Count < 2)
                ended = true;

        }
        else if (netPlay.netSession.SessionState ==
            NetworkSessionState.Ended)
                ended = true;
```

```
            if (ended)
            {
                Game1.menu.EndGame();
                netPlay.netSession.Dispose();
                netPlay.hosting = false;
                netPlay.joined = false;
            }
        }
    }
}

public void NewGame()
{
    if (netPlay.hosting)
        netPlay.netSession.StartGame();
}
```

The GotResult() method is called whenever an asynchronous result is completed. We'll leave it empty for the time being. We're handling our asynchronous results in Update() anyway.

```
private void GotResult(IAsyncResult result)
{
    //
}
}
```

Keeping NetConnect happy and updated will allow us to make and maintain network connections.

Sending and Receiving Game Messages

While we're already technically passing data back and forth over a network, we haven't yet sent any game messages. *Messages* are chunks of data that keep everyone informed. We'll be sending character and particle data in our messages.

As you probably know, sending data over a network is much more time- and resource-consuming than just working with it locally. For this reason, we'll be packing our data into smaller data types when sending it. For example, 32-bit floats can become 16-bit shorts or 8-bit bytes, yielding a fairly quick, dirty, and effective size improvement.

When we pack up our data to send as a message, we can delimit it such that the reader on the other end knows what to do with the data. For instance, our message can look like this:

- Character

  - 128 bits of character data

- Particle
  - Blood particle
  - 64 bits of particle data
- Particle
  - Bullet particle
  - 80 bits of particle data
- End message

Assuming we parse everything correctly, we'll know exactly how many bits to read per object to update on the reading end. If we get anything just slightly off, however, we'll end up with bizarrely skewed numbers and probably crashes, so it's important to be careful. An example of a message is shown in Figure 12-5.

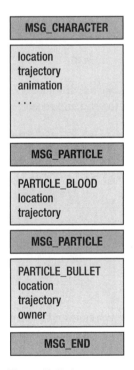

Figure 12-5. *A game message*

Network Game Interaction

The following is our NetGame class, which concerns itself with message composing, sending, receiving, and parsing:

```
public class NetGame
{
    NetPlay netPlay;

    public const byte MSG_SERVER_DATA = 0;
    public const byte MSG_CLIENT_DATA = 1;
    public const byte MSG_CHARACTER = 2;
    public const byte MSG_PARTICLE = 3;
    public const byte MSG_END = 4;

    PacketWriter writer;
    PacketReader reader;

    float frame;

    public float frameTime;
```

Our constructor, besides taking a reference to our overarching NetPlay class, initializes our PacketReader and PacketWriter. We'll be using the writer and reader to send and receive messages, respectively.

```
    public NetGame(NetPlay _netPlay)
    {
        netPlay = _netPlay;

        writer = new PacketWriter();
        reader = new PacketReader();
    }

    public void Update(Character[] c, ParticleManager pMan)
    {
```

LocalNetworkGamer gamer will handle all of our reading and writing; gamer can send and receive messages. The GetGamer() function is defined later. Its purpose is to find the LocalNetworkGamer at player index 1.

```
        LocalNetworkGamer gamer = GetGamer();
        if (gamer == null)
            return;
```

We're updating every frame, but we don't want to send data every frame. If you think of the Internet as a large series of tubes, we need to send the data just fast enough so that it doesn't clog up on one end. If we send too much data, it will not fit in the pipe. If we send too little data at too great a speed, it will just pile up somewhere. The goal is to get the perfect amount across with the perfect timing, so that the players don't notice anything whatsoever. That's a little easier said than done. Since we're just testing a basic game, we don't need to concern ourselves with the problem. If you plan on making this game available over the Live platform, this *is* a problem you will need to tackle.

For the time being, we'll set it up to send data every 0.05 second, or at 20 frames per second. This is too fast for most, if not all, Live matches, but will work fine for System Link.

```
frame -= frameTime;
if (frame < 0f)
{
    frame = .05f;

    if (netPlay.hosting)
    {
        if (c[0] != null)
        {
            writer.Write(MSG_SERVER_DATA);
```

As the host, we'll send data about our own character as well as every non-null character other than index 1. The character at index 1 is controlled by the client. This is a fairly simple client/server setup, in that the clients all report to a single server, and then the server relays data back to all the clients. This works in most cases; however, you may find that a more peer-to-peer setup works better.

```
c[0].WriteToNet(writer);

for (int i = 2; i < c.Length; i++)
    if (c[i] != null)
        c[i].WriteToNet(writer);
```

After our characters have been written, we'll write particles, finish off with an end-message byte, and send our data off with SendDataOptions.None, meaning we don't care if it reaches its destination or it arrives at its destination out of order.

```
pMan.NetWriteParticles(writer);

writer.Write(MSG_END);
gamer.SendData(writer, SendDataOptions.None);
        }
    }
    if (netPlay.joined)
    {
        if (c[1] != null)
        {
            writer.Write(MSG_CLIENT_DATA);
```

Likewise, our client writes the character only at index 1 (himself), as well as any particles he may have spawned (more on the particles in the "Particle Net Data" section later in this chapter).

```
                    c[1].WriteToNet(writer);

                    pMan.NetWriteParticles(writer);

                    writer.Write(MSG_END);
                    gamer.SendData(writer, SendDataOptions.None);
                }

            }

        }
```

If any data has been sent to us and is ready for processing, gamer.IsDataAvailable will be true.

```
        if (gamer.IsDataAvailable)
        {
            NetworkGamer sender;
            gamer.ReceiveData(reader, out sender);

            if (!sender.IsLocal)
            {
                byte type = reader.ReadByte();
```

Here's a tricky bit: it's the host's responsibility to send out data on all currently active (non-null) characters. So, in order to handle character death, we'll set a flag in all characters to false and check it again after processing the update. Any character not updated by the message will be presumed dead and made null.

```
                if (netPlay.joined)
                {
                    for (int i = 0; i < c.Length; i++)
                        if (i != 1)
                            if (c[i] != null)
                                c[i].receivedNetUpdate = false;
                }
```

We enter a while loop in which we process each portion of the incoming message until we read a MSG_END. All bit-by-bit processing is done within the classes that are updated.

```
                bool end = false;
                while (!end)
                {
                    byte msg = reader.ReadByte();
                    switch (msg)
                    {
                        case MSG_END:
                            end = true;
                            break;
                        case MSG_CHARACTER:
```

When we read a character, we'll read off the first three fields from this method before passing the reader to the character to finish processing the update. These three fields— defID, team, and ID—are used to create the character if this is the first time the reader has seen the character.

```
int defID = NetPacker.SbyteToInt
    (reader.ReadSByte());
int team = NetPacker.SbyteToInt
    (reader.ReadSByte());
int ID = NetPacker.SbyteToInt
    (reader.ReadSByte());

if (c[ID] == null)
{
    c[ID] = new Character(new Vector2(),
        Game1.charDef[defID],
        ID, team);
}

c[ID].ReadFromNet(reader);

c[ID].receivedNetUpdate = true;
break;
case MSG_PARTICLE:
    byte pType = reader.ReadByte();
    bool bg = reader.ReadBoolean();
```

This is the first time we use NetPacker, which we'll define in the next section. As we've said, essentially, NetPacker's function is to pack and unpack big data types into small data types. Here, we see an 8-bit signed byte (Sbyte) being turned into a 32-bit integer. This will be fine as long as we never have any defID, team, or ID fields greater than 127. It's easy to just use 32-bit integers for everything in our game, but when bandwidth is at a premium, we take what we can get!

For parsing particles, we first read the type and a bit to specify whether it's a background particle (remember that we use this field for our AddParticle() method).

```
switch (pType)
{
    case Particle.PARTICLE_NONE:
        //
        break;
    case Particle.PARTICLE_BLOOD:
        pMan.AddParticle(new
            Blood(reader), bg, true);
        break;
    case Particle.PARTICLE_BLOOD_DUST:
        pMan.AddParticle(new
            BloodDust(reader), bg, true);
        break;
```

```
                            case Particle.PARTICLE_BULLET:
                                pMan.AddParticle(new
                                    Bullet(reader), bg, true);
                                break;
                            ...
                            case Particle.PARTICLE_SMOKE:
                                pMan.AddParticle(new
                                    Smoke(reader), bg, true);
                                break;
                            default:
                                //Error!
                                break;
                        }
                        break;
                }
            }
```

We're being a bit sneaky here: particles are sent only when they are created. All particles that aren't owned by the client are created and sent by the host, while all particles that *are* owned by the client (for example, bullets that the client spawns) are sent from the client to the server. At the same time, it's important for the server to abort any client-owned particles that the game might try to spawn outside a network read. Likewise, the client must abort all particle spawns that it does not own unless they come through the network.

The client will iterate through its characters again to see if any have not been updated in the last update, killing off those that have not been updated.

```
            if (netPlay.joined)
            {
                for (int i = 0; i < c.Length; i++)
                    if (i != 1)
                        if (c[i] != null)
                            if (c[i].receivedNetUpdate == false)
                            {
                                c[i] = null;
                            }
            }
        }
    }
}
```

Finally, here's our GetGamer() method. It uses a bit of trickery to figure out which LocalNetworkGamer is at player index 1.

```
private LocalNetworkGamer GetGamer()
{
    foreach (LocalNetworkGamer gamer in
            netPlay.netSession.LocalGamers)
```

```
            if (gamer.SignedInGamer.PlayerIndex == PlayerIndex.One)
                return gamer;
        return null;
    }


}
```

Data Packing

Now we get to NetPacker, whose function is to turn big data types into small data types and vice versa. It works fine as long as the data we're looking at does not go beyond the bounds of the smaller data types.

Take a look at the first function, TinyFloatToByte() and its counterpart, ByteToTinyFloat():

```
class NetPacker
{
    public static byte TinyFloatToByte(float f)
    {
        f *= 255f;
        if (f > 255f) f = 255f;
        if (f < 0f) f = 0f;
        return (byte)f;
    }

    public static float ByteToTinyFloat(byte b)
    {
        float f = (float)b;
        return f / 255f;
    }

    public static short IntToShort(int i)
    {
        if (i > short.MaxValue) i = short.MaxValue;
        if (i < short.MinValue) i = short.MinValue;
        return (short)i;
    }

    public static int ShortToInt(short s)
    {
        return (int)s;
    }

    public static sbyte IntToSbyte(int i)
    {
        if (i > sbyte.MaxValue) i = sbyte.MaxValue;
```

```
        if (i < sbyte.MinValue) i = sbyte.MinValue;
        return (sbyte)i;
    }

    public static int SbyteToInt(sbyte s)
    {
        return (int)s;
    }
```

We use this only for floats that range in size from 0f to 1f inclusive. We expand the value such that 0f becomes 0 and 1f becomes 255 in TinyFloatToByte(), and do the opposite in ByteToTinyFloat(). Assuming our original float value was within the 0f to 1f range, we'll lose only a tiny amount of precision but save 24 bits of bandwidth.

We're also handling small floats, medium (mid) floats, and big floats. Because the range of a short is –32767 and 32767, our value conversion ranges are as shown in Table 12-1.

Table 12-1. *NetPacker Conversion Ranges*

Type	Min Value	Max Value
Big float	–32767	32767
Mid float	–6553	6553
Small float	–1638	1638
Tiny float	0	1

If we keep using the best conversions (we'll have to play it by ear), we'll maximize bandwidth efficiency and minimize precision loss.

```
    public static short BigFloatToShort(float f)
    {
        if (f > short.MaxValue) f = short.MaxValue;
        if (f < short.MinValue) f = short.MinValue;
        return (short)f;
    }

    public static float ShortToBigFloat(short s)
    {
        return (float)s;
    }

    public static short MidFloatToShort(float f)
    {
        f *= 5f;
        if (f > short.MaxValue) f = short.MaxValue;
        if (f < short.MinValue) f = short.MinValue;
        return (short)f;
    }
```

```
    public static float ShortToMidFloat(short s)
    {
        return (float)(s) / 5f;
    }

    public static short SmallFloatToShort(float f)
    {
        f *= 20f;
        if (f > short.MaxValue) f = short.MaxValue;
        if (f < short.MinValue) f = short.MinValue;
        return (short)f;
    }

    public static float ShortToSmallFloat(short s)
    {
        return (float)(s) / 20f;
    }
}
```

Character Net Data

Let's move on to the write and read functions for Character. We'll be sending references to a packet reader and writer for ReadFromNet() and WriteToNet(), respectively. Here's WriteToNet():

```
public void WriteToNet(PacketWriter writer)
{
    writer.Write(NetGame.MSG_CHARACTER);

    writer.Write(NetPacker.IntToSbyte(charDef.defID));
    writer.Write(NetPacker.IntToSbyte(team));
    writer.Write(NetPacker.IntToSbyte(ID));

    writer.Write(NetPacker.BigFloatToShort(loc.X));
    writer.Write(NetPacker.BigFloatToShort(loc.Y));

    writer.Write(NetPacker.IntToShort(anim));
    writer.Write(NetPacker.IntToShort(animFrame));
    writer.Write(NetPacker.MidFloatToShort(frame));

    writer.Write(NetPacker.IntToSbyte(state));
    writer.Write(NetPacker.IntToSbyte(face));

    writer.Write(NetPacker.BigFloatToShort(trajectory.X));
    writer.Write(NetPacker.BigFloatToShort(trajectory.Y));
```

```
    writer.Write(keyRight);
    writer.Write(keyLeft);

    writer.Write(NetPacker.IntToShort(HP));
}
```

Take a look at how `ReadFromNet()` differs from `WriteToNet()`:

```
public void ReadFromNet(PacketReader reader)
{
    loc.X = NetPacker.ShortToBigFloat(reader.ReadInt16());
    loc.Y = NetPacker.ShortToBigFloat(reader.ReadInt16());

    anim = NetPacker.ShortToInt(reader.ReadInt16());
    animFrame = NetPacker.ShortToInt(reader.ReadInt16());
    animName = charDef.GetAnimation(anim).name;
    frame = NetPacker.ShortToMidFloat(reader.ReadInt16());

    state = NetPacker.SbyteToInt(reader.ReadSByte());
    face = NetPacker.SbyteToInt(reader.ReadSByte());

    trajectory.X = NetPacker.ShortToBigFloat(reader.ReadInt16());
    trajectory.Y = NetPacker.ShortToBigFloat(reader.ReadInt16());

    keyRight = reader.ReadBoolean();
    keyLeft = reader.ReadBoolean();

    HP = NetPacker.ShortToInt(reader.ReadInt16());

    receivedNetUpdate = true;
}
```

We're starting by reading the location data, because from `NetGame`, we already read the first four items. First, we read the message type, before our `switch` block, and then the next three for use in a case where we needed to spawn a new character.

There's a bit of noticeable waste here. Fields like `defID`, `team`, and `ID` don't change every frame, if ever. If we wanted to optimize more, we would include these as a separate message. This could get a bit hairy though. We would need to flag new characters to make sure we send out this data, we would need to account for special cases where packets arrived out of order and the recipient received the character location data before the character ID data, and so on and so forth.

Particle Net Data

Getting our particles in shape is a much uglier task. We broke down our strategy for dealing with particles in a multiplayer setting a few pages earlier, but let's lay it down again in a series of scenarios:

Client adds particle that client owns: This happens when the client fires bullets, swings his wrench, or creates any other particle where owner = 1. The client spawns the particle and flags it for a network send. At the next network write, the client sends the particle and unchecks its flag, signifying that it no longer needs to be sent. The server receives and spawns the particle.

Client adds particle that client does not own: This happens when the client's game tries to spawn explosions, blood, and so on its own. For instance, if a bullet hits a zombie, the game will try to spawn blood. However, if the server doesn't think the bullet hit the zombie, we don't want blood being spawned on the client and not on the server. The server is final arbiter for particles that the client does not own. The client does not spawn the particle. Hopefully, at the next network update, the client will receive the particle data that it tried to spawn. This time, because the data is from a network source, the client *will* create the particle.

Server adds particle that client owns: This happens when a client tries to create a particle, like firing a bullet, on the server machine. Because we're constantly updating all characters on both machines, and because the FireTrig() call in the character is called from the update, a client updated on the host will attempt to fire bullets if in the right animation. However, if there's a bit of a network hiccup, the server could end up seeing the client skip over the fire frame or hit it twice, so we want to make sure we spawn bullet particles only when the client sends them. In this case, the server does not spawn the particle. Again, hopefully at the next network update, the server will receive the particle data from the client and create it.

Server adds a particle that client does not own: This happens when the server spawns anything that is not owned by the client. The server spawns the particle and flags it for a network send. At the next network write, the server sends the particle and unchecks its flag, signifying that it no longer needs to be sent. The client receives and spawns the particle.

The big omission in this is that particle data is sent only at creation and is not updated. We figured we could get away with this for now—we don't have any particles change trajectory mid-flight. If we included homing rockets, collectable items, or anything else that lingered for longer than a second, we would definitely need to implement some sort of particle-updating messaging functionality.

To allow particles to be sent and received, we'll need particle-specific code in every particle class. We'll put a virtual NetWrite() method in the base Particle class, which will be over-loaded from each class that extends Particle, and as you may have noticed from the NetGame code, we'll be making a new constructor for every type of particle that will accept a PacketReader.

We'll also define some constant values for our particle types. We use these from NetGame as well. Let's start in Particle.

```
public const byte PARTICLE_NONE = 0;
public const byte PARTICLE_BLOOD = 1;
public const byte PARTICLE_BLOOD_DUST = 2;
public const byte PARTICLE_BULLET = 3;
public const byte PARTICLE_FIRE = 4;
```

```
public const byte PARTICLE_FOG = 5;
public const byte PARTICLE_HEAT = 6;
public const byte PARTICLE_HIT = 7;
public const byte PARTICLE_MUZZLEFLASH = 8;
public const byte PARTICLE_ROCKET = 9;
public const byte PARTICLE_SHOCKWAVE = 10;
public const byte PARTICLE_SMOKE = 11;

...

public bool netSend;

...

public virtual void NetWrite(PacketWriter writer)
{
    writer.Write(NetGame.MSG_PARTICLE);
    writer.Write(PARTICLE_NONE);
    writer.Write(background);
}
```

Let's take a look at how `Blood`, a class that extends `Particle`, must now be changed to be net-friendly. First off, we'll overload the constructor. The previous constructor accepted location; trajectory; red, green, blue, and alpha values; size; and icon. The overloaded constructor accepts a `PacketReader` which, when read, will reveal all of these values.

```
public Blood(Vector2 loc,
    Vector2 traj,
    float r,
    float g,
    float b,
    float a,
    float size,
    int icon)
{
    this.loc = loc;
    ...
}

public Blood(PacketReader reader)
{
    this.loc =
        new Vector2(
        NetPacker.ShortToBigFloat(reader.ReadInt16()),
        NetPacker.ShortToBigFloat(reader.ReadInt16()));

    this.traj =
        new Vector2(
```

```
        NetPacker.ShortToBigFloat(reader.ReadInt16()),
        NetPacker.ShortToBigFloat(reader.ReadInt16())));

    this.r = NetPacker.ByteToTinyFloat(reader.ReadByte());
    this.g = NetPacker.ByteToTinyFloat(reader.ReadByte());
    this.b = NetPacker.ByteToTinyFloat(reader.ReadByte());
    this.a = NetPacker.ByteToTinyFloat(reader.ReadByte());

    this.size = NetPacker.ShortToSmallFloat(reader.ReadInt16());
    this.flag = NetPacker.SbyteToInt(reader.ReadSByte());

    this.owner = -1;
    this.exists = true;
    this.rotation = GlobalFunc.GetAngle(new Vector2(), traj);
    this.frame = Rand.getRandomFloat(0.3f, 0.7f);
}
```

As with our characters, we do a bit of extra writing here. We need to specify the message type, particle type, and background bit. When we did our reading in the constructor, we just started at the location because the previous three items are read in NetGame.

```
public override void NetWrite(PacketWriter writer)
{
    writer.Write(NetGame.MSG_PARTICLE);
    writer.Write(Particle.PARTICLE_BLOOD);
    writer.Write(background);
    writer.Write(NetPacker.BigFloatToShort(loc.X));
    writer.Write(NetPacker.BigFloatToShort(loc.Y));

    writer.Write(NetPacker.BigFloatToShort(traj.X));
    writer.Write(NetPacker.BigFloatToShort(traj.Y));

    writer.Write(NetPacker.TinyFloatToByte(r));
    writer.Write(NetPacker.TinyFloatToByte(g));
    writer.Write(NetPacker.TinyFloatToByte(b));
    writer.Write(NetPacker.TinyFloatToByte(a));

    writer.Write(NetPacker.SmallFloatToShort(size));
    writer.Write(NetPacker.IntToSbyte(flag));
}
```

Let's take a look at another one:

```
public Fog(PacketReader reader)
{
    this.loc =
        new Vector2(
        NetPacker.ShortToBigFloat(reader.ReadInt16()),
        NetPacker.ShortToBigFloat(reader.ReadInt16())));
```

```
        this.traj = new Vector2(80f, -30f);
        this.size = Rand.getRandomFloat(6f, 8f);
        this.flag = Rand.getRandomInt(0, 4);
        this.owner = -1;
        this.exists = true;
        this.frame = (float)Math.PI * 2f;
        this.additive = true;
        this.rotation = Rand.getRandomFloat(0f, 6.28f);
    }


    public override void NetWrite(PacketWriter writer)
    {
        writer.Write(NetGame.MSG_PARTICLE);
        writer.Write(Particle.PARTICLE_FOG);
        writer.Write(background);
        writer.Write(NetPacker.BigFloatToShort(loc.X));
        writer.Write(NetPacker.BigFloatToShort(loc.Y));
    }
```

All Fog really needed was location data.

Because all of the particles have different constructors and need to be constructed with different data, we (*groan*) must add this overloaded constructor/overloaded NetWrite() combo for every last particle. What's more, one misstep along the way will mess up everything. If we try to read the wrong amount of bits, every subsequent read will have an incorrect offset, leading to weird performance (most likely in the form of crashes). When we implemented this, we started with just Fire, then tried to implement another one, caused a crash, fixed the crash, and moved on. One suggestion to change this would be to keep track of how many bits we have read in and at what offset the new particle needs to be. This way, we could fix reading errors as they happen. However, because of time issues, we will just get down and dirty while hoping we haven't made a mistake.

We need to update ParticleManager. First off, we add an overload to AddParticle() to allow us to add a particle specified as sent through the network.

```
public void AddParticle(Particle newParticle, bool background)
{
    AddParticle(newParticle, background, false);
}


public void AddParticle(Particle newParticle, bool background,
    bool netSent)
{
    for (int i = 0; i < particle.Length; i++)
    {
        if (particle[i] == null)
        {
            particle[i] = newParticle;
            particle[i].background = background;
```

Here's where we handle the scenarios laid out a few pages ago. It looks much shorter in code!

```
        if (!netSent)
        {
            if (Game1.netPlay.joined)
            {
                if (particle[i].GetOwner() == 1)
                    particle[i].netSend = true;
                else
                    particle[i] = null;
            }
            else if (Game1.netPlay.hosting)
            {
                if (particle[i].GetOwner() != 1)
                    particle[i].netSend = true;
                else
                    particle[i] = null;
            }
        }
        break;
    }
  }
}
```

We'll send off any particles flagged for a send in NetWriteParticles(), and then unflag them.

```
public void NetWriteParticles(PacketWriter writer)
{
    for (int i = 0; i < particle.Length; i++)
        if (particle[i] != null)
        {
            if (particle[i].netSend)
            {
                particle[i].NetWrite(writer);
                particle[i].netSend = false;
            }
        }
}
```

We'll need to round up a few more odds and ends before everything is ready for prime time. We need to add player 2's health to the HUD. We need to give player 2 a different skin so that we don't end up with two clones running around together. We should turn off bucket monster spawning from the client side. Lastly, we need to plug everything into Game1.

Adding the Second Player to the HUD

In HUD.Draw(), we modify our heart-drawing algorithm a little to turn it into a loop that allows for two players. Remember our floating HP value that we used for a smoothly adjusting health bar? We had only one. We need two. All we need to do is declare it as a float array of size 2 and change all affected code (Update() would be a good place to start).

Our heart-drawing algorithm in HUD.Draw() is modified like this:

```
for (int p = 0; p < Game1.players; p++)
{
    float fProg = fHP[p] / (float)character[p].MHP;
    float prog = (float)character[p].HP / (float)character[p].MHP;
    fProg *= 5f;
    prog *= 5f;
    for (int i = 0; i < 5; i++)
    {
        float r =
            (float)Math.Cos((double)heartFrame * 2.0 +
            (double)i) * .1f;
```

Here's a new bit: we're using t to hold each heart's x coordinate. Player 1's hearts come from the left of the screen and are left-justified; player 2's hearts come from the right.

```
        float t = (p == 0 ?
            66f + (float)i * 32f :
            Game1.screenSize.X - 66f - (float)i * 32f);

        sprite.Draw(spritesTex, new Vector2(t, 66f),
            new Rectangle(i * 32, 192, 32, 32),
            new Color(new Vector4(0.5f, 0f, 0f, .25f)),
            r, new Vector2(16f, 16f), 1.25f,
            SpriteEffects.None, 1f);

        float ta = fProg - (float)i;


        if (ta > 1f) ta = 1f;
        if (ta > 0f)
        {
```

Here's a tremendously ugly draw call:

```
            sprite.Draw(spritesTex, new Vector2(t, 66f),
                (p == 0 ?
                new
                Rectangle(i * 32, 192, (int)(32f * ta), 32)
                :
                new
```

```
            Rectangle(i * 32 + (int)(32f * (1f - ta)),
                192, (int)(32f * ta), 32)
            ),
            new Color(new Vector4(1f, 0f, 0f, .75f)),
            r, new Vector2(16f
            - (p == 1 ? 32f * (1f - ta) : 0f), 16f), 1.25f,
            SpriteEffects.None, 1f);
    }

    ta = prog - (float)i;
    if (ta > 1f) ta = 1f;
    if (ta > 0f)
        ...
}
```

The two big conditionals involve the source rectangle and the center vector. The first conditional chooses between the rectangle we were using originally (for player 1), in which the width scales as the heart changes sizes, and a rectangle for player 2, in which the x coordinate shifts *and* the width scales.

The second conditional is required for player 2's heart. This causes the center to shift as well. While changing the width of the hearts on player 1's health bar involved changing only the source rectangle width, doing this for player 2 involves changing the source rectangle width and x coordinate, as well as the x coordinate of the center vector.

Giving the Second Player a Skin

We need to get a new skin for player 2. We'll call him Esteban. Esteban is a well-seasoned zombie smasher. He wears a hoodie and looks slightly emo. We made some new images: head, torso, and legs. He can use a wrench and revolver as well for now. The new images are shown in Figure 12-6.

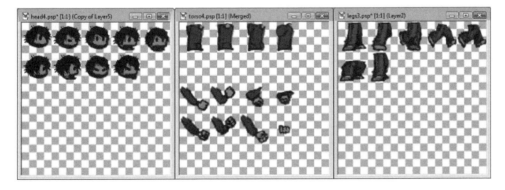

Figure 12-6. *Player 2 images*

We'll add these files to our Content project and load them from Game1 as normal. We called them head4.png, torso4.png, and legs3.png.

In Character.Draw(), we'll just hard-code the skin change. Esteban is exactly the same character as Guy, only with a skin swap, so the change can really be this superficial:

```
if (ID == 1 && Game1.players == 2)
{
    switch (t)
    {
        case 0:
            texture = headTex[3];
            break;
        case 1:
            texture = torsoTex[3];
            break;
        case 2:
            texture = legsTex[2];
            break;
    }
}
```

Plugging Everything into the Game

To turn off bucket monster spawning, we just add the following to the beginning of Bucket.Update().

```
if (Game1.netPlay.joined)
    return;
```

Lastly, we'll make the necessary changes in Game1. We need to update the scroll value to follow the correct player (host follows Guy; client follows Esteban) and make sure our input is sent to the correct player (host to index 0; client to index 1). We'll make some changes in UpdateGame():

```
int idx = 0;
if (netPlay.joined)
    idx = 1;

if (character[idx] != null)
{
    scroll += ((character[idx].loc -
        new Vector2(400f, 400f)) - scroll) * frameTime * 20f;
}

...
```

```
if (map.transOutFrame <= 0f)
{
    pManager.UpdateParticles(frameTime, map, character);

    if (gameType == GameType.Solo)
    {
        if (character[0] != null)
            character[0].DoInput(0);
    }
    else if (gameType == GameType.Arena)
    {
        if (netPlay.hosting)
            if (character[0] != null)
                character[0].DoInput(0);
        if (netPlay.joined)
            if (character[1] != null)
                character[1].DoInput(0);
    }
```

Finally, we'll make sure to keep netPlay updated from Update(); otherwise, our whole network machine won't get off the ground. Because this game is in the habit of doing wonky things with frameTime, we give netPlay an unaltered value as soon as we get it, and then carry on with our manipulation.

```
frameTime = (float)gameTime.ElapsedGameTime.TotalSeconds;
netPlay.netGame.frameTime = frameTime;

frameTime *= 1.3f;

if (slowTime > 0f)
{
    slowTime -= frameTime;
    frameTime /= 10f;
}

netPlay.Update(character, pManager);
```

Once everything is plugged in, we should be ready to roll. You will not be blown away by performance, and we aren't set up to handle some odd situations, but it's a fantastic start for 30 pages of networking crash course. Guy and Esteban battle it out with some monsters in Figure 12-7. (OK, they're not really battling it out, but you get the idea.)

Figure 12-7. *Network play in action*

Conclusion

We've implemented a fairly rough, if functional, networking engine for Zombie Smashers XNA. It doesn't have any prediction, smoothing, or optimal sending strategy, but it's as good a place to start as any.

To recap, we added hosting functionality to our menu system. We implemented a network connection management class to allow us to create, find, and join sessions and maintain a current session. And we implemented a network game management class to facilitate message sending and receipt over our character and particle classes.

There are a number of ways to improve on our networking system. We'll leave you with a few ideas:

Implement more efficient sending: You can check `NetworkGamer.RoundTripTime` to get a rough estimate of how often you can send data before choking up the system.

Send less: We use a lot of cosmetic particles, like fire and smoke from the torch and map fog. If you spawn these from the map with `netSent = true`, they'll be spawned independently on the client and server side with no sending in between. You'll save on transmitting a bit of data, without losing any information.

Smooth movement: Here's a pretty sneaky strategy that was implemented in The Dishwasher game: keep two separate vectors for character location—one for the true location and one that sort of plays catch-up with the true location. As you get updates from the other side of the network, you'll immediately update the true location (which you'll use for all game logic), but the draw location will set its location to a weighted average of the previous draw location and the new true location. This will make performance look a bit smoother.

Predict movement: If your character is moving left with a trajectory of –100, and packets take 100 milliseconds to arrive, you can assume that by the time you get the packet, the character has moved –100 × 0.1 on the remote machine.

All of these items involve varying degrees of complexity (heck, you could write a thesis on prediction algorithms), but you have a good start, so it should be fairly easy to experiment in network land.

A Parting Word

Well, here we are at the end of the last chapter in the book.

We've built a fairly robust infrastructure for what could be an amazing game. We have a neat character format and editor that give us the means to create beautifully animated characters with a high level of interactivity. We have a versatile map format that allows us to create rich maps with parallax scrolling, collision data, and a simple yet extremely functional scripting language.

We implemented side-scrolling game play (with collision detection); a particle engine and numerous cool-looking particle effects; sound effects and music; snazzy, next-gen postprocessing (including heat haze!); and rudimentary networking.

Now you're on your own.

You have a great start. You can work with Zombie Smashers XNA, adding new skins, monsters, maps, and so on. This is a good place to begin to get a feel for the techniques and styles we've used.

Once you have a handle on the capabilities and strengths of the project's codebase (which, if you really pored over the text, could be as early as now!), you can get to work on a new game using what we've covered here—as long as it's 2D. Nowadays, when the market is awash with AAA first-person shooters developed by teams of hundreds, it's easy to think of 2D as restricted. You'll just have to remind yourself that the video game industry once thrived on a flat plane. What major obstacles will we have to clear to pay homage to great design *sans* the third dimension? Here are some ideas:

2D fighter (Street Fighter 2): This would be the easiest implementation. You would just need to create new attack animations and tie them to different buttons—`attack` and `second` would now be jab, `strong`, `fierce`, `short`, `front`, and `roundhouse` (assuming Street Fighter 2 attack names).

Platform-happy side-scroller (Mario): There was a time when cutesy platformers ruled! Coins were collected, gaps were jumped, and goombas were stomped—all while an Italian protagonist walked a perilous line. Our game (which uses The Dishwasher: Dead Samurai as a model) is a combat action-intensive type, but you could easily modify the engine to place emphasis on careful footing, puzzles, timing, and all of that good stuff.

Side-scrolling shooter (Contra): You might want to make the map size a little larger. The big hurdle you would need to overcome involves animating separate parts of a character separately—the legs need to be able to move independently from the torso. If you're not shooting, your hero can be in a full-body running animation, but as soon as you open fire, the hero's torso, arms, head, and gun must enter a shooting animation, while still attached to legs.

Top-down adventure (Zelda): For the animation, you could do as in the original Zelda and have only four ways for a character to face: backward, left, right, or front. For every animation (such as `run` and `attack`), you would have three variants: back, side, and front. You could just flip sides for left and right facings. A convention you could use would be to append a facing suffix to every animation; for example, you would have `runb`, `runs`, and `runf` for run back, run side, and run front.

Multiplayer-intensive game: This is deliberately ambiguous, but we're really imagining a deathmatch using a Contra clone or a dungeon crawler (you can't make an MMORPG, but how about a Diablo clone?) using our top-down adventure concept. This is probably the most cumbersome to implement (remember that you need one machine, Silver Live account, and XNA Creators Club membership per instance of the game). If you have a small development team (read: roommates), this is much more doable. If you have a large, well-funded development team, why are you reading this book?

Of course, there are many ways to make a game. The ones we suggest here are those that have been cloned again and again over the ages. Sticking with an age-honored formula won't earn you originality points, but you can inject a bit of character—that thing that *only you* can provide—into whatever project you produce.

Game development is an art that takes time to hone and perfect. You will never see success if you don't put yourself on the line and try out ideas. Many of your ideas may fail, but when you get your first success, it will feel that much better. In time, you'll start producing masterpieces that you can just fire up and lose a few hours at a time playing. And you might just learn a thing or two about yourself.

Good luck!

APPENDIX A

■ ■ ■

Designing the Wraith
Our Freaky Awesome Skeleton
Monster

This appendix will lay out the process of creating the wraith characters for our game, as rapidly conceptualized in Figure A-1.

Figure A-1. *The wraith: the concept*

Wraiths are large, undead skeleton creatures with rocket-launching chainsaw arms. They soak up a lot more damage than zombies and cannot be tossed into the air for an air combo. Often, they won't react to damage at all, meaning you won't be able to interrupt their fearsome chainsaw swing with a well-timed attack. To defeat the wraith, our hero must be patient, quick, and precise.

Wraith Graphics

We'll start with some graphics. We'll use the setup shown in Figure A-2. We have a few head icons in head3; a bit of spine, some arms, and our wraith shawl in torso3; and our chainsaw/rocket launcher and some "swish" effects in weapon2.

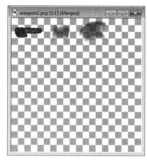

Figure A-2. *Wraith images*

Save the images as PNGs from whatever image editor you use (Paint.NET works just fine). Place them into the gfx folders in the Content projects for CharacterEditor and ZombieSmashers.

In CharacterEditor, add the projects to the solution from Solution Explorer. Then edit LoadContent() to load our new imagery:

```
legsTex = new Texture2D[1];
torsoTex = new Texture2D[3];
headTex = new Texture2D[3];
weaponTex = new Texture2D[2];
```

Wraith Animation

We can now play with the new wraith graphic palette and assemble some wraith animation frames. We put him together as shown in Figure A-3. We set up the following animations for him:

- idle

- run (he sort of hovers)

- fly (he won't be airborne often; only when spawned in air)

- land

- attack (he winds up his chainsaw and *slams!*)

- second (he fires off a rocket)

- init

- hit

- diehit (he dies in flames)

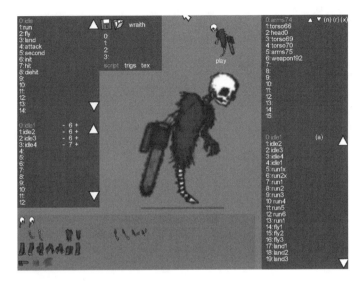

Figure A-3. *Wraith in the character editor*

We won't need some animations, such as jhit, jmid, and jfall, because this guy is going to be a biggie—he won't be lifted into the air by uppercuts, kicks, and so on.

We'll be able to specify that the wraith is a big guy in the script by defining a new command: nolifty (pronounced "no-liftee"), which means "I cannot be lifted!" Imagine coming across some terribly large boss character in our game, smacking him with a wrench uppercut, and sending the guy two stories into the air. It would look ridiculous, right? Hence, we'll specify any character who looks too big to knock into the air as being/having nolifty.

The initialization script for the wraith goes as follows:

```
hp 200
ai wraith
size 140
speed 75
nolifty
```

He's a tough guy who can soak up a bit of damage and doesn't move quickly.

We'll add some new triggers:

```
public const int TRIG_CHAINSAW_DOWN = 21;
public const int TRIG_CHAINSAW_UPPER = 22;
public const int TRIG_ROCKET = 23;
public const int TRIG_FIRE_DIE = 24;
```

We have two chainsaw attack triggers, a fire rocket trigger, and a "fire die" trigger for the fire that is emitted by a dying wraith. Our big chainsaw swing attack for the attack animation is shown in Figure A-4. Figure A-5 shows our creature firing a rocket in his second animation. And our wraith is dying in flames in Figure A-6, in our diehit animation.

Figure A-4. *Wraith attack*

Figure A-5. *Wraith secondary attack*

Figure A-6. *Wraith dies in flames!*

We created some new sounds to go with this, like explode, saw, and launch, adding them to the XACT project and the Wraith character definition script.

Wraith AI

Back in ZombieSmashers, we can start by creating an AI class for our wraith. The wraith will just move toward its target, chainsawing or firing rockets.

```
class Wraith : AI
{
    public override void Update(Character[] c, int ID, Map map)
    {
        me = c[ID];
```

```
        if (jobFrame < 0f)
        {
            float r = Rand.getRandomFloat(0f, 1f);
            if (r < 0.6f)
            {
                job = JOB_MELEE_CHASE;
                jobFrame = Rand.getRandomFloat(2f, 4f);
                FindTarg(c);
            }
            else
            {
                job = JOB_SHOOT_CHASE;
                jobFrame = Rand.getRandomFloat(1f, 2f);
                FindTarg(c);
            }

        }

        base.Update(c, ID, map);
    }
}
```

Particles: Rockets and Shockwaves

We'll be doing a bit of work with particles to give our wraith some rockets. We need a Rocket particle class and a Shockwave particle class. The rocket will travel in a sort of swervy, sinusoidal pattern, exploding on impact with a wall or character. As the rocket travels, it leaves a contrail of fire and smoke. Also, we don't actually need to *draw* the rocket—a contrail is enough.

The Rocket class, including the network-friendly constructor overload and NetWrite() overload, looks like this:

```
class Rocket : Particle
{
    public Rocket(Vector2 loc, Vector2 traj, int owner)
    {
        this.loc = loc;
        this.traj = traj;
        this.owner = owner;
        this.frame = 4f;
        this.exists = true;
    }

    public Rocket(PacketReader reader)
    {
        this.loc =
            new Vector2(
```

```
                NetPacker.ShortToBigFloat(reader.ReadInt16()),
                NetPacker.ShortToBigFloat(reader.ReadInt16()));

        this.traj =
            new Vector2(
            NetPacker.ShortToBigFloat(reader.ReadInt16()),
            NetPacker.ShortToBigFloat(reader.ReadInt16()));

        this.owner = NetPacker.SbyteToInt(reader.ReadSByte());

        this.frame = 4f;
        this.exists = true;
    }

    public override void NetWrite(PacketWriter writer)
    {
        writer.Write(NetGame.MSG_PARTICLE);
        writer.Write(Particle.PARTICLE_ROCKET);
        writer.Write(background);
        writer.Write(NetPacker.BigFloatToShort(loc.X));
        writer.Write(NetPacker.BigFloatToShort(loc.Y));

        writer.Write(NetPacker.BigFloatToShort(traj.X));
        writer.Write(NetPacker.BigFloatToShort(traj.Y));

        writer.Write(NetPacker.IntToSbyte(owner));
    }

    public override void Update(float gameTime, Map map,
        ParticleManager pMan, Character[] c)
    {
        if (HitManager.CheckHit(this, c, pMan))
            frame = 0f;

        traj.Y = (float)Math.Sin((double)frame * 13.0) * 150f;

        if (map.CheckParticleCol(loc))
        {
            this.frame = 0f;
            pMan.MakeExplosion(loc, 1f);
        }

        pMan.AddParticle(new Fire(loc, -traj / 8f,
            .5f, Rand.getRandomInt(0, 4)));
        pMan.AddParticle(new Smoke(loc,
            Rand.getRandomVector2(-20f, 20f, -50f, 10f)
            - traj / 10f,
```

```
            1f, .8f, .6f, 1f, .5f,
            Rand.getRandomInt(0, 4)));
        pMan.AddParticle(new Heat(loc,
            Rand.getRandomVector2(-20f, 20f, -50f, -10f),
            Rand.getRandomFloat(.5f, 2f)));

        base.Update(gameTime, map, pMan, c);
    }
}
```

When the rocket collides with the map collision map, it triggers a `ParticleManager`. `MakeExplosion()`, which creates some fire, smoke, and two shockwaves: a refracting one and a visible one.

Our `Shockwave` class follows.

```
class Shockwave : Particle
{
    public Shockwave(Vector2 loc,
        bool refract,
        float size)
    {
        this.loc = loc;

        this.size = size;
        this.owner = -1;
        this.exists = true;
        this.frame = .5f;
        this.refract = refract;
    }

    public Shockwave(PacketReader reader)
    {
        this.loc =
            new Vector2(
            NetPacker.ShortToBigFloat(reader.ReadInt16()),
            NetPacker.ShortToBigFloat(reader.ReadInt16()));

        this.size = NetPacker.ShortToMidFloat(reader.ReadInt16());
        this.refract = reader.ReadBoolean();

        this.owner = -1;
        this.exists = true;
        this.frame = .5f;
    }
```

```
public override void NetWrite(PacketWriter writer)
{
    writer.Write(NetGame.MSG_PARTICLE);
    writer.Write(Particle.PARTICLE_SHOCKWAVE);
    writer.Write(background);
    writer.Write(NetPacker.BigFloatToShort(loc.X));
    writer.Write(NetPacker.BigFloatToShort(loc.Y));

    writer.Write(NetPacker.MidFloatToShort(size));
    writer.Write(refract);
}
```

We can draw a shockwave with `refract` on or off. When `refract` is on, we'll just draw a donut in bright red; when it's off, we'll draw a filled circle in translucent white.

```
public override void Draw(SpriteBatch sprite, Texture2D spritesTex)
{
    Rectangle sRect = new Rectangle(
        128
        + (refract ? 0 : 64),
        128, 64, 64);

    a = frame * (refract ? 1f : 0.5f);

    float gb = (refract ? 0f : 1f);

    sprite.Draw(spritesTex, GameLoc(), sRect, new Color(
        new Vector4(1f, gb, gb, a)),
        rotation + frame * 16f, new Vector2(32.0f, 32.0f),
        size * (.5f - frame) * 2f,
        SpriteEffects.None, 1.0f);

}
}
```

The sprites image has been updated to include our donut and circle at 128, 128 and 192, 128, respectively, as shown in Figure A-7.

We'll be creating a refracting and nonrefracting shockwave, some fire, and some smoke from `ParticleManager.MakeExplosion()`. The method also plays a sound, shakes up the screen, and uses our blast effect.

```
public void MakeExplosion(Vector2 loc, float mag)
{
    for (int i = 0; i < 8; i++)
        AddParticle(new Smoke(loc,
            Rand.getRandomVector2(-100f, 100f,
            -100f, 100f),
```

```
        1f, .8f, .6f, 1f,
        Rand.getRandomFloat(1f, 1.5f),
        Rand.getRandomInt(0, 4)));
for (int i = 0; i < 8; i++)
    AddParticle(new Fire(loc,
        Rand.getRandomVector2(-80f, 80f, -80f, 80f),
        1f, Rand.getRandomInt(0, 4)));

AddParticle(new Shockwave(loc, true, 25f));
AddParticle(new Shockwave(loc, false, 10f));
Sound.PlayCue("explode");
QuakeManager.SetQuake(.5f);
QuakeManager.SetBlast(1f, loc);
}
```

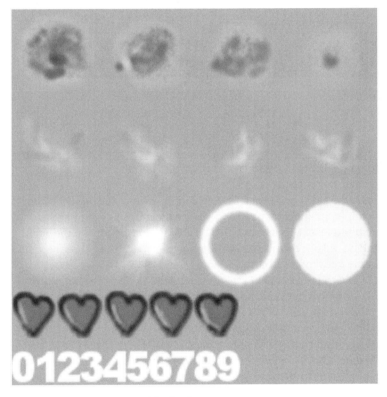

Figure A-7. *Sprites image with shockwave*

Our shockwave in action is shown in Figure A-8.

Figure A-8. *Shockwave in action*

Hit Logic

We'll need to add some functionality to HitManager.CheckHit() to implement the nolifty status, rocket strikes, and chainsaw smashes.

The way that we'll set up the nolifty character will primarily prevent the monster from being lifted into the air by uppercut attacks, but also will cause the monster's animation to sometimes not be affected by attacks. This means you'll be able to smash away on the wraith for a couple of seconds, and he will be reacting to every hit, but then for the next three seconds, he will be able to attack in the midst of your barrage.

We'll add a flag to the Character class called stunFrame, which will decrease at a rate of 1f per second if above 0f. If stunFrame is between 0f and 3f, the monster won't be affected by attacks.

We get the previous state and previous location of the wraith. If we don't want him lifted, we'll check to see if he is currently airborne and previously grounded; if this is the case, we return him to his previous state. Also, we now need to check for noAnim before every trajectory and animation change to prevent us from moving characters that shouldn't be moving.

```
int pState = c[i].state;
Vector2 pLoc = c[i].loc;

bool noAnim = false;
if (c[i].stunFrame > 0f &&
    c[i].stunFrame < 3f)
    noAnim = true;
if (c[i].noLifty)
```

```
{
    if (c[i].stunFrame <= 0f ||
        · c[i].stunFrame > 5.2f)
        c[i].stunFrame = 5.5f;
}

if (typeof(Bullet).Equals(p.GetType()))
{
    ...
}
else if (typeof(Rocket).Equals(p.GetType()))
{
    pMan.MakeExplosion(p.GetLoc(), 1f);
    hVal *= 5f;
    if (!noAnim)
    {
        c[i].trajectory.X = (p.GetTraj().X > 0f ? 600f : -600f);
        c[i].SetAnim("jhit");
        c[i].SetJump(300f);
    }
    Game1.slowTime = 0.25f;
    r = true;
}
else if (typeof(Hit).Equals(p.GetType()))
{
    ...
    if (!noAnim)
    {
        c[i].SetAnim("idle");
        c[i].SetAnim("hit");
    }
    ...

    switch (p.GetFlag())
    {
        ...
        case Character.TRIG_WRENCH_SMACKDOWN:
        case Character.TRIG_CHAINSAW_DOWN:
            hVal *= 15f;
            pMan.MakeBloodSplash(p.GetLoc(),
                new Vector2(-50f * tX, 150f));
            c[i].SetAnim("jfall");
            c[i].SetJump(-900f);

            Game1.slowTime = 0.125f;
            QuakeManager.SetQuake(.5f);
```

```
                    QuakeManager.SetBlast(.5f, p.GetLoc());
                    break;
                ...
        }
}
if (c[i].state == Character.STATE_AIR)
{
    ...
    if (c[i].noLifty)
    {
        if (pState == Character.STATE_GROUNDED)
        {
            c[i].loc = pLoc;
            c[i].state = pState;
            c[i].SetAnim("hit");
        }
        if (c[i].trajectory.X > 300f)
            c[i].trajectory.X = 300f;
        if (c[i].trajectory.X < -300f)
            c[i].trajectory.X = -300f;
    }
}
```

This leaves a few odds and ends, like adding and loading wraith graphics to ZombieSmashers, adding wraith.zdx to our project, and loading the character definition in Initialize():

```
charDef[CharDef.CHAR_DEF_WRAITH] = new CharDef("chars/wraith",
    CharDef.CHAR_DEF_WRAITH);
```

Also, there are a couple of places where we tied a string to an object for scripting purposes; we used this for the character script AI command and the map monster spawning commands. In Script, we'll add a new case:

```
case Script.COMMAND_AI:
    switch (line.GetSParam())
    {
        case "zombie":
            character.ai = new Zombie();
            break;
        case "wraith":
            character.ai = new Wraith();
            break;
        ...
    }
    break;
```

Likewise, in `MapScript`, we add a case to `GetMonsterFromString()`:

```
public static int GetMonsterFromString(String m)
{
    switch (m)
    {
        case "wraith":
            return CharDef.CHAR_DEF_WRAITH;
        ...
    }
    return CharDef.CHAR_DEF_ZOMBIE;
}
```

We're now able to add wraiths from map scripts. We added a new map and linked it to the current ones. We put in some nice water and a bucket full of wraiths. You can see the new map and wraith in action in Figure A-9.

Figure A-9. *Wraith in action!*

That should wrap it up!

This appendix should have helped you get a better handle on what goes into creating a new character. We've created graphics, animation, and new particle effects; and incorporated everything into a neat chainsaw-wielding creature.

Storage
Saving Your Settings

This appendix will show you how to get a storage device, read from it, and write to it.

In Windows, it's easy enough to just read from and write to a saves folder in your game folder. On the Xbox 360, you can't do this. You must use a special object called a *storage container*, which resides in a *storage device*. A storage device can be a hard drive or memory unit. If both are present, the user is prompted to choose.

Once you have your storage device and opened a storage container, file reading and writing is fairly simple.

Managing Devices and Containers

We'll start with the Store class, which we'll use for all storage management functionality. If you've read Chapter 12, you may notice some similarities between this class and NetConnect.

We'll set up the class as a sort of common gateway for all reading/writing functionality, and then we'll implement a Settings class for reading and writing game settings (of which we have one, but really, who's counting?).

Starting at the class level, we'll declare our StorageDevice, which will be a hard drive, memory unit, or null (meaning the device search failed).

```
public class Store
{
    public StorageDevice device;
    IAsyncResult deviceResult;
    public bool pendingDevice;

    public StorageContainer container;
    bool containerOpen;

    public const int STORE_SETTINGS = 0;
    public const int STORE_GAME = 1;
```

```
private string[] storeStr = {
    "settings.sav",
    "game.sav"
};
```

Have you ever played an Xbox 360 game that asked you where you would like to save files? A dashboard blade pops out, letting you select the storage device. This is an *asynchronous* operation, meaning that the rest of the game doesn't grind to a halt while you select the device. We'll be using this technique here, and that's why we've declared IAsyncResult deviceResult. While we're waiting on our device result, pendingDevice will be set to true.

We'll call GetDevice() from Game1 during initialization. This will pop out the device selector blade and give the player a chance to pick the device. If the player has only one storage device, he won't see a selector blade, but the operation will still do its stuff asynchronously.

```
public void GetDevice()
{
    deviceResult = Guide.BeginShowStorageDeviceSelector(
        PlayerIndex.One, null, null);
    pendingDevice = true;
}
```

We'll call Update() from Game1.Update(). All this will do is attempt to follow up on our asynchronous device retrieval. If we just got the device, we'll read our game settings.

```
public void Update()
{
    if (pendingDevice)
    {
        if (deviceResult.IsCompleted)
        {
            device =
                Guide.EndShowStorageDeviceSelector(deviceResult);
            pendingDevice = false;
            Read(STORE_SETTINGS);
        }
    }
}
```

In attempting to read or write, a couple of things could have gone wrong. We could still be in our asynchronous device finding operation, the user could have closed the device selector blade (giving us a null device), or the device could have been detached. CheckDeviceFail() checks for these issues. We'll use this function before any reads or writes.

```
private bool CheckDeviceFail()
{
    if (pendingDevice)
        return true;
    if (device == null)
        return true;
```

```
    if (!device.IsConnected)
        return true;
    return false;
}
```

We need to open our container only once for all writes and reads within the same device. This next function does just that:

```
private void OpenContainer()
{
    if (!containerOpen)
        container = device.OpenContainer("ZombieSmashersXna");
    containerOpen = true;
}
```

Our Write() function uses our device and container to get a path. Then it creates a FileStream using this path and writes to it. We use a BinaryWriter that we can just pass along to whatever object we're using to save. Here, we've implemented only the Settings object, which will ultimately be a public static at the Game1 class level.

```
public void Write(int type)
{
    if (CheckDeviceFail())
        return;

    OpenContainer();

    string fileName = Path.Combine(container.Path,
        storeStr[STORE_SETTINGS]);

    FileStream file =
        File.Open(fileName, FileMode.OpenOrCreate,
        FileAccess.Write);

    BinaryWriter writer = new BinaryWriter(file);

    switch (type)
    {
        case STORE_SETTINGS:
            Game1.settings.Write(writer);
            break;
    }

    file.Close();

}
```

Likewise, our Read() function does almost the same thing. Just substitute "read" for "write" in all cases, and we're good!

```
public void Read(int type)
{
    if (CheckDeviceFail())
        return;

    OpenContainer();

    string fileName = Path.Combine(container.Path,
        storeStr[STORE_SETTINGS]);

    FileStream file;
    if (!File.Exists(fileName))
    {
        return;
    }
    else
        file = File.Open(fileName, FileMode.Open, FileAccess.Read);

    BinaryReader reader = new BinaryReader(file);

    switch (type)
    {
        case STORE_SETTINGS:
            Game1.settings.Read(reader);
            break;
    }

    file.Close();

}
}
```

Reading and Writing

There isn't much left to do. We just need to create a Settings class and plug everything in. We'll only use one setting: rumble. This will determine whether our controller vibrates to accentuate things like gunshots, explosions, and the like. Up until now, rumble was on by default.

```
public class Settings
{
    public bool rumble = true;

    public bool Rumble
    {
        get { return rumble; }
        set { rumble = value; }
    }
```

```
    public void Write(BinaryWriter writer)
    {
        writer.Write(rumble);
    }

    public void Read(BinaryReader reader)
    {
        rumble = reader.ReadBoolean();
    }
}
```

Had we implemented a SaveGame class (we have the structure in place to do so from within Store at least), we could have created a more complex example, but we can make do with this one.

Bringing It All Together

In Game1, we'll declare our Store and Settings as public statics:

```
public static Store store;
public static Settings settings;
```

We'll initialize them and start trying to get the storage device in Initialize():

```
...
base.Initialize();

store = new Store();
settings = new Settings();
store.GetDevice();
```

Don't forget that our store likes to be updated! If we don't call any updates, our asynchronous device retrieval will appear to never complete. In the Game1.Update() function, throw this:

```
store.Update();
```

In Menu, we need to add the user interface to let us turn rumble on and off. In Update(), we have a big switch block that normally does transitions whenever the player hits A or Start. We'll modify one of the cases to cause the game to write the settings when Back is pressed and toggle rumble when the rumble options are selected.

```
case Level.Options:
    switch (option[selItem])
    {
        case Option.Back:
            Transition(Level.Main);
            Game1.store.Write(Store.STORE_SETTINGS);
            break;
```

```
        case Option.RumbleOn:
            Game1.settings.Rumble = false;
            break;
        case Option.RumbleOff:
            Game1.settings.Rumble = true;
            break;
    }
    break;
```

We put this content together between Chapter 10 (which does *most* of the work on the main menu) and Chapter 12 (which adds a multiplayer level to the main menu), so we definitely snuck in a bit of extra functionality on this menu. We added the `RumbleOn` and `RumbleOff` items to the `Option` enumerator, added some items to the graphic, as shown in Figure B-1. We also added the following `case` to the `switch` block in `PopulateOptions()`:

```
case Level.Options:
    if (Game1.settings.Rumble)
        option[0] = Option.RumbleOn;
    else
        option[0] = Option.RumbleOff;
    option[1] = Option.Back;
    totalOptions = 2;
    break;
```

Figure B-1. *Options image*

That should square away our user interface.

In QuakeManager, we need to make sure it doesn't set rumble when rumble has been disabled in the global settings:

```
public static void SetRumble(int i, int motor, float val)
{
    if (Game1.settings.rumble)
        rumble[i].SetVal(motor, val);
}
```

With everything in place, we'll have a working options menu that properly saves settings, as shown in Figure B-2.

Figure B-2. *Options menu*

Index

You Need the Companion eBook

Your purchase of this book entitles you to buy the companion PDF-version eBook for only $10. Take the weightless companion with you anywhere.

We believe this Apress title will prove so indispensable that you'll want to carry it with you everywhere, which is why we are offering the companion eBook (in PDF format) for $10 to customers who purchase this book now. Convenient and fully searchable, the PDF version of any content-rich, page-heavy Apress book makes a valuable addition to your programming library. You can easily find and copy code—or perform examples by quickly toggling between instructions and the application. Even simultaneously tackling a donut, diet soda, and complex code becomes simplified with hands-free eBooks!

Once you purchase your book, getting the $10 companion eBook is simple:

❶ Visit **www.apress.com/promo/tendollars/**.

❷ Complete a basic registration form to receive a randomly generated question about this title.

❸ Answer the question correctly in 60 seconds, and you will receive a promotional code to redeem for the $10.00 eBook.

Offer valid through 03/22/09.